Lecture Notes in Computer Scier

Commenced Publication in 1973
Founding and Former Series Editors:
Gerhard Goos, Juris Hartmanis, and Jan van Leeuwen

Markus Müller-Olm

Variations
on Constants

Flow Analysis of Sequential and Parallel Programs

 Springer

Author

Markus Müller-Olm
Westfälische Wilhelms-Universität Münster
Institut für Informatik, FB 10
Einsteinstraße 62, 48149 Münster, Germany
E-mail: mmo@denethor.uni-muenster.de

Library of Congress Control Number: 2006933227

CR Subject Classification (1998): D.2.4, D.2, D.3, F.3

LNCS Sublibrary: SL 2 – Programming and Software Engineering

ISSN   0302-9743
ISBN-10   3-540-45385-7 Springer Berlin Heidelberg New York
ISBN-13   978-3-540-45385-7 Springer Berlin Heidelberg New York

Springer is a part of Springer Science+Business Media

springer.com

© Springer-Verlag Berlin Heidelberg 2006
Printed in Germany

Typesetting: Camera-ready by author, data conversion by Boller Mediendesign
Printed on acid-free paper   SPIN: 11871743   06/3142   5 4 3 2 1 0

Foreword

By its nature, automatic program analysis is the art of finding adequate compromises. Originally, in the 1970s, program analysis aimed at deriving preconditions for typically obviously correct optimizing program transformations. Heuristics for loop optimizations were popular, which in particular concerned the treatment of multi-dimensional arrays. The limits of these heuristics-based approaches became apparent when looking at the combined effects of optimizations – in particular in the context of concurrency. Since then, the loss of confidence in optimizing compilers has been fought by semantics-based methods that come with explicitly stated power and limitations.

A particularly natural and illustrative class of program analyses aims at detecting program constants, i.e. occurrences of program expressions which are guaranteed to evaluate to the same value in every run. This problem is essentially as hard as program verification in its full generality, though there are interesting subclasses which can be solved effectively or even efficiently.

Markus Müller-Olm investigates particularly interesting variations of such classes which are characterized by varying strengths of interpretation and by increasingly complex data and control structures. In particular, he considers in detail three main classes of problems:

– The purely sequential situation, where his ideal theoretic treatment of polynomial constants is really outstanding. It is a delight to follow the elegant algebraic development!
– The treatment of copy constants for fork-join parallel programs. This turns out to be very hard already in restricted settings like acyclic programs, and becomes undecidable in the context of procedures.
– A variation of the second class, where he waives the usual atomicity properties during execution. At first sight it is really surprising that this drastically simplifies the analysis problem. However, a closer look reveals that the decrease in algorithmic complexity goes hand in hand with a decrease in quality – as the waived atomicity is vital for a decent control of parallel computation.

Markus Müller-Olm succeeds in significantly improving the known results for the scenarios considered. However, what makes the book very special is the impressive firework of elaborate methods and powerful techniques.

Everybody working in the field will profit from passing from scenario to scenario and experiencing Markus Müller-Olm's mastership of choosing the adequate means for each of the considered analysis problems: one leaves with a deep understanding of the inherent underlying differences and in particular of the complexity of modern programming concepts in terms of the hardness of the implied analysis problem.

July 2006   Bernhard Steffen

Preface

Computer science is concerned with design of programs for a wide range of purposes. We are, however, not done once a program is constructed. For various reasons, programs need to be *analyzed* and *processed* after their construction. First of all, we usually write programs in high-level languages and before we can execute them on a computer they must be translated into machine code. In order to speed up computation or save memory, optimizing compilers perform program transformations relying heavily on the results of program analysis routines. Secondly, due to their ever-increasing complexity, programs must be validated or verified in order to ensure that they serve their intended purpose. *Program analysis* (in a broad sense) is concerned with techniques that automatically determine run-time properties of given programs prior to run-time. This includes flow analysis, type checking, abstract interpretation, model checking, and similar areas.

By Rice's theorem [79, 31], every non-trivial semantic question about programs in a universal programming language is undecidable. At first glance, this seems to imply that automatic analysis of programs is impossible. However, computer scientists have found at least two ways out of this problem. Firstly, we can use *weaker formalisms* than universal programming languages for modeling systems such that interesting questions become decidable. Important examples are the many types of automata studied in automata theory and Kripke structures (or labeled transition systems) considered in model checking. Secondly, we can work with *approximate analyses* that do not always give a definite answer but may have weaker (but sound) outcomes. Approximate analyses are widely used in optimizing compilers.

An interesting problem is to assess the *precision* of an approximate analysis. One approach is to consider an abstraction of programs or program behavior that gives rise to weaker but sound information and to prove that the analysis yields exact results with respect to this abstraction (cf. Fig. 0.1). The loss of precision can then be attributed to and measured by the employed abstraction. This scheme has been used in the literature in a number of scenarios [40, 86, 43, 87, 88, 24].

The scheme of Fig. 0.1 allows us to make meaningful statements on approximate analysis problems independently of specific algorithms: by devising abstractions of programs, we obtain well-defined weakened analysis problems

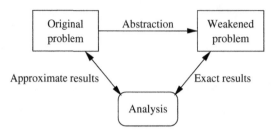

Fig. 0.1. Using an abstraction to assess the precision of an approximate analysis.

and we can classify these problems with the techniques of complexity and recursion theory. The purpose of such research is twofold: on the theoretical side, we gain insights on the trade-off between efficiency and precision in the design of approximate analyses; on the practical side, we hope to uncover potential for the construction of more precise (efficient) analysis algorithms.

In this monograph we study weakened versions of constant propagation. The motivation for this choice is threefold. Firstly, the constant-propagation problem is easy to understand and of obvious practical relevance. Hence, uncovering potential for more precise constant-propagation routines is of intrinsic interest. Secondly, there is a rich spectrum of natural weakened constant-propagation problems. On the one hand, we can vary the set of algebraic operators that are to be interpreted by the analysis. On the other hand, we can study the resulting problems in different classes of programs (sequential or parallel programs, with or without procedures, with or without loops etc.). Finally, results for the constant-propagation problem can often be generalized to other analysis questions. For instance, if as part of the abstraction we decide not to interpret algebraic operators at all, which leads to a problem known as *copy-constant detection*, we are essentially faced with analyzing transitive dependences in programs. Hence, results for copy-constant detection can straightforwardly be adapted to other problems concerned with transitive dependences, like faint-code elimination and program slicing.

In this monograph we combine techniques from different areas such as linear algebra, computable ring theory, abstract interpretation, program verification, complexity theory, etc. in order to come to grips with the considered variants of the constant-propagation problem. More generally, we believe that combination of techniques is the key to further progress in automatic analysis, and constant-propagation allows us to illustrate this point in a theoretical study.

Let us briefly outline the main contributions of this monograph:

A hierarchy of constants in sequential programs. We explore the complexity of constant-propagation for a three-dimensional taxonomy of constants in sequential imperative programs that work on integer variables. The first dimension restricts the set of interpreted integer expressions. The second dimension distinguishes between *must-* and *may-constants*. May-constants appear in two variations: single- and multiple-valued. May-constants are closely related to reachability. In the third dimension we distinguish between programs with and without loops. We succeed in classifying the complexity of the problems almost completely (Chapter 2). Moreover, we develop (must-)constant-propagation algorithms that interpret completely all integer operators except for the division operators by using results from linear algebra and computational ring theory (Chapter 3).

Limits for the analysis of parallel programs. We study propagation of copy constants in parallel programs. Assuming that base statements execute atomically, a standard assumption in the program verification and analysis literature, we show that copy-constant propagation is undecidable, PSPACE-complete, and NP-complete if we consider programs with procedures, without procedures, and without loops, respectively (Chapter 4). These results indicate that it is very unlikely that recent results on efficient exact analysis of parallel programs can be generalized to richer classes of dataflow problems.

Abandoning the atomic execution assumption. We then explore the consequences of abandoning the atomic execution assumption for base statements in parallel programs, which is the more realistic setup in practice (Chapters 5 to 9). Surprisingly, it turns out that this makes copy-constant detection, faint-code elimination and, more generally, analysis of transitive dependences decidable for programs with procedures (Chapter 8) although it remains intractable (NP-hard) (Chapter 9). In order to show decidability we develop a precise abstract interpretation of sets of runs (program executions) (Chapter 7). While the worst-case running time of the developed algorithms is exponential in the number of global variables, it is polynomial in the other parameters describing the program size. As well-designed parallel programs communicate on a small number of global variables only, there is thus the prospect of developing practically relevant algorithms by refining our techniques.

These three contributions constitute essentially self-contained parts that can be read independently of each other. Figure 0.2 shows the assignment of the chapters to these parts and indicates dependences between the chapters. For clarity, transitive relationships are omitted.

Throughout this monograph we assume that the reader is familiar with the basic techniques and results from the theory of computational complexity [72, 36], program analysis [70, 2, 30, 56], and abstract interpretation [14, 15]. A brief introduction to constraint-based program analysis is provided in Appendix A.

Acknowledgments

This monograph is a revised version of my habilitation thesis (*Habilitationsschrift*), which was submitted to the Faculty of Computer Science (*Fach-*

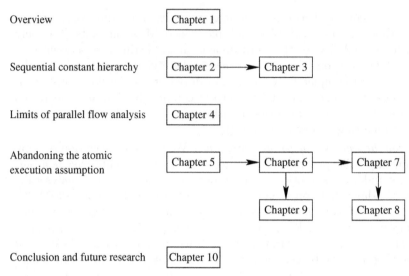

Fig. 0.2. Dependence between the chapters.

bereich Informatik) of Dortmund University in August 2002 and accepted in February 2003. I would like to thank Bernhard Steffen, head of the research group on Programming Systems and Compiler Construction at Dortmund University, in which I worked from 1996, for continual advice and support in many ways. I am also grateful to Oliver Rüthing and Helmut Seidl for our joint work. I thank all three and Jens Knoop for many helpful discussions and Hardi Hungar for insightful comments on a draft version. I thank the referees of my habilitation thesis, Javier Esparza, Neil Jones, and Bernhard Steffen, for their time and enthusiasm.

From October 2001 until March 2002 I worked at Trier University, which allowed me to elaborate the third part free from teaching duties. I thank Helmut Seidl and the DAEDALUS project, which was supported by the European FP5 programme (RTD project IST-1999-20527), for making this visit possible.

Dortmund, June 2005   Markus Müller-Olm

Table of Contents

1. Introduction

Constant propagation is one of the most widely used optimizations in practice (cf. [2, 30, 56]). Its goal is to replace expressions that always yield a unique constant value at run-time by this value. This transformation can both speed up execution and reduce code size by replacing a computation or memory access by a load-constant instruction. Often constant propagation enables powerful further program transformations. An example is branch elimination: if the condition guarding a branch of a conditional can be identified as being constantly false, the whole code in this branch is dynamically unreachable and can be removed.

The term *constant propagation* is somewhat reminiscent of the technique used in early compilers: copying the value of constants in programs (like in $x := 42$) to the places where they are used. The associated analysis problem, to identify expressions in the programs that are constant at run-time, is more adequately called *constant detection*. However, in the literature the term constant propagation is also used to denote the detection problem. We use the term constant propagation in informal discussions but prefer the term constant detection in more formal contexts.

Constant propagation is an instance of an automatic program analysis. There are fundamental limitations to program analysis deriving from undecidability. In particular, constant detection in full generality is undecidable. Here is a simple reduction for a prototypic imperative programming language. Suppose we are given a program P and assume that **new** is a variable not appearing in P. Consider the little program:

$$\mathbf{read}(\mathbf{new}) \,;\, P \,;\, \mathbf{write}(\mathbf{new}) \,.$$

If P does not terminate, **new** can be replaced by any constant in the write statement for trivial reasons, otherwise this transformation is unsound because the read-statement can read an arbitrary value. Thus, in order to solve the constant detection problem in its most general form, we have to solve the halting problem.

Similar games can be played in every universal programming language and for almost any interesting analysis question. Hence, the best we can hope for is approximate algorithms. An approximate analysis algorithm does not always give a definite answer. An approximate constant-detection algorithm,

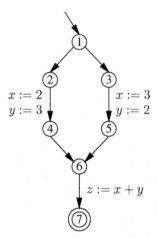

Fig. 1.1. A constant not detected by standard constant propagation.

for instance, detects some but in general not all constants in a program. The standard approach to constant propagation called *simple constant propagation*, for instance, does not detect that z is a constant of value 5 at node 7 in the flow graph in Fig. 1.1; cf. Appendix A. It is important that an approximate analysis algorithm only errs on one side and that this is taken into account when the computed information is exploited. This is called the *soundness* of the algorithm. We take soundness for granted in the discussion that follows.

Undecidability of the halting problem implies that it is undecidable whether a given program point can be reached in some execution of the program or not. We have seen above by the example of constant detection that this infects almost every analysis question. It is therefore common to abstract guarded branching to non-deterministic branching in order to ban this fundamental cause of undecidability. This abstraction is built into the use of the MOP-solution (see Appendix A) as the semantic reference point in dataflow analysis. This is: instead of the 'real' executions, we take all executions into account that at each branching point choose an arbitrary branch irrespective of the guard. Clearly, this abstraction makes reachability of program points decidable. Most analysis questions encountered in practice (and all the ones we are interested in in this monograph) ask for determining a property valid in all executions of the programs. For such questions information that is determined after guarded branching is abstracted to non-deterministic branching is valid, because more executions are considered. Adopting this abstraction, we work with non-deterministic programs in this monograph. Non-deterministic programs represent deterministic programs in which guarded branching has been abstracted to non-deterministic branching.

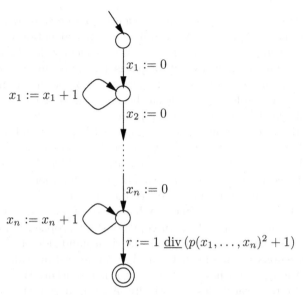

Fig. 1.2. Undecidability of constant detection; the reduction of Reif and Lewis.

A Hierarchy of Integer Constants in Sequential Programs

The abstraction to non-deterministic branching does not solve all the problems with undecidability. Constant detection, for instance, remains undecidable for programs working on integer variables and a full signature of integer operators. Independent proofs of this fact have been given by Hecht [30] and by Reif and Lewis [78]. We briefly recall the construction of Reif and Lewis. It is based on a reduction from Hilbert's famous tenth problem, whether a multivariate polynomial has a zero in the natural numbers. This is known to be an undecidable problem [50]. Assume given a polynomial $p(x_1, \ldots, x_n)$ in n variables $x_1, \ldots, x_n$ with natural coefficients different from the zero polynomial and consider the (non-deterministic) program in Figure 1.2. The initialization and the loop choose an arbitrary natural value for the x_i. If the chosen values constitute a zero of $p(x_1, \ldots, x_n)$, then $p(x_1, \ldots, x_n)^2 + 1 = 1$ and r is set to 1. Otherwise, $p(x_1, \ldots, x_n)^2 + 1 \geq 2$ such that r is set to 0. Therefore, r is a constant of value 0 at the end of the program if and only if $p(x_1, \ldots, x_n)$ does not have a natural zero. This result shows us that we cannot even hope for algorithms that detect all constants in non-deterministic programs.

On the other hand there are well-known and well-defined classes of constants that can be detected, even efficiently. A simple example are *copy constants* [20]. Roughly speaking, a variable x is a copy constant either if it is assigned a constant value (e.g., through $x := 42$) or if it is assigned the value of another copy constant (e.g., in $y := 42 \, ; x := y$). All other forms of assignments (e.g. $x := y + 1$) are (conservatively) assumed to make x

non-constant [83]. Copy constants can efficiently be detected by a standard dataflow analysis; cf. Appendix A. Also if we restrict attention to programs without loops, even general constant detection is clearly decidable because there are only finitely many execution paths reaching any given program point and we can inspect all paths in succession. But even in this setting the problem is intractable; recently it has been shown to be co-NP-hard [42]. Another decidable class of constants are *finite constants* [89].

These results motivate our considerations in Chapter 2 and 3 where we examine the borderline of intractability and undecidability more closely. To this end, we investigate the constant propagation problem for integers with respect to a three-dimensional taxonomy. The first dimension is given by the distinction between arbitrary and loop-free flow graphs.

The second dimension introduces a hierarchy of weakened versions of the constant-propagation problem. In copy-constant propagation only non-composite expressions are interpreted on the right hand side of assignments; all other expressions are assumed to produce non-constant values. We are interested in the question how far we can go in restricting the expressions that are interpreted exactly less drastically. A natural way of relaxing this restriction is to fix a sub-signature of integer operators and to require that all expressions built from operators of this sub-signature are interpreted fully. All but one of the classes studied in Chapter 2 are given in this way. More specifically, we investigate the following natural sub-signatures of the full integer signature and use the following names for the corresponding classes of constants:

1. the empty signature gives rise to *copy constants*;
2. the signature $\{+, -\}$ gives rise to *Presburger constants*.
3. the signature $\{+, -, *\}$ gives rise to *polynomial constants*; and
4. the full integer signature $\{+, -, *, \underline{\text{div}}, \underline{\text{mod}}\}$ gives rise to *full integer constants*.[1]

The one remaining class is the class of *linear constants* which has previously been studied in the literature [83]. It lies between the classes of copy constants and Presburger constants. In linear-constant detection all expressions of the form $a * x + b$, where a and b are integers and x is a program variable, are interpreted in addition to non-composite expressions.

Finally, in the third dimension we vary the general nature of the constant-propagation problem. Besides the standard *must-constancy* problem we consider the less frequently addressed problem of *may-constancy*. Essentially, this problem asks if a variable may evaluate to a given constant c at a given program point in some program execution. Inspired by the work of Muth and Debray [69] we further distinguish between a *single-value* and a

---

[1] The results remain valid if we abandon the $\underline{\text{mod}}$ operator. Note that $\underline{\text{mod}}$ can be expressed by the other operators by means of the identity $x \underline{\text{mod}} y = x - x * (x \underline{\text{div}} y)$ for $x \geq 0$, $y > 0$.

multiple-value variant, where in the latter case the values of multiple variables are checked simultaneously. While the most prominent application of must-constant propagation is compile-time simplification of expressions, both must- and may-variants are equally well suited for eliminating unnecessary branches in programs. Furthermore, the may-variant leads to insight in the complexity of (may-)aliasing of array elements. It has also strong connections to reachability analysis, a topic that has found much attention in recent years in the model checking community.

Combination of the second and third dimension of the taxonomy gives rise to 15 different classes of constants. We succeed in almost completely characterizing the complexity of detecting these classes of constants in general (non-deterministic) flow graphs as well as in loop-free flow graphs. Only two questions remain open, both concern general flow graphs: (1) we miss an upper bound for linear may-constants and (2) the upper and lower bound for polynomial must-constants do not coincide.

Constant Propagation Via Effective Weakest Preconditions

There are two motivations for research that classifies the complexity for subclasses of analysis problems. On the theoretical side, we hope to increase our understanding of the tradeoff between efficiency and precision for analysis problems that can be solved only approximately. On the practical side, we hope to uncover potential for construction of more powerful analysis algorithms. Indeed, perhaps the most interesting results of our study of the constant taxonomy are the following two findings that uncover algorithmic potential (Chapter 3).

The first finding is that the detection of Presburger constants is tractable, i.e. can be done in polynomial time; the second is that polynomial constants are decidable. The latter result is particularly interesting because full constants are undecidable as we have seen above. So the division operator is identified as the source of non-decidability. For showing decidability of polynomial constants we apply results from computable ring theory.

The detection algorithms for Presburger and polynomial constants proposed in this monograph use an indirect three phase approach. In the first phase a candidate value is computed that is verified in the second and third phase by means of a *symbolic weakest-precondition computation*. The algorithms are obtained by instantiating a generic algorithm for the construction of approximate constant-propagation algorithms that are complete with respect to evaluation of a subset of expressions. We describe the general algorithmic idea of constant propagation via symbolic weakest-precondition computation and analyze the demands for making this general algorithmic idea effective. Assertions are represented by affine subspaces of $\mathbb{Q}^n$ for Presburger constants and by ideals in the polynomial ring $\mathbb{Z}[x_1, \ldots, x_n]$ for polynomial constants.

Limits for the Analysis of Parallel Programs

While the first part is concerned with analysis of *sequential* programs, the bulk of this monograph is concerned with analysis of *parallel* programs. Automatic analysis of parallel programs is known as a notoriously hard problem. A well-known obstacle is the so-called *state-explosion problem*: the number of (control) states of a parallel program grows exponentially with the number of parallel components. Some results that are rather surprising in view of the state-explosion problem have been the starting point for the considerations in this monograph: certain basic but important dataflow-analysis problems can still be solved completely and efficiently for programs with a fork/join kind of parallelism. Let us briefly report on these results before we describe our contribution.

Knoop, Steffen, and Vollmer [44] show that *bit-vector analyses*, which comprise, e.g., live/dead variables, available expressions, and reaching definitions [56], can efficiently be performed on such programs. Knoop shows in [41] that a simple variant of constant detection, that of so-called *strong constants*, is tractable as well. These papers restrict attention to the *intraprocedural* problem, in which each procedure body is analyzed separately with worst case assumption on called procedures. Seidl and Steffen [85] generalize these results to the interprocedural case in which the interplay between procedures is taken into account and to a slightly more extensive class of dataflow problems called *gen/kill problems*. These papers extend the fixpoint computation technique common in data flow analysis to parallel programs.

Another line of research applies automata-theoretic techniques that originally have been developed for the verification of so-called *PA-processes (Process-Algebra Processes)* [5, 51, 7, 47], a certain class of infinite-state processes combining sequentiality and parallelism. Specifically, Esparza and Knoop [18], and Esparza and Podelski [19] demonstrate how live variables analysis can be done and indicate that other bit-vector analyses can be approached in a similar fashion.

Can these results be generalized further to considerably richer classes of dataflow problems? For answering this question we investigate the complexity of exact copy-constant detection in parallel programs. Intuitively, copy-constant detection which is closely related to analysis of static dependences represents the next level of difficulty of dataflow problems beyond gen/kill problems. In the sequential setting, copy-constant are detected by a *distributive* dataflow framework on a lattice with chain height two and can thus—by a classic result of Kildall [40, 56]—completely and efficiently be solved by a fixpoint computation.

We show in Chapter 4 by means of a reduction from the halting problem for two-counter machines that copy-constant detection is undecidable in parallel programs with procedures (parallel interprocedural analysis). Moreover, we show PSPACE-completeness in case that there are no procedure calls (parallel intraprocedural analysis), and co-NP-completeness if also loops are abandoned (parallel acyclic analysis). The latter results rely on reductions from the intersection problem for regular and star-free regular expressions, respectively. These results render the possibility of complete and efficient dataflow algorithms for parallel programs for more extensive classes of analyses unlikely even for loop-free programs, as it is generally believed that the inclusions $P \subseteq (\text{co-})NP \subseteq PSPACE$ are proper.

Let us be a bit more specific about the setting in which these results are obtained. We consider a prototypic language of explictly parallel programs. The threads operate on a shared memory via assignment statements of a very restricted form:[2] constant assignments $x := 0$ and $x := 1$ for two distinct constants 0 and 1, and copying assignments $x := y$. Any sensible concurrent programming language that allows threads to access a shared memory provides such statements and therefore our hardness results are applicable to many scenarios. The language allows us to form composed statements by means of *sequential composition* ;, *parallel composition* $\|$, and *non-deterministic branching* $\sqcap$. Moreover, there is a *loop construct* **loop** π **end**, that executes the loop body π an indefinite number of times. The non-deterministic branching and indefinite loop constructs are chosen in accordance with the abstraction of guarded to non-deterministic branching mentioned above. Parallelism is understood in an interleaving fashion; assignment statements are assumed to execute atomically.

In the *intraprocedural* setting we consider analysis in statements of the form described above; in the *loop-free* case we abandon the loop statement. In the *interprocedural* setting we consider programs consisting of procedures, the body of which consist of statements of the form outlined above. Of course, procedures may also (recursively) call each other. A terminological remark is in order here. Whenever we speak of interprocedural analysis, we implicitly imply that the analysis takes properly into account the call/return behavior of procedures, i.e., we always assume that a dynamic instance of a procedure entered at a certain call site returns to that same call sites. In the traditional parlance of the flow-analysis literature one says that only *realizable paths* are considered and that the analysis is *context-sensitive*. In the literature also so-called *context-insensitive interprocedural analyses* are considered. Such analyses do not properly mirror the call/return behavior but pessimistically assume that a procedure called at a certain call site may return to any other call site. Clearly, this leads to sound but in general less precise analysis results. In this monograph we always imply that interprocedural problems only involve realizable paths. Thus, we reserve the term *interprocedural* analysis or problem for *context-sensitive interprocedural* analysis or problem, respectively.

---

[2] Just for presentational convenience and clarity two other types of basic statements are considered in addition: the do-nothing statement **skip** and write-statements **write**(e).

The results of Chapter 4 should be contrasted with complexity and undecidability results of Taylor [91] and Ramalingam [77] who consider *synchronization-dependent* dataflow analyses of parallel programs, i.e. analyses that are precise with respect to the synchronization structure of programs. Taylor and Ramalingam largely exploit the strength of rendezvous-style synchronization, while we exploit interference only here and no kind of synchronization. Our results thus point to a much more fundamental limitation in dataflow analysis of parallel programs.

In order to perform our reductions without relying on synchronization we use a subtle technique involving re-initialization of variables. In all reductions programs are constructed in such a way that certain *well-behaved runs* simulate some intended behavior, e.g., the execution sequences of the given two-counter machine in the undecidability proof. But we cannot avoid that the constructed programs have also certain runs that bear no correspondence to the behavior to be simulated. One would use synchronization to exclude such *spurious runs* but in the absence of synchronization primitives this is not possible. In order to solve this problem, we ensure by well-directed re-initialization of variables that the spurious runs do not contribute to propagation of the information that is to be determined by the analysis. Intuitively, one may interpret this as a kind of "internal synchronization".

The prototypic framework poses only rather weak requirement such the results apply to many concurrent programming languages. One additional remark concerning the parallel composition operator is in order here. It is inherent in the definition of parallel composition that $\pi_1 \parallel \pi_2$ terminates if and when both threads π_1 and π_2 terminate (like, for instance, in OC-CAM [33]). This means that there is an implicit synchronization between π_1 and π_2 at the termination point. However, as explained in Section 4.6, the hardness results remain valid without this assumption. Therefore, they also apply to languages like JAVA in which spawned threads run and terminate independently of the spawning thread.

Abandoning the Atomic Execution Assumption

Another standard assumption turns out to be more critical: atomic execution of assignments. The idealization that assignments execute atomically is quite common in the literature on program verification as well as in the theoretical literature on flow analysis of parallel programs. However, in a multi-processor environment where a number of concurrently executing processes access a shared memory, this is often an unrealistic assumption. The reason is that assignments are broken into smaller instructions before execution. This is explained in more detail in Chapter 6.

Surprisingly, the reductions of Chapter 4 break down when the atomic execution assumption for assignment statements is abandoned. Without this assumption the subtle game of re-initialization of variables that is crucial for putting the reductions to work can no longer be played. This is illustrated by means of an example program in Section 6.2. Of course, this does not imply that the hardness results are no longer valid: there could be reductions employing other techniques. But we can indeed show, that interprocedural detection of copy constants and faint-code elimination becomes decidable. Specifically, we develop EXPTIME-algorithms for these problems. Recall that these problems are undecidable under the assumption that assignments execute atomically. So, the (unrealistic) idealization from program verification "atomic execution of assignment statements" that presumably simplifies matters actually increases the difficulty of these problems from the program analysis point of view: amazingly, these problems become more tractable if we adopt a less idealized, more realistic view of execution. The presentation of these results is spread over Chapters 5 to 8 as it is technically somewhat involved. In the following we give a high-level overview and introduction to these chapters.

In our algorithms we apply the constraint-based approach to program analysis. Constraint-based program analysis provides a framework to develop analyses and argue about their correctness and completeness. Put in a nutshell, the idea is to set up constraint systems that characterize sets of program executions and to perform the analysis by solving these constraint systems over a lattice of abstract values. Appendix A explains this in more detail.

Constraint-based analysis of *parallel programs* has been pioneered by Seidl and Steffen [85]. In order to come to grips with parallel composition, new operators on run sets are used that are not needed in systems for sequential programs. The new operators are an interleaving operator $\otimes$ and prefix and postfix operators *pre* and *post*. In general, it is not possible to give adequate interpretations of these new operations for arbitrary dataflow frameworks. Seidl and Steffen show, however, that for gen/kill dataflow problems this can be done. Note that the copy-constant framework does *not* belong to this class.

In Chapter 5 we define parallel flow graphs, furnish them with an operational semantics, and define constraint systems characterizing various sets of runs: same-level and inverse-same-level runs, reaching and terminating runs, and bridging runs. For the moment, we still assume atomic execution of base statements. While same-level and reaching runs are already found in Seidl and Steffen's exposition, and they indicate that inverse-same-level and terminating runs can be obtained by duality, bridging runs are new. Moreover, in contrast to Seidl and Steffen we relate the constraint systems to the underlying operational semantics instead of postulating them. In our opinion this clarifies what exactly is specified by the constraint systems. It also helped to uncover and correct a subtle error in their treatment of non-reachable program points. While an understanding of the other sets of runs is not needed in the remainder of this introduction, we must explain bridging runs.

In a bridging run we are given two program points u and v. A bridging run from a program point u to another program point v is a sequence of atomic actions that can bring us from a configuration in which control is at program point u to a configuration in which control is at program point v. Why are we interested in bridging runs? We call a pair of program variables (x, y) a *dependence* and say that a given run *exhibits* the dependence (x, y) if the value of y after the run depends on the value of x before the run, where we judge dependences syntactically. If we are able to determine the dependences exhibited by bridging runs then we can use this information to indirectly answer certain program analysis questions. In particular, this information suffices to detect copy constants and faint code.

In Chapter 6 we explain why atomic execution is not a realistic assumption on program execution and motivate and define a non-standard interpretation for the operators and constants used in the constraint systems for parallel programs. This non-standard interpretation captures non-atomic execution of base statements. The idea is to break base statements into atomic actions of smaller granularity and to use an interleaving semantics on these atomic actions. By interpreting the constraint systems from Chapter 5 with the new interpretation, we get run sets that capture non-atomic execution of base statements. These run sets are taken as the reference semantics for judging the precision of our algorithms for copy-constant detection and faint-code elimination.

Unfortunately, we cannot obtain the dependences of the interleaving $R_1 \otimes R_2$ of two (non-atomic) run sets from the dependences of the two run sets R_1 and R_2: we can invent run sets that have the same dependences but behave differently when interleaved with other run sets. Therefore, we need a more informative abstract domain that records more information than just dependences. This domain is the topic of Chapter 7. Here we give a rough description of the underlying ideas.

The basic idea is to collect not just dependences but *dependence sequences*. A dependence sequence of a run is a sequence of dependences that can be exhibited successively by the run. For example, the run $r_1 = \langle c := b, e := d \rangle$ has $\langle (b, c), (d, e) \rangle$ as one of its dependence sequences. This dependence sequence plays a dual role: it captures, on the one hand, the potential of r_1 to exhibit the dependence (b, e) if its environment can fill the 'gap' between c and d (e.g., if the environment can perform the run $r_2 = \langle d := c \rangle$) and, on the other hand, its potential to successively fill the 'gaps' (b, c) and (d, e) in a run of the environment (e.g., in $r_3 = \langle b := a, d := c, f := e \rangle$). This idea needs to be refined further in order to allow a proper propagation through all the operators: we must also collect information about transparency of runs. This leads to the notion of *dependence traces*. Moreover, we need to ensure finiteness of the domain in order to ensure that least fixpoints can be computed effectively. The latter problem is solved by introducing first, a subsumption order on dependence traces and, secondly, a notion of shortness of dependence traces. We then work with antichains (with respect to the subsumption order) of short dependence traces. In Chapter 7 we show that one can define on this abstract domain operations that are both sound and precise abstractions of the corresponding operations on non-atomic run sets.

By solving the constraint system for bridging runs over the abstract domain introduced in Chapter 5, we can determine in particular the dependences exhibited by bridging runs. As mentioned, this information can be used to detect copy constants and eliminate faint code. Algorithms based on this idea that solve these problems are developed in Chapter 8 and their running time is analyzed. These algorithms prove that we can detect copy constants and eliminate faint code in parallel programs completely, if we abandon the assumption that base statements execute atomically.

The algorithms run in exponential time, which raises the question whether there are also efficient algorithms for these problems. In Chapter 9 we show by means of a reduction from the well-known SAT-problem that the answer is 'no', unless P=NP. Unlike the reductions in Chapter 4, this reduction relies only on active propagation along copying assignments but not on well-directed re-initialization. It applies independently of the atomicity assumption for base statements. In the conclusions, Chapter 10, we sketch possible remedies and discuss directions for future research that may still lead to algorithms of practical interest.

2. A Hierarchy of Constants

Constant propagation aims at detecting expressions in programs that always yield a unique constant value at run-time. Replacing constant expressions by their value is one of the most widely used optimizations in practice (cf. [2, 30, 56]). Unfortunately, the constant propagation problem is undecidable even if the interpretation of branches is completely ignored, like in the common model of non-deterministic flow graphs where every program path is considered executable. This has been proved independently by Hecht [30] and by Reif and Lewis [78]. We discussed Reif and Lewis' proof in the introduction. Here we briefly recall Hecht's proof because we will encounter variants of his construction later in this chapter. It is based on the Post correspondence problem.

A Post correspondence system consists of a set of pairs $(u_1, v_1), \ldots, (u_k, v_k)$ with $u_i, v_i \in \{0, 1\}^*$. The correspondence system has a solution, if and only if there is a sequence $i_1, \ldots, i_n$ such that $u_{i_1} \cdot \ldots \cdot u_{i_n} = v_{i_1} \cdot \ldots \cdot v_{i_n}$. Figure 2.1 illustrates Hecht's reduction. The variables x and y are used as decimal numbers representing strings in $\{0, 1\}^*$. For each pair of the correspondence system a distinct branch of the loop appends the strings u_i and v_i to x and y, respectively. This is achieved by shifting the digits of x and y by $|u_i|$ and $|v_i|$ places first by multiplying them with $10^{|u_i|}$ and $10^{|v_i|}$, where $|u_i|$ and $|v_i|$ are the length of u_i and v_i. Afterwards, we add u_i and v_i where we identify u_i and v_i with the decimal number they represent. It is easy to see that $x - y$ always evaluates to a value different from 0, if the Post correspondence problem has no solution.[1] In this case the expression 1 $\underline{\text{div}}$ $((x - y)^2 + 1)$ always evaluates to 0. But if the Post correspondence system is solvable, the expression $x - y$ can have the value 0 such that 1 $\underline{\text{div}}$ $((x - y)^2 + 1)$ can evaluate to 1. Thus, r is constant (with value 0), if and only if the Post correspondence problem is not solvable. To exclude r from being constantly 1 in the case that the Post correspondence system is universally solvable, r is set to 0 by a bypassing assignment statement.

On the other hand, constant detection is certainly decidable for *acyclic*, i.e., loop-free, programs. But even in this setting the problem is intractable; it has been shown to be co-NP-hard [42] recently. This result is based on

---

[1] Note that the initialization of x and y with 1 avoids a problem with leading zeros.

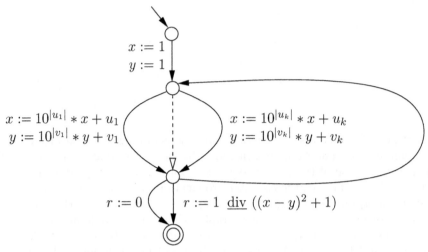

Fig. 2.1. Undecidability of constant propagation: the reduction of Hecht.

a polynomial-time reduction of the co-problem of 3-SAT, the *satisfiability* problem for clauses which are conjunctions consisting of three negated or unnegated Boolean variables (cf. [22, 72]). An instance of 3-SAT is solvable if there is a variable assignment such that every clause is satisfied.

The reduction is illustrated in Figure 2.2 for a 3-SAT instance over the Boolean variables $\{b_1, \ldots, b_k\}$:

$$\underbrace{(b_3 \vee \overline{b_5} \vee b_6)}_{c_1} \wedge \ldots \wedge \underbrace{(b_2 \vee \overline{b_3} \vee b_5)}_{c_n}.$$

For each Boolean variable b_i two integer variables x_i and $\overline{x_i}$ are introduced that are initialized by 0. The idea underlying the reduction is the following: each path of the program chooses a witnessing literal in each clause by setting the corresponding variable to 1. If this can be done without setting both x_i and $\overline{x_i}$ for some i then we have found a satisfying truth assignment, and vice versa. On such a path the expression $x_1\overline{x_1} + \ldots + x_k\overline{x_k}$ evaluates to 0 and, consequently, both r_1 and r_2 are set to 0. On all other paths the value of $x_1\overline{x_1} + \ldots + x_k\overline{x_k}$ differs from 0 but stays in the range $\{1, \ldots, k\}$ which implies that variable r_2 is set to 1. Similarly to the undecidability reduction of Figure 2.1 the bypassing assignment $r_1 := 1$ avoids that r_1 is constantly 0 in the case that all runs induce satisfying truth assignments. Summarizing, r_2 is a constant (of value 1), i.e., evaluates to 1 on every program path if and only if the underlying instance of 3-SAT has no solution.

Note that both reductions presented so far crucially depend on an operator like integer division (or modulo) which is capable of projecting many different values onto a single one.

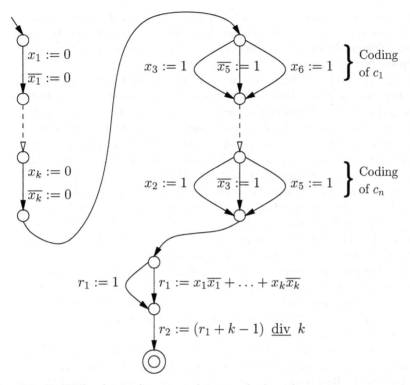

Fig. 2.2. Co-NP-hardness of constant detection for loop-free programs

The purpose of this and the following chapter is to examine the borderline of intractability and undecidability more closely. To this end, we investigate the constant detection problem for non-deterministic flow graphs working on integers with respect to a three-dimensional taxonomy. This taxonomy has been introduced in a conference paper [60] where also the reductions of this chapter have first been presented.

The first dimension of the taxonomy is given by the distinction between arbitrary and loop-free flow graphs. The second dimension introduces a hierarchy of weakened versions of the constant propagation problem. In these variants only assignment statements whose right hand side belongs to a given subset S of expressions are interpreted exactly. Assignment statements of other form are conservatively interpreted as non-deterministic assignments. We consider expression sets S that are given by restricting the set of integer operators that are allowed in expression building. We consider signatures without operators (*copy constants*), with operators restricted to the set $\{+, -\}$ (*Presburger constants*), operators restricted to $\{+, -, *\}$ (*polynomial constants*), and the standard signature, i.e., the one with operators $+, -, *, \underline{\text{div}}, \underline{\text{mod}}$ (*full constants*). Moreover, we consider linear expressions in one variable, i.e., expressions of the form $x := ay + b$ because the associated class of constants, *linear constants*, has previously been studied in the literature [83]. Obviously, the class of linear constants lies between copy constants and Presburger constants.

Finally, in the third dimension we vary the general nature of the constant detection problem. Besides the standard *must-constancy* problem we also consider the less frequently addressed problem of *may-constancy* here. Essentially, this problem asks if a variable may evaluate to a given constant d at some given program point. Inspired by work of Muth and Debray [69] we further distinguish between a *single value* and a *multiple value* variant, where in the latter case the values of multiple variables are questioned simultaneously. Muth and Debray introduced the single and multiple value variants as models for independent-attribute and relational-attribute dataflow analyses [37]. May-constant detection, in particular the multiple value variant, is closely related to reachability of program, a problem that has found much attention recently in the model checking community.

While the most prominent application of must-constant detection is the *compile-time simplification* of expressions, the must- and may-variants are equally well suited for eliminating unnecessary branches in programs. Furthermore, the may-variant has some interesting consequences for the complexity of (may-)aliasing of array elements.

In this chapter we introduce this taxonomy of constants formally, discuss the results that are known or obvious and present a number of new intractability and undecidability results that sharpen previous results. In the next chapter we show decidability of polynomial must-constants and polynomial-time decidability of Presburger must-constants.

2.1 A Taxonomy of Constants

2.1.1 Flow Graphs

Let $X = \{x_1, \ldots, x_n\}$ be a finite set of variables and Expr a set of expressions over X; the precise nature of expressions is immaterial at the moment. A (deterministic) assignment is a pair consisting of a variable and an expression written in the form $x := t$; the set of assignment statements is denoted by Asg. A non-deterministic assignment statement consists of a variable and is written $x :=?$; the set of non-deterministic assignment statements is denoted by NAsg.

A (non-deterministic) flow graph is a structure $G = (N, E, A, \mathbf{s}, \mathbf{e})$ with finite node set N, edge set $E \subseteq N \times N$, a unique start node $\mathbf{s} \in N$, and a unique end node $\mathbf{e} \in N$. We assume that each program point $u \in N$ lies on a path from $\mathbf{s}$ to $\mathbf{e}$. The mapping $A : E \rightarrow$ Asg $\cup$ NAsg $\cup$ {**skip**} associates each edge with a deterministic or non-deterministic assignment statement or with the statement **skip**. Edges represent the branching structure and the statements of a program, while nodes represent program points. The set of successors of program point $u \in N$ is denoted by $Succ[u] = \{v \mid (u, v) \in E\}$.

A *path* reaching a given program point $u \in N$ is a non-empty sequence of edges $p = \langle e_1, \ldots, e_k \rangle$ with $e_i = (u_i, v_i) \in E$ such that $u_1 = \mathbf{s}$, $v_k = u$, and $v_i = u_{i+1}$ for $1 \leq i < k$. In addition $p = \varepsilon$, the empty sequence, is a path reaching the start node $\mathbf{s}$. We write $R[u]$ for the set of paths reaching u.

Let Val be a set of values. A mapping $\sigma : X \to$ Val that assigns a value to each variable is called a *state*; we write $\Sigma = \{\sigma \mid \sigma : X \to$ Val$\}$ for the set of states. For $x \in X$, $d \in$ Val and $\sigma \in \Sigma$, we write $\sigma[x \mapsto d]$ for the state that maps x to d and coincides for the other variables with σ. We assume a fixed interpretation for the operators used in terms and we assume that the value of term t in state σ, which we denote by t^σ, is defined in the standard way.

In order to accommodate non-deterministic assignments we interpret statements by relations on Σ rather than functions. The relation associated with assignment statement $x := t$ is $[\![x := t]\!] \stackrel{\text{def}}{=} \{(\sigma, \sigma') \mid \sigma' = \sigma[x \mapsto t^\sigma]\}$; the relation associated with non-deterministic assignment $x :=?$ is $[\![x :=?]\!] \stackrel{\text{def}}{=} \{(\sigma, \sigma') \mid \exists d \in$ Val $: \sigma' = \sigma[x \mapsto d]\}$; and the relation associated with **skip** is the identity: $[\![\mathbf{skip}]\!] \stackrel{\text{def}}{=} \{(\sigma, \sigma') \mid \sigma = \sigma'\}$. This local interpretation of statements is straightforwardly extended to paths $p = \langle e_1, \ldots, e_k \rangle \in E^*$: $[\![p]\!] = [\![A(e_1)]\!] ; \ldots ; [\![A(e_k)]\!]$, where ; denotes relational composition. We obtain the set of states $S[u]$, which are possible at a program point $u \in N$ as follows: $S[u] \stackrel{\text{def}}{=} \{\sigma \mid \exists \sigma_0 \in \Sigma, p \in R[u] : (\sigma_0, \sigma) \in [\![p]\!]\}$. The state σ_0 represents the unknown initial state—the state in which the program is started—which models the input to the program.

2.1.2 May- and Must-Constants

In this section we define when a variable x is a constant at a program point u in a given flow graph. We distinguish between must-constants and the less frequently considered class of may-constants. May-constants come in two variants: as single and multiple value may-constants. We provide formal definitions as well as some typical application scenarios. For simplicity, we restrict attention to constancy of variables in our formal framework. In practice also constancy of expressions is of interest. Our definitions can straightforwardly be extended to this more general case and in discussing applications we assume that this has been done. All our results apply also to this more general setting as constancy of expressions is easily reduced to constancy of variables: if we are interested in constancy of an expression e at a program point u we can add an assignment $v := e$ to a new variable v at u and question for constancy of v.

Must-Constants A variable $x \in X$ is a *must-constant* at a program point $u \in N$ if

$$\exists d \in \text{Val } \forall \sigma \in S[u] : \sigma(x) = d .$$

The problem of *must-constant detection* is to determine for a given variable x and program point u, whether x is a must-constant, and, if so, what the value of the constant is.

Must-constancy information can be used in various ways. The most important application is the *compile-time simplification* of expressions. Furthermore, information on must-constancy can be exploited in order to eliminate conditional branches. For instance, if there is a condition $e \neq d$ situated at an edge leaving node n and e is determined a must-constant of value d at node n, then this branch is not executable (cf. Figure 2.3(a)) and may be removed. Since (must-)constant detection and the elimination of unexecutable branches mutually benefit from each other, approaches for *conditional constant propagation* were developed taking this effect into account [93, 9].

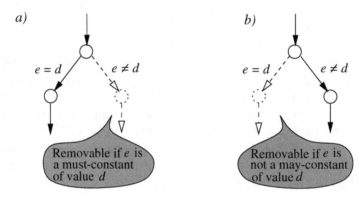

Fig. 2.3. Constancy information used for branch elimination.

May-Constants Complementary to must-constancy, a variable $x \in X$ is a *may-constant* of value $d \in \mathbb{Z}$ at a program point $u \in N$ if

$$\exists \sigma \in S[u] : \ \sigma(x) = d \, .$$

Note that opposed to the must-constancy definition here the value of the constant is given as an additional input parameter. There is a natural *multiple value* extension of the notion of may-constancy. Given variables $x_1, \ldots, x_k$ and values $d_1, \ldots, d_k \in \mathbb{Z}$ the corresponding multiple value may-constancy problem is defined by:

$$\exists \sigma \in S[u] : \ \sigma(x_1) = d_1 \ \wedge \ \ldots \ \wedge \ \sigma(x_k) = d_k \, .$$

While may-constancy information cannot be used for expression simplification, it has also some valuable applications. Most obvious is a complementary branch elimination transformation. If an expression e is not a may-constant of value d at node n then any branch that is guarded by the condition $e = d$ is unexecutable (cf. Figure 2.3(b)).

May-constancy information is also valuable for reasoning about aliasing of array elements. This can be used, for instance, for parallelization of code or for improving the precision of other analyses by excluding a worst-case treatment of assignments to elements in an array. Figure 2.4 gives such an example in the context of constant propagation. Here the assignment to x can be simplified towards $x := 6$, only if the assignment to $a[i]$ does not influence $a[0]$. This, however, can be guaranteed if i is not a may-constant of value 0 at the corresponding program node.

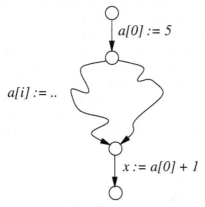

Fig. 2.4. Using array alias information from may-constant detection in the context of must-constant propagation.

2.1.3 Weakened Constant Detection Problems

We can weaken the demands for a constant detection algorithm as follows: we select a certain subset of expressions $S \subseteq$ Expr that are interpreted precisely and assume conservatively that assignments whose right hand side does not belong to S assign an arbitrary value to their respective target variable. This can be made formal as follows.

For a given flow graph $G = (N, E, A, \mathbf{s}, \mathbf{e})$ and subset of expressions $S \subseteq$ Expr, let $G_S = (N, E, A_S, \mathbf{s}, \mathbf{e})$ be the flow graph with the same underlying graph but with the following weakened edge annotation:

$$A_S(e) = \begin{cases} x :=?, & \text{if } A(e) = (x := t) \text{ and } t \notin S \\ A(e), & \text{otherwise}. \end{cases}$$

A variable $x \in X$ is called an *S-must-constant (S-may-constant)* at program point $u \in N$ in flow graph G if it is a must-constant (may-constant) at u in the weakened flow graph G_S. The *detection problem for S-must-constants (S-may-constants)* is the problem of deciding for a given set of variables X, flow graph G, variable x, and program point u whether x is an S-must-constant (S-may-constant) at u in G. Clearly, if x is an S-must-constant at u it is also a must-constant at u. Similarly, if x is not an S-may-constant at u it is not a may-constant at u. In both cases the reverse implication does not hold in general. Thus, an analysis that solves a weakened constant-detection problem yields sound information for must-constancy and non-may-constancy in the original flow graph.

We should emphasize two points about the above framework that make the construction of S-constant-detection algorithms more challenging. Firstly, in contrast to the setup in [60], we allow assignment statements, the right hand side of which do not belong to S. They are interpreted as non-deterministic assignments. Forbidding them is adequate for studying lower complexity bounds for analysis questions, which is the main concern of [60]. It is less adequate when we are interested in algorithms because in practice we want to detect S-constants in the context of other code.

Secondly, a variable can be an S-constant although its value statically depends on an expression that is not in S. As a simple example consider the flow graph in Fig. 2.5 and assume that the expressions 0 and $y - y$ belong to S but e does not.

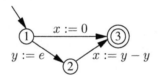

Fig. 2.5. Static dependency and S-constancy: variable x is an S-constant at program point 3 although it statically depends on the uninterpreted expression e.

Because $y - y$ equals 0 for any value $y \in \mathbb{Z}$, an S-must-constant detection algorithm must identify x as a must-constant (of value 0) at program point 3, although the value of x at program point 3 statically depends on the uninterpreted expression e. Besides cancellation through subtraction such effects arise through multiplication with terms evaluating to zero. Hence, S-constant detection algorithms must handle arithmetic properties of the expressions in S. Of course, in real programs cancellation through arithmetic properties may not be as obvious as in this example.

There are at least two other natural definitions for a notion of S-constant propagation:

1. We can study constant propagation in flow graphs whose edge annotation is restricted to assignments from $S \cup \{\textbf{skip}\}$; this is the setup in [60].
2. We can treat the effect of assignments whose right hand side does not belong to S more pessimistically: if the value of x at u statically depends on an uninterpreted assignment, we may define that

− x is not a must-constant at u and that
− x is a may-constant at u for any value d.
This definition also leads to a conservative approximation of must- and non-may constancy, but is weaker than our definition as demonstrated by the above example.

From all the potential definitions our definition requires most from an S-constant-propagation algorithm. Firstly, it must handle more inputs than with Definition 1. Secondly, an S-constant-propagation algorithm in the sense of 2 can easily be obtained from an algorithm in our sense. We only need to combine it in a straightforward way with a static dependence analysis. The latter can be performed by a cheap bit-vector analysis [30, 56]. On the other hand, Definition 1 poses in principle the strongest requirements for hardness considerations. Fortunately, all our reductions use only statements from $S \cup \{\mathbf{skip}\}$. Therefore, all our results apply to all three definitions.

2.1.4 Classes of Integer Constants

To study weakened versions of constant-detection problems is particularly interesting for programs computing on the integers, i.e., if Expr is the set of integer expressions formed from integer constants and variables with the standard operators $+, -, *, \underline{\mathrm{div}}, \underline{\mathrm{mod}}$: we have seen above that the general constant-detection problem is undecidable in this case.

We introduce now weakened classes of integer constants. Except for linear constants these classes are induced by considering only a fragment of the standard signature. While the first two classes are well-known in the field of (must-) constant propagation and the class of Presburger constants is closely related to the class of invariants considered in [39], we are not aware of any work devoted to the fragment of polynomial constants prior to our conference papers [60, 62].

Copy Constants. S-constants with respect to the set $S = X \cup \mathbb{Z}$, i.e., the set of non-composite expressions, are known as *copy constants* [20]. This is due to the fact that constants can only be produced by assignments $x := c$ and be propagated by assignments of the form $x := y$.

Linear Constants. S-constants with respect to the set $S = \{a * x + b \mid a, b \in \mathbb{Z}, x \in X\} \cup X \cup \mathbb{Z}$ are known as *linear constants* [83].

Presburger Constants. A *Presburger constant* is an S-constant for the set S of integer expressions that can be built from the operators $+$ and $-$. We decided for this term because in Presburger arithmetics integer operations are also restricted to addition and subtraction. Note, however, that the complexity issues in deciding Presburger formulas and Presburger constants are of a completely different nature, since in the context of constant detection the problem is mainly induced by paths in flow graphs and not by a given logical formula. We call S-constants with respect to the set

$S = \{c_0 + \sum_{i=1}^{k} c_i * x_i \mid c_j \in \mathbb{Z}, x_i \in X\}$ *affine constants*. As far as expressiveness is concerned Presburger expressions and affine expressions coincide because multiplication with constants can be simulated by iterated addition. Affine expressions can, however, be more succinct. Nevertheless, all our results on Presburger constants equally apply to affine constants and from now on we do not distinguish these two classes of constants.

Polynomial Constants. If all expressions built from the operators $+, -, *$ are interpreted, the resulting constants are called *polynomial constants* as this signature allows just to write multi-variate polynomials. Formally, polynomial constants are S-constants with respect to the set $S = \mathbb{Z}[x_1, \ldots, x_n]$, the set of multi-variate polynomials in the variables $x_1, \ldots, x_n$ with coefficients in $\mathbb{Z}$.

2.2 Known Results

Table 2.1 summarizes the complexity results that are known or obvious. Problems that have a polynomial-time algorithm are emphasized in a light shade of grey, those that are decidable though intractable in a dark shade of grey, and the undecidable fields are filled black. White fields represent problems where the complexity and decidability is unknown or at least, to the best of our knowledge, undocumented. In the following we briefly comment on these results.

For an unrestricted signature we already presented Hecht's undecidability proof for must-constants and the co-NP-hardness result for the acyclic counterpart. It is also well-known that the must-constant detection problem is distributive [30], if all right-hand side expressions are either constant or represent a one-to-one function in $\mathbb{Z} \to \mathbb{Z}$ depending on a single variable (see the remark on page 206 in [86] for a similar observation). Hence the class of linear constants defines a distributive dataflow problem, which guarantees that the standard maximum fixed-point iteration strategy over $\mathbb{Z} \cup \{\bot, \top\}$ computes the exact solution in polynomial time.[2]

The may-constancy problem for copy constants has recently been examined by Muth and Debray [69]. It is easy to see that the single value case can be dealt with in polynomial-time: the number of values that a variable may possess at a program point (via copy or constant assignments) is bounded by the number of constant assignments in the program. Hence one can determine the may-copy-constants by collecting at each program point for all of the variables the set of possible values from this set. Formally, this can be achieved by computing the union-over-all-path solution in a union-distributive dataflow framework over the lattice $\{\sigma \mid \sigma : Var \to 2^{\mathbb{Z}_G}\}$, where $\mathbb{Z}_G$ denotes the set

---

[2] Sagiv, Reps and Horwitz [83] give an alternative procedure for detecting linear constants by solving a graph reachability problem on the *exploded supergraph* of a program. They additionally show that with this method linear constant detection can be solved precisely even for interprocedural control flow.

Table 2.1. Complexity of constant detection: known results.

| | | Must–Constants | May–Constants | |
			single value	multiple value
acyclic control flow	Copy Constants	P	P	**NP–complete** Muth & Debray [69]
	Linear Constants	P Sharir & Pnueli [86]		
	Presburger Constants			
	+,–,* Constants			
	Full Constants	**Co–NP hard** Knoop & Rüthing [42]		
unrestricted control flow	Copy Constants	P	P	**PSPACE–compl.** Muth & Debray [69]
	Linear Constants	P Sharir & Pnueli [86]		
	Presburger Constants			
	+,–,* Constants			
	Full Constants	**undecidable** Hecht [30]		

of constant right-hand sides in the flow graph G under consideration and the order on functions is the pointwise lift of subset inclusion on $2^{\mathbb{Z}_G}$.

The multiple value problem has been shown NP-complete in the acyclic case and PSPACE-complete in the presence of unrestricted control flow by Muth and Debray [69]. For proving NP-hardness and PSPACE-hardness they use reductions from 3-SAT and the acceptance problem for polynomial-space-bounded Turing machines, respectively. It is worth mentioning that the number of variables questioned simultaneously for constancy in these reductions is not bounded by a fixed constant. Finally, since Muth and Debray do not consider any kind of arithmetics, all other fields in the may-constancy column remain open.

In the following we aim at successively filling the white parts in Table 2.1. To this end, we start with providing new undecidability results and then prove a number of new intractability results. Positive results for the classes of Presburger and polynomial must-constants are presented in Chapter 3.

2.3 New Undecidability Results

Hecht's construction sketched in Fig. 2.1 can easily be adapted for proving undecidability of Presburger may-constants. The only modification is to replace the two assignment to r in Figure 2.1 by a single assignment $r := x - y$. As argued before, x may equal y immediately after leaving the loop, if and only if the instance of the Post correspondence problem has a solution. Hence, in this case $x - y$ may evaluate to 0.

Theorem 2.3.1. *Deciding single valued may-constancy at a program point is undecidable for the class of Presburger constants.*

This construction can be modified further to obtain a stronger undecidability result for the class of multiple value may-constants. Here we have:

Theorem 2.3.2. *Deciding multiple valued may-constancy at a program point is undecidable for the class of linear constants. This even holds if only two values are questioned.*

The idea is to substitute the difference $x - y$ in the assignment to r by a loop which simultaneously decrements x and y. It is easy to see that $x = 0 \land y = 0$ may hold at the end of the resulting program if and only if x may equal y at the end of the main loop.

Complexity of Array Aliasing. The previous two undecidability results have immediate implications for array aliasing, which complements similar results known in the field of pointer induced aliasing [46]. As a consequence of Theorem 2.3.1 we have:

Corollary 2.3.1. *Deciding whether $A[i]$ may alias $A[c]$ for a one-dimensional array A, integer variable i and integer constant c is undecidable, even if i is computed only using the operators $+$ and $-$.*

Theorem 2.3.2 provides a negative result for array accesses with linear index calculations.

Corollary 2.3.2. *Let c_1, c_2 be integer constants and i, j integer variables. Determining whether $A[i, j]$ may alias $A[c_1, c_2]$ for a two-dimensional array A is an undecidable problem even if i, j are computed only with linear assignments of the form $x := a\,y + b$.*

Clearly, x may equal y at the end of the loop in Hecht's construction if and only if the given Post correspondence system has a solution. Thus, the problem to decide whether an array access $A[x]$ may alias another access $A[y]$ just after the loop is also undecidable. This gives us the following result for one-dimensional arrays.

Theorem 2.3.3. *Let i, j be integer variables. Determining whether $A[i]$ may alias $A[j]$ for a one-dimensional array A is an undecidable problem even if i, j are computed only with linear assignments of the form $x := a\,y + b$.*

It should be noted that traditional work on array dependences like the omega test [74, 76] is restricted to scenarios where array elements are addressed by affine functions depending on some index variables of possibly nested for-loops. In this setting the aliasing problem can be stated as an integer linear programming problem which can be solved effectively. In contrast, our results address the more fundamental issue of aliasing in the presence of arbitrary loops.

2.4 New Intractability Results

After having marked off the range of undecidability we prove in this section some intractability results.

We start by strengthening the result on the co-NP-hardness of must-constant detection for acyclic control flow. Here the construction of Figure 2.2 can be modified such that the usage of integer division is no longer necessary. Basically, the trick is to use multiplication by 0 as the projective operation, i.e. as the operation with the power to map many different values onto a single one. In the construction of Figure 2.2 this requires the following modifications (cf. Fig. 2.6).

All variables are now initialized by 1 and the part reflecting the clauses sets the corresponding variables to 0. Finally, the assignments to r_1 and r_2 are substituted by a single assignment $r := (x_1 + \overline{x}_1) \cdot \ldots \cdot (x_k + \overline{x}_k)$ that is bypassed by another assignment $r := 0$. It is easy to see that the instance of 3-SAT has no solution if and only if on every path both x_i and $\overline{x_i}$ are set to 0 for some $i \in \{1, \ldots, k\}$. This, however, guarantees that at least one factor of the right-hand side expression defining r is 0 which then ensures that r is a must-constant of value 0. Finally, the branch performing the assignment $r := 0$ assures that r cannot be a must-constant of any other value. Thus, we have:

Theorem 2.4.1. *Deciding polynomial must-constants in acyclic programs is co-NP-hard.*

On the other hand, it is not hard to see that the problem of must-constant propagation is in co-NP for acyclic control flow. To this end, one has to prove that the co-problem, i.e., checking non-constancy at a program point, is in NP, which is easy to see: a non-deterministic Turing machine can guess two paths through the program witnessing two different values. Since each path is of linear length in the program size and the integer operations can be performed in linear time with respect to the sum of the lengths of the decimal

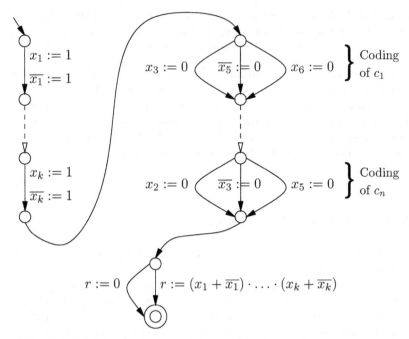

Fig. 2.6. Co-NP-hardness of polynomial constants for acyclic programs.

representation of their inputs, this can be done in polynomial time. Hence we have:

Theorem 2.4.2. *Must-constant propagation is in co-NP when restricted to acyclic control flow.*

Next we are going to show that the problem addressed by Theorem 2.4.1 gets presumably harder without the restriction to acyclic control flow.

Theorem 2.4.3. *Detecting polynomial must-constants in arbitrary flow graphs is PSPACE-hard.*

Theorem 2.4.3 is proved by means of a polynomial time reduction from the language-universality problem of non-deterministic finite automata (NFA) (cf. remark to Problem AL1 in [22]). This is the question whether an NFA $\mathcal{A}$ over an alphabet X accepts the universal language, i.e., whether $L(\mathcal{A}) = X^*$. Without loss of generality, let us consider an NFA $\mathcal{A} = (X, S, \delta, s_1, F)$, where $X = \{0, 1\}$ is the underlying alphabet, $S = \{1, \ldots, k\}$ the is set of states, $\delta \subseteq S \times X \times S$ is the transition relation, s_1 is the start state, and $F \subseteq S$ is the set of accepting states. The polynomial time reduction to a constant propagation problem is depicted in Figure 2.7.

For every state $i \in \{1, \ldots, k\}$ a variable s_i is introduced. The idea of the construction is to guess an arbitrary input word letter by letter. While this is

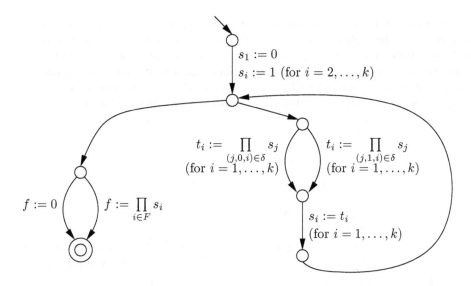

Fig. 2.7. PSPACE-hardness of polynomial must-constants.

done, it is ensured by appropriate assignments that each variable s_i holds 0 if and only if the automaton can be in state i after reading the word guessed so far. This implies that $\prod_{i \in F} s_i$ is 0 for all words if and only if $\mathcal{A}$ accepts the universal language.

Initially, only the start state variable s_1 is set to 0 as 1 is the only state which is reachable under the empty word. The central part of the program is a loop which guesses a next alphabet symbol. If we decide, for instance, for 0, then, for each i, an auxiliary state variable t_i is set to 0 by the assignment $t_i := \prod_{(j,0,i) \in \delta} s_j$, if and only if one of its 0-predecessors is recognized reachable by the word guessed so far.[3] After all the variables t_i have been set in this way their values are copied to the variables s_i. When the loop is exited which can happen after an arbitrary word has been guessed, it is checked whether the guessed word is accepted. Like before, the direct assignment $f := 0$ has the purpose to ensure that constant values different from 0 are impossible. Therefore, f is a must-constant (of value 0) at the end of the program, if and only if the underlying automaton accepts the universal language $\{0, 1\}^*$.

The final reduction in this section addresses the complexity of linear may-constants. Here we have:

Theorem 2.4.4. *Deciding linear may-constants is NP-hard.*

Again we employ a polynomial time reduction from 3-SAT which however differs from the ones seen before. The main idea here is to code a set of

---

[3] The auxiliary state variables t_i are introduced in order to avoid overwriting state variables which are still used in consecutive assignments.

satisfied clauses by a number interpreted as a bit-string. For example, in an instance with three clauses the number 100 would indicate that clause two is satisfied, while clauses zero and one are not. To avoid problems with carry-over effects, we employ a $(k + 1)$-adic number representation where k is the number of variables in the 3-SAT instance. With this coding we can use linear assignments to set the single "bits" corresponding to satisfied clauses.

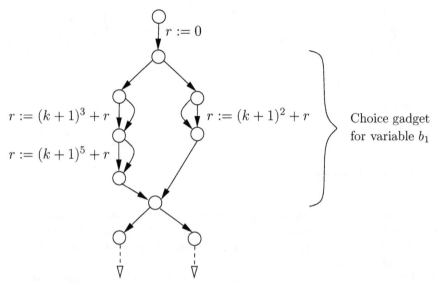

Fig. 2.8. NP-hardness of linear may-constant detection.

To illustrate our reduction let us assume an instance of 3-SAT with Boolean variables $\{b_1, \ldots, b_k\}$ and clauses $c_0, \ldots, c_{n-1}$, where the literal b_1 is contained in c_3 and c_5, and the negated literal $\neg b_1$ is contained in c_2 only. Then this is coded in a program as depicted in Figure 2.8. We have a non-deterministic choice part for each Boolean variable b_i. The left branch sets the bits for the clauses that contain b_i and the right branch those for the clauses that contain $\overline{b_i}$. Every assignment can be bypassed by an empty edge in case that the clause is also made true by another literal. It is now easy to see that r is a may-constant of value $\underbrace{1 \ldots 1}_{n\ times}$ (in $(k + 1)$-adic number representation) if and only if the underlying instance of 3-SAT is satisfiable.

On the other hand, it is easy to see that detecting may-constancy is in NP for acyclic control flow, since a non-deterministic Turing machine can guess a witnessing path for a given constant in polynomial time. Thus, we have:

Theorem 2.4.5. *May-constant propagation is in NP when restricted to acyclic control flow.*

Table 2.2. Complexity of constant detection: preliminary summary.

		Must-Constants	May-Constants	
			single value	multiple value
acyclic control flow	Copy Constants			
	Linear Constants			NP complete
	Presburger Constants			
	+,-,* Constants	Co-NP compl.		
	Full Constants			
unrestricted control flow	Copy Constants			PSPACE-compl.
	Linear Constants		NP-hard	
	Presburger Constants			undecidable
	+,-,* Constants	PSPACE-hard		
	Full Constants			

2.5 Summary

The decidability and complexity results of this chapter are summarized in Table 2.2. Note that hardness results propagate from a class of constants to more comprehensive classes of constants, i.e., downwards in the table, and vice versa for easiness results. Moreover, hardness results for acyclic control flow propagate to unrestricted control flow which explains the NP-hardness entry for linear constants and unrestricted control flow.

The table shows that we have already gone a good deal of the way towards classifying the complexity of the problems in our taxonomy of constant propagation. In the next chapter we complement the negative results of this chapter by positive results. Specifically, we attack Presburger and polynomial must-constant propagation.

3. Deciding Constants by Effective Weakest Preconditions

One goal of classifying the complexity of weakened versions of program-analysis problems is to uncover potential for more precise analysis algorithms. As witnessed by the white space in Table 2.2, three questions remained open in the complexity classification of the previous chapter: there is no result for Presburger must-constants and there are no upper bounds for polynomial must-constants and Presburger may-constants. In this chapter we provide answers for two of these questions that uncover algorithmic potential. We show that Presburger must-constants can be detected in polynomial time and that polynomial must-constants are decidable by developing corresponding algorithms. These classes are interesting from a practical point of view because the operators $+, -, *$ are very frequently used, e.g., for computing memory addresses of array components. As we consider must-constants throughout this chapter, we omit the qualifying prefix 'must' in the following.

The two algorithms share the same basic algorithmic idea. The main ingredient is effective computation of the weakest precondition of a certain assertion. In this computation, assertions are represented by appropriate mathematical structures. In order to emphasize similarity of the algorithms and to enable application to other scenarios, we develop a generic framework for development of S-constant detection algorithms in Section 3.3. Afterwards, we show how to apply it to detection of Presburger and polynomial constants. In the algorithm for Presburger constants, which is discussed in Section 3.4, assertions are represented by affine subspaces of $\mathbb{Q}^n$, where n is the number of variables in the underlying flow graph and well-known results from linear algebra are exploited. In the algorithm for polynomial constants presented in Section 3.7, assertions are represented by the set of zeros of ideals of $\mathbb{Z}[x_1, \ldots, x_n]$, the ring of multi-variate polynomials in the variables $x_1, \ldots, x_n$ with coefficients in $\mathbb{Z}$. Here we rely on results from computable ring theory in order to compute with ideals. We recall these less known results in Section 3.5 and describe some additional observations in Section 3.6.

In order to allow the reader to develop some intuition for the algorithms before following the technical generic description in Section 3.3, we provide a more illustrative and informal description of the Presburger constant- propagation algorithm beforehand (Section 3.2). Before that we illustrate the power of the algorithms by discussing some examples of Presburger and polynomial constants (Section 3.1).

3.1 Presburger and Polynomial Constants

Presburger constants are already beyond the scope of standard algorithms. Consider, for instance, the two example flow graphs in Figure 3.1.

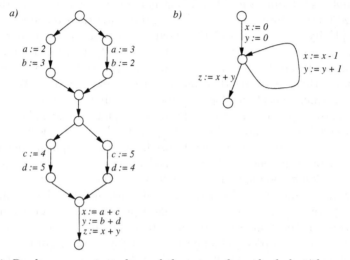

Fig. 3.1. Presburger constants beyond the scope of standard algorithms.

Part (a) extends the classic example that the standard constant propagation algorithm, so-called *simple constant propagation*, is non-distributive (cf. [30]). In this flow graph, z is a constant of value 14 at the end of the program. However, none of its operands is constant, although both are defined outside of any conditional branch. Simple constant propagation works by a forward propagation of variable assignments of the form $\delta : X \rightarrow \mathsf{Val} \cup \{\bot, \top\}$ where X is the set of program variables and Val is the value domain. It takes the meet of variable assignments at join points. Already at the join point of the first diamond this algorithm computes a variable assignment with $\delta(a) = \delta(b) = \bot$ because the variables are assigned different values in the two branches and there is no way to recover from this loss of precision.

Part (b) shows a small loop that simultaneously decrements x and increments y. Obviously, z is a (Presburger) constant of value 0 at the end of the program. However, this example is also outside the scope of any standard algorithm and even outside the scope of Knoop and Steffen's EXPTIME algorithm for finite constants [89] because no finite unfolding of the loop suffices to identify z as a constant. We should mention that Karr's algorithm [39], which is briefly discussed in the conclusions of this chapter, is able to identify z as a constant.

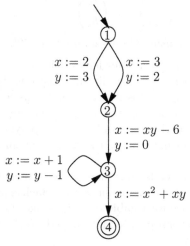

Fig. 3.2. A polynomial constant not detected by standard algorithms.

In Fig. 3.2, variable x is a (polynomial) constant of value 0 at node 4. For similar reasons as above, no standard algorithms can handle this example. Because constancy depends on the multiplications in the terms $xy - 6$ and $x^2 + xy$ neither our Presburger constant-detection algorithm nor Karr's algorithm can handle this example, in contrast to our algorithm for polynomial constants.

3.2 Presburger-Constant Detection at a Glance

For Presburger-Constant Detection we employ techniques known from linear algebra. We use a backward analysis propagating sets of *linear equations* describing *affine vector spaces* (over $\mathbb{Q}$).

The Dataflow Framework. Given a set of program variables $X = \{x_1, \ldots, x_n\}$ a linear equation is of the following form: $\sum_i a_i x_i = b$, where $a_i, b \in \mathbb{Q}$, $i = 1, \ldots, n$. Since at most n of these linear equations are linearly independent, an affine vector space can always be described by means of a linear equation system $Ax = b$ where A is a $k \times n$-matrix over $\mathbb{Q}$, $1 \leq k \leq n$, and $b \in \mathbb{Q}^k$. The affine vector sub-spaces of $\mathbb{Q}^n$ are partially ordered by set inclusion. This results in a (complete) lattice where the length of chains is bounded by $n+1$ as any affine space strictly contained in another affine space has a smaller dimension (the summand 1 accounts for the empty space).

The Meet Operation. The meet of two affine vector spaces represented by the equations $A_1 x = b_1$ and $A_2 x = b_2$ can be computed by normalizing the equation

$$\begin{pmatrix} A_1 \\ A_2 \end{pmatrix} x = \begin{pmatrix} b_1 \\ b_2 \end{pmatrix}$$

which can be done efficiently using Gauss-elimination [72].

Local Transfer Functions. The local transfer functions of affine assignments perform a backward substitution on the linear equations. For instance, the equation $3x + y = 10$ is backward-substituted along the assignment $x := 2u - 3v + 5$ towards $3 \, (2 \, u - 3 \, v + 5) + y = 10$ which then can be "normalized" towards $y + 6 \, u - 9 \, v = 5$. Clearly, this can be done in polynomial time. After this normalization, the resulting equation system is again simplified using Gauss-elimination.

A linear equation that depends on x like $3x + y = 10$ cannot be generally valid after a non-deterministic assignment $x :=?$. Such equations are thus transformed along $x :=?$ to unsatisfiable equations like $0 \, x = 1$. Equations that are independent of x are propagated unchanged. Non-affine assignments are treated in the same way.

The Overall Procedure. Our backward dataflow analysis can be regarded as a demand-driven analysis which works separately for each variable x and program point u. Conceptually, it is organized in three phases:

Phase 1: Guess an arbitrary cycle-free path from the start node to u, for instance using depth-first search, and compute the value c of x on this path using, e.g., the value 0 as initial value of all variables.

Phase 2: Solve the backward dataflow analysis where initially the program point u is annotated by the affine vector space described by the linear equation $x = c$ and all other program points by the universal affine space, i.e., the one given by the empty equation system, i.e., the equation system with zero equations.

Phase 3: The guess generated in Phase 1 is proved, if and only if the start node is still associated with the universal affine vector space.[1]

The completeness of the algorithm is a consequence of the distributivity of the analysis. Obviously, the guessed equation $x = c$ is true iff the backward substitution along every path originating at the start node yields a universally valid constraint at the start node. Since this defines the meet-over-all-paths solution of our dataflow framework the algorithmic solution is guaranteed to coincide if the transfer functions are distributive, which is immediate from the definition.

The algorithm can also be understood from a program verification point of view. By Phase 1, c is the only candidate value for x being constant at

---

[1] In practice, one may already terminate with the result of non-constancy of x whenever a linear equation system encountered during the analysis is unsolvable.

u. Phase 2 effectively computes the weakest (liberal) precondition of the assertion $x = c$ at program point n. Clearly, x is a constant at u if and only if the weakest liberal precondition of $x = c$ is universally valid. This point of view is elaborated in the remainder of this chapter.

As mentioned, the length of the chains appearing at the program points during Phase 2 of the analysis is bounded by $n + 1$, where n is the number of variables. Any change at a node can trigger a re-evaluation at its predecessor nodes. Therefore, we have at most $e \cdot (n + 1)$ Gaussian elimination steps, where $e = |E|$ denotes the number of edges in the flow graph. Each Gaussian elimination performs at most $\mathcal{O}(n^3)$ arithmetic operations [72]. Thus, the complete dataflow analysis for a single occurrence of a program variable performs at most $\mathcal{O}(e \cdot n^4)$ arithmetic operations. For an exhaustive analysis that computes constancy information for any left-hand side occurrence of a variable the estimation becomes $\mathcal{O}(p \cdot e \cdot n^4)$, where p denotes the number of program points in the flow graph.

Theorem 3.2.1. *Presburger (must-)constants can be detected with polynomially many arithmetic operations.* □

In order to achieve a truly polynomial running time, we must ensure in addition that the length of all the numbers appearing in this computation are polynomially bounded. For this we argue similarly as in [64]. It is well-known that the numerators and denominators of the numbers appearing in a Gaussian elimination over $\mathbb{Q}$ are determinants of minors of the original matrix [72, Problem 11.5.3]. Therefore, their size is polynomially bounded in the length of the numbers in the original matrices. In our algorithm these numbers are obtained via propagation of the linear equation $x = c$. Thus, it suffices to show that the length of the numbers in the propagated equations is polynomially bounded.

For this, we observe first that Phase 1 of the algorithm evaluates at most $|N|$ assignment statements with an affine right hand side in order to determine the candidate value c. This implies that the length of the (binary or decimal) representation of c is polynomially bounded in the size of the input program. The crucial idea to keep numbers small enough in the second phase is to avoid propagating "simplified" equations that are achieved through Gaussian elimination. Thus, whenever we observe that a propagated linear equation a is not yet implied by the equations stored for a program point u, we propagate the equation a itself via the ingoing edges to the predecessors of u instead of some "simplified" equation. As a consequence, all the numbers in the matrices on which Gaussian elimination is done are obtained by at most $e \cdot (n + 1)$ backwards propagation steps from the linear equation $x = c$. As in each step an affine expression appearing as a right hand side of an assignment in the given program is substituted for a variable, the size of the resulting numbers stays polynomially bounded as well.

Summarizing, we have:

Theorem 3.2.2. *Presburger (must-)constants can be detected in polynomial time.* □

We now illustrate our algorithm by means of the example of Figure 3.1.

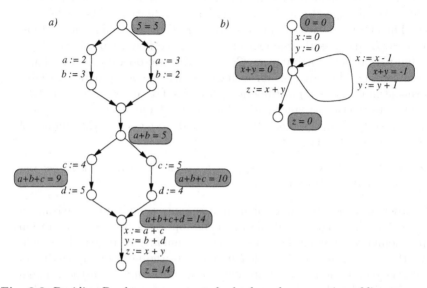

Fig. 3.3. Deciding Presburger constants by backward propagation of linear equations.

The emphasized annotation of Figure 3.3 contains the linear equations resulting from the initial guess $z = 14$ (in Figure 3.3(a)) and $z = 0$ (in Figure 3.3(b)), respectively. It should be noted that for the sake of presentation we did not display the equations for every program point. The particular power of this technique results from the normalization performed on the linear equations which provides a handle to cope with arithmetic properties like commutativity and associativity to a certain extent. For instance, the equation $a + b = 5$ in Figure 3.3(a) is the uniform result of two different intermediate equations.

Let us briefly discuss the modifications for polynomial constant propagation. We use more expressive equations of the form $p(x_1, \ldots, x_n) = 0$, where $p(x_1, \ldots, x_n)$ is a multi-variate polynomial with coefficients in $\mathbb{Z}$. A collection of such equations represents the set of zeros of an ideal in $\mathbb{Z}[x_1, \ldots, x_n]$. Exploiting results from computable ring theory we can effectively compute with such equations. In particular, we use Gröbner bases as canonic representation of ideals and the Buchberger algorithm for simplification. While polynomial assignments are handled analogously to affine assignments by backward substitution, the treatment of non-deterministic assignments needs a refinement.

The reason is that an equations that depends on x can still be generally valid for all values of x for certain values of other variables. The equation $x\,y = 0$, for instance, is valid after $x :=?$ if $y = 0$ is valid before.

After this informal presentation of the algorithms we are now ready for the more formal generic description.

3.3 A Generic Algorithm

We assume the formal framework of Section 2.1. Suppose we are given a variable $x \in X$ and a program point $w \in N$. In this chapter we describe a generic algorithm for deciding whether x is an S-constant at w or not. While standard constant propagation works by forward propagation of variable assignments, we use a three phase algorithm that employs a backwards propagation of assertions, as we have seen in Section 3.2. For the moment we can think of assertions as predicates on states as in program verification.

Phase 1: In the first phase we follow an arbitrary cycle-free path from **s** to w, for instance using depth-first search, and compute the value c, referred to as the *candidate value*, that x holds after this path is executed. This implies that, if x is a constant at w, it must be a constant of value c.

Phase 2: In the second phase we compute the weakest precondition for the assertion $x = c$ at program point w in G_S by means of a backwards dataflow analysis.

Phase 3: Finally, we check whether the computed weakest precondition for $x = c$ at w is **true**, i.e., is valid for all states.

It is obvious that this algorithm is correct. The problem is that Phase 2 and 3 are in general not effective. However, as only assignments of a restricted form appear in G_S, the algorithm becomes effective for certain sets S, if assertions are represented appropriately. In the remainder of this section we analyze the requirements for adequate representations. For this purpose, we first characterize weakest preconditions in flow graphs.

Semantically, an *assertion* is a subset of states $\phi \subseteq \Sigma$. Given an assertion ϕ and a statement s, the *weakest precondition* of s for ϕ, $\mathsf{wp}(s)(\phi)$, is the largest assertion ϕ' such that execution of s from all states in ϕ' is guaranteed to terminate only in states in ϕ.[2] The following identities for the weakest precondition of assignment and skip statements are well-known:

$$\mathsf{wp}(x := e)(\phi) \stackrel{\text{def}}{=} \phi[e/x] \stackrel{\text{def}}{=} \{\sigma \mid \sigma[x \mapsto e^\sigma] \in \phi\}$$

$$\mathsf{wp}(x :=?)(\phi) \stackrel{\text{def}}{=} \forall x(\phi) \stackrel{\text{def}}{=} \{\sigma \mid \forall d \in \mathbb{Z} : \sigma[x \mapsto d] \in \phi\}$$

$$\mathsf{wp}(\mathbf{skip})(\phi) \stackrel{\text{def}}{=} \phi$$

---

[2] In the sense of Dijkstra [17] this is the weakest *liberal* precondition as it does not guarantee termination. For simplicity we omit the qualifying prefix "liberal" in this chapter.

These identities characterize weakest preconditions of basic statements. Let us now consider the following more general situation in a given flow graph $G = (N, E, A, \mathbf{s}, \mathbf{e})$: we are given an assertion $\phi \subseteq \Sigma$ as well as a program point $w \in N$ and we are interested in the weakest precondition that guarantees validity of ϕ whenever execution reaches w. The latter can be characterized as follows.

Let $W_0[w] = \phi$ and $W_0[u] = \Sigma$ and consider the following equation system consisting of one equation for each program point $u \in N$:

$$\mathbf{W}[u] = W_0[u] \cap \bigcap_{v \in Succ[u]} \mathsf{wp}(A(u,v))(\mathbf{W}[v]). \qquad (3.1)$$

By the Knaster-Tarski fixpoint theorem, this equation system has a largest solution (w.r.t. subset inclusion) because $\mathsf{wp}(s)$ is monotonic. By abuse of notation, we denote the largest solution by the same letter $\mathbf{W}[u]$. For each program point $u \in N$, $\mathbf{W}[u]$ is the weakest assertion such that execution starting from u with any state in $\mathbf{W}[u]$ guarantees that ϕ holds whenever execution reaches w. In particular, $\mathbf{W}[\mathbf{s}]$ is the weakest precondition for validity of ϕ at w. The intuition underlying equation (3.1) is the following: firstly, $W_0[u]$ must be implied by $\mathbf{W}[u]$ and, secondly, for all successors v, we must guarantee that their associated condition $\mathbf{W}[u]$ is valid after execution of the statement $A(u, v)$ associated with the edge (u, v); hence $\mathsf{wp}(A(u, v))(\mathbf{W}[v])$ must be valid at u too.

For two reasons, the above equation system cannot be solved directly in general: firstly, because assertions may be infinite sets of states they cannot be represented explicitly; secondly, there are infinitely long descending chains of assertions such that we cannot guarantee that standard fixpoint iteration terminates.

In order to construct an algorithm that detects S-constants we represent assertions by the members of a lattice $(\mathbb{D}, \sqsubseteq)$. For Presburger constants $\mathbb{D}$ is the set of affine spaces of $\mathbb{Q}^n$ and for polynomial constants the set of ideals in $\mathbb{Z}[x_1, \ldots, x_n]$. We then simulate the iterative fixpoint computation for $\mathbf{W}$ on the members of lattice $\mathbb{D}$. In order to ensure termination, we require that $\mathbb{D}$ has no infinite ascending chains. In order to ensure that the computed result represents $\mathbf{W}$ *precisely*, we make sure (1) that the start value W_0 is represented precisely and (2) that the operations on $\mathbb{D}$ mirror the operations on assertions precisely. These requirement are detailed below. Note that it is a non-trivial fact that we can find such a lattice $\mathbb{D}$ for a certain set S of expressions: if, for instance, S is the set of all integer expressions, such a lattice cannot exist, because this would imply decidability of must-constancy.

Let us assume that $\gamma : \mathbb{D} \to 2^{\Sigma}$ captures how the lattice element represent assertions. First of all, we require

(a) $\mathbb{D}$ has no infinite decreasing chains, i.e., there is no infinite chain $d_1 \sqsupseteq d_2 \sqsupseteq d_3 \sqsupseteq \ldots$.

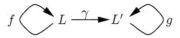

Fig. 3.4. Situation in the Transfer Lemma.

This guarantees that maximal fixpoints of monotonic functions can effectively be computed by standard fixpoint iteration. Secondly, we suppose

(b) γ is universally conjunctive, i.e., $\gamma(\sqcap X) = \bigsqcap\{\gamma(d) \mid d \in X\}$ for all $X \subseteq \mathbb{D}$.

The most important reason for this assumption is that it ensures that we can validly compute on representations without losing precision: if we precisely mirror the equations characterizing weakest preconditions on representations, the largest solution of the resulting equation system on representations characterizes the representation of the weakest precondition by the following well-known lemma. It appears in the literature (for the dual situation of least fixpoints) under the name *Transfer Lemma* [4] or *μ-Fusion Rule* [49].

Lemma 3.3.1 (Transfer Lemma). *Suppose L, L' are complete lattices, $f : L \to L$ and $g : L' \to L'$ are monotonic functions and $\gamma : L \to L'$ (cf. Fig. 3.4).*
If γ is universally conjunctive and $\gamma \circ f = g \circ \gamma$ then $\gamma(\nu f) = \nu g$, where νf and νg are the largest fixpoints of f and g, respectively. $\square$

We must mirror all the object occurring in the equation system characterizing weakest preconditions on representations precisely. Firstly, we must represent the start value, W_0. The fact that γ is universally conjunctive implies that $\gamma(\top) = \Sigma$, i.e., the top value of $\mathbb{D}$ is a precise representation of Σ. In addition, we require:

(c) Assertion $x = c$ can be represented precisely: for each $x \in X$, $c \in \mathsf{Val}$ we can effectively determine $d_{x=c} \in \mathbb{D}$ with $\gamma(d_{x=c}) = \{\sigma \in \Sigma \mid \sigma(x) = c\}$.

Secondly, we need effective representations for the operators appearing in equations. Requirement (b) implies that the meet operation of $\mathbb{D}$ precisely abstracts intersection of assertions. In order to enable effective computation of intersections, we require in addition:

(d) for given $d, d' \in \mathbb{D}$, we can effectively compute $d \sqcap d'$.

By induction this implies that we can compute finite meets $d_1 \sqcap \ldots \sqcap d_k$ effectively.

The only remaining operations on assertions are the weakest precondition transformers of basic statements. We must represent $\mathsf{wp}(x := t)$ for expressions $t \in S$, which is the substitution operator $(\cdot)[t/x]$ on assertions. As the S-constant detection algorithm computes the weakest precondition in weakened flow graph G_S, assignments $x := t$ with $t \notin S$ do not occur.

(e) There is a computable substitution operation $(\cdot)[t/x] : \mathbb{D} \to \mathbb{D}$ for each $x \in X$, $t \in S$, which satisfies $\gamma(d[t/x]) = \gamma(d)[t/x]$ for all $d \in \mathbb{D}$.

Obviously, wp(**skip**), the identity, is precisely represented by the identity on R. Thus, it remains to represent wp($x :=?$):

(f) There is a computable projection operation $proj_i : \mathbb{D} \to \mathbb{D}$ for each variable $x_i \in X$ such that $\gamma(proj_i(d)) = \forall x_i(\gamma(d))$ for all $d \in \mathbb{D}$.

Finally, we need the following in order to make Phase 3 of the algorithm effective.

(g) Assertion true is decidable, i.e., there is a decision procedure that decides for a given $d \in \mathbb{D}$, whether $\gamma(d) = \Sigma$ or not.

If, for a given set $S \subseteq$ Expr, we can find a lattice satisfying requirements (a)–(g), we can effectively execute the three phase algorithm from the beginning of this section by representing assertions by elements from this lattice. This results in a detection algorithm for S-constants.

In this chapter we are interested in detection of Presburger and polynomial constants. Thus, from now on, let Val $= \mathbb{Z}$.

3.4 Detection of Presburger Constants

Before we turn attention to detection of polynomial constants let us explain that the detection algorithm for Presburger constants that has informally been presented in Section 3.2 is an instance of the generic algorithm described in Section 3.3. Let $S = \{c_0 + \sum_{i=1}^{n} c_i x_i \mid c_0, \ldots, c_n \in \mathbb{Z}\}$. In the algorithm of Section 3.2 assertions are represented by affine vector spaces in $\mathbb{Q}^n$. In addition we need the empty set for representing the assertion false $= \emptyset$. Thus, $\mathbb{D} = \{z + U \mid z \in \mathbb{Q}^n, U$ is a subspace of $\mathbb{Q}^n\} \cup \{\emptyset\}$. For the remainder of this section, we adopt the convention to consider the empty set an affine space. We write 0 for a matrix or vector with zero entries and rely on the context to resolve the ambiguity inherent in this convention.

The order on $\mathbb{D}$ is set union: $\sqsubseteq = \subseteq$. From linear algebra we know that the intersection of arbitrary affine spaces is again an affine space. Thus, $(\mathbb{D}, \sqsubseteq)$ is a complete lattice with intersection as its meet operation. Note, however, that the join operation of this lattice, $\sqcup$, is different from set union $\cup$ because the union of affine spaces is in general not an affine space. The join of a family $\mathcal{A} \subseteq \mathbb{D}$ is the smallest affine space that contains all members of $\mathcal{A}$: $\bigsqcup \mathcal{A} = \bigcap \{B \in \mathbb{D} \mid \forall A \in \mathcal{A} : A \subseteq B\}$.

The representation mapping $\gamma : \mathbb{D} \to 2^\Sigma$ is defined by

$$\gamma(d) := \{\sigma \in 2^\Sigma \mid (\sigma(x_1), \ldots, \sigma(x_n)) \in d\}.$$

As we are using affine subspaces of $\mathbb{Q}^n$ to represent assertions for integer variables, the representation mapping γ does two things. Firstly, it transfers the tuple representation to a state representation which is merely an isomorphic transformation. Secondly, it selects the integer tuples from the given affine space $d \subseteq \mathbb{Q}^n$.

From linear algebra we know that all affine spaces $z + U \in \mathbb{D}$ can be represented by a matrix $A \in \mathbb{Q}^{k \times n}$ with $k \leq n$ and a (column) vector $b \in \mathbb{Q}^k$, such that $z + U = \{x \in \mathbb{Q}^n \mid Ax = b\}$. The empty set can also be represented by a matrix and a vector, e.g., by $A = (0, \ldots, 0)$ and $b = (1)$. In the concrete algorithm the elements of $\mathbb{D}$ are represented in this way by a matrix A and a vector b but this further representation step is suppressed in this section. We show, however, that all the needed operations on affine spaces can efficiently be performed on their representation by a matrix and a vector. Conceptually, it is simpler to consider the affine spaces themselves as representations because they are ordered. On pairs (A, b) we have only the *pre*-order induced by their interpretation as affine spaces:

$$(A, b) \leq (A', b') \quad :\Leftrightarrow \quad \{x \mid Ax = b\} \subseteq \{x \mid A'x = b'\}.$$

Thus, in order to cover this further representation step also, we would need a more general description of the generic algorithm that permits pre-orders as representations. While it is not hard to develop this more general framework it would obscure the presentation.

Let us now show that the requirements of the generic algorithm are satisfied:

(a) For dimension reasons a properly decreasing chain of affine spaces can have at most length $n + 1$.
(b) That the representation mapping γ is universally conjunctive is obvious from the definition.
(c) For $x_i \in X$ and $c \in \mathbb{Z}$, define $d_{x_i=c} \stackrel{\text{def}}{=} \{(c_1, \ldots, c_n) \in \mathbb{Q}^n \mid c_i = c\}$. Obviously, this set can be represented by the matrix $A = (a_{1j}) \in \mathbb{Q}^{1n}$ defined by $a_{1i} = 1$ and $a_{1j} = 0$ if $j \neq i$ and the vector $b = (c)$: $d_{x_i=c} = \{x \in \mathbb{Q}^n \mid Ax = b\}$. This also shows that $d_{x_i=c}$ is indeed an affine space.
(d) If we are given two affine spaces $d_1 = \{x \in \mathbb{Q}^n \mid A_1x = b_1\} \in \mathbb{D}$ and $d_2 = \{x \in \mathbb{Q}^n \mid A_2x = b_2\} \in \mathbb{D}$ we can effectively determine a representation of $d_1 \sqcap d_2 = d_1 \cap d_2$ by normalizing the following equation via Gauss elimination:

$$\begin{pmatrix} A_1 \\ A_2 \end{pmatrix} x = \begin{pmatrix} b_1 \\ b_2 \end{pmatrix}.$$

(e) Suppose we are given $x_s \in X$ and $e = c_0 + \sum_{i=1}^n c_i x_i \in S$. For $x = (x_i) \in \mathbb{Q}^n$, let us write $x[e/x_s]$ for the vector $y = (y_i) \in \mathbb{Q}^n$ with $y_s = c_0 + \sum_{i=1}^n c_i x_i$ and $y_i = x_i$ for $i \neq s$. We define the substitution operator $(\cdot)[e/x_s] : \mathbb{D} \to \mathbb{D}$ by $d[e/x_s] = \{x \in \mathbb{Q}^n \mid x[e/x_s] \in d\}$. This definition directly reflects the definition of substitution on assertions. Therefore, the following lemma is obvious.

Lemma 3.4.1 (Adequacy). $\gamma(d)[e/x_s] = \gamma(d[e/x_s])$.   □

The following lemma shows that and how the substitution operator can (efficiently) be computed on representations of affine spaces via matrices and vectors. It also implies that $d[e/x_s]$ is indeed an affine space and thus ensures that $(\cdot)[e/x_s]$ is well-defined. The lemma formalizes the backwards substitution and subsequent normalization on linear equations in the informal explanation of the local transfer functions of affine assignments in Section 3.2.

Suppose we are given $A = (a_{ij}) \in \mathbb{Q}^{k \times n}$ and $b = (b_i) \in \mathbb{Q}^k$ such that $d = \{x \in \mathbb{Q}^n \mid Ax = b\}$.

Lemma 3.4.2 (Computation). Let $A' = (a'_{ij}) \in \mathbb{Q}^{k \times n}$ with $a'_{is} := a_{is}c_s$ and $a'_{ij} := a_{ij} + a_{is}c_j$ for $j \neq s$, and $b' = (b'_i) \in \mathbb{Q}^k$ with $b'_i := b_i - a_{is}c_0$.

Then: $d[e/x_s] = \{x \in \mathbb{Q}^n \mid A'x = b'\}$.

Proof. Let $x \in \mathbb{Q}^n$ and $y = x[e/x_s]$. By the definitions, $x \in d[e/x_s]$ if and only if $Ay = b$. By the definition of matrix multiplication this is the case if and only if for all i, $1 \leq i \leq k$,

$$\sum_{j=1}^{n} a_{ij}y_j = b_i . \tag{3.2}$$

As the sum on the left hand side can be rewritten as follows

$$\sum_{j=1}^{n} a_{ij}y_j = \sum_{\substack{j=1 \\ j \neq s}}^{n} a_{ij}x_j + a_{is}\left(c_0 + \sum_{j=1}^{n} c_j x_j\right) = \sum_{j=1}^{n} a'_{ij}x_j + a_{is}c_0 ,$$

Equation (3.2) holds if and only if $\sum_{j=1}^{n} a'_{ij}x_j = b_i - a_{is}c_0 = b'_i$. Consequently, $x \in d[e/x_s]$ if and only if $A'x = b'$. □

(f) Suppose we are given $x_s \in X$. We define the projection operator $proj_{x_s} : \mathbb{D} \to \mathbb{D}$ on representations of affine spaces as follows: if $d = \{x \in \mathbb{Q}^n \mid Ax = b\} \in \mathbb{D}$ then

$$proj_{x_s}(d) = \begin{cases} d & \text{if } a_{is} = 0 \text{ for all } i \in \{1, \dots, k\} \\ \emptyset & \text{otherwise} . \end{cases}$$

This definition is motivated by the following intuition: a vector $x = (x_i) \in \mathbb{Z}^n$ (or $x \in \mathbb{Q}^n$, this doesn't make any difference) satisfies all the linear equations described by $Ax = b$ for arbitrary variation of x_s (in $\mathbb{Z}$ or $\mathbb{Q}$) if and only if all equations are independent of x_s. A formalization of this intuition yields:

Lemma 3.4.3 (Adequacy). $\forall x_s(\gamma(d)) = \gamma(proj_{x_s}(d))$. □

We leave the formal proof, which is similar to the proof of Lemma 3.4.5 below, to the reader.

It is also not hard to show that the above definition is independent of the representation by a matrix A and vector b. The crucial lemma, the proof of which is also left to the reader, is this:

Lemma 3.4.4 (Well-definedness). *Let $A = (a_{ij}) \in \mathbb{Q}^{k \times n}$, $b \in \mathbb{Q}^k$, $A' = (a'_{ij}) \in \mathbb{Q}^{k' \times n}$, and $b' \in \mathbb{Q}^{k'}$. Suppose $\{x \mid Ax = b\} = \{x \mid A'x = b'\} \neq \emptyset$. Then: $a_{is} = 0$ for all $i = 1, \ldots, k$ if and only if $a'_{is} = 0$ for all $i = 1, \ldots, k'$.* □

It is immediate from its definition that and how the projection operator can efficiently be computed on the representation of an affine space via a matrix A and a vector b. We only need to check whether the s'th row of A is constantly 0; if this is the case, d is left unchanged by the projection such that $proj_{x_s}(d)$ is again represented by A and b; otherwise the projection of d is empty and we can use, e.g., $A = (0, \ldots, 0)$ and $b = (1)$ for representing $proj_{x_s}(d)$ because $\emptyset = \{x \in \mathbb{Q}^n \mid (0, \ldots, 0)x = 1\}$.

(g) In order to check whether an affine space $d = \{x \in \mathbb{Q}^n \mid Ax = b\} \in \mathbb{D}$ given by matrix A and column vector b represents Σ we need only check whether all entries of A and b are zero as witnessed by the following lemma. Obviously this condition can efficiently be decided from A and b.

Lemma 3.4.5 (Test for true). *$\gamma(\{x \in \mathbb{Q}^n \mid Ax = b\}) = \Sigma$ if and only if $A = 0$ and $b = 0$.*

Proof. By definition of γ, we have $\gamma(\{x \mid Ax = b\}) = \Sigma$ if and only if $Ad = b$ for all $d \in \mathbb{Z}^n$. We show that the latter condition holds if and only if $A = 0$ and $b = 0$.

If, on the one hand, $A = 0$ and $b = 0$, then we clearly have $Ad = 0 = b$ for all $d \in \mathbb{Z}^n$. If, on the other hand, $Ad = b$ holds for all $d \in \mathbb{Z}^n$, we have, first of all, $b = A0 = 0$. Moreover, all entries of A must be zero: If A has a non-zero entry, say $a_{i,j}$, then the j'th component of its application to the vector $d = (d_k)$ with $d_i = 1$ and $d_k = 0$ for $k \neq i$ would be $a_{ij} \neq 0 = b_j$. □

3.5 A Primer on Computable Ideal Theory

They key idea for the detection of polynomial constants is to represent an assertion by the zeros of an ideal in the polynomial ring $\mathbb{Z}[x_1, \ldots, x_n]$ and to apply techniques from computable ideal theory. While a full introduction to this area is beyond the scope of this monograph, we recall in this section the facts needed and make some additional observations in Section 3.6. Accessible introductions can be found in standard textbooks on computer algebra. The case of polynomial rings over fields is covered, e.g., by [16, 23, 95], while

[55] treats the more general case of polynomial rings over rings, that is of relevance here, as $\mathbb{Z}$ is an integral domain but not a field.

Recall that $\mathbb{Z}$ together with addition and multiplication forms a commutative ring, i.e., a structure $(R, +, \cdot)$ with a non-empty set R and two inner operations $+$ and $\cdot$ such that $(R, +)$ is an Abelian group, $\cdot$ is associative and commutative, and the distributive law $a \cdot (b + c) = a \cdot b + a \cdot c$ is valid for all $a, b, c \in R$. On the set of polynomials, $\mathbb{Z}[x_1, \ldots, x_n]$, we can define addition and multiplication operations in the standard way; this makes $\mathbb{Z}[x_1, \ldots, x_n]$ a commutative ring as well.

A non-empty subset $I \subseteq R$ of a ring R is called an *ideal* if $a + b \in I$ and $r \cdot a \in I$ for all $a, b \in I$, $r \in R$. The ideal *generated* by a subset $B \subseteq R$ is

$$\langle B \rangle = \{ r_1 \cdot b_1 + \ldots + r_k \cdot b_k \mid r_1, \ldots, r_k \in R, b_1, \ldots, b_k \in B \},$$

and B is called a *basis* or *generating system* of I if $I = \langle B \rangle$. An ideal is called *finitely generated* if it has a finite basis $B = \{b_1, \ldots, b_m\}$. Hilbert's famous basis theorem tells us that $\mathbb{Z}[x_1, \ldots, x_n]$ is *Noetherian*, since $\mathbb{Z}$ is Noetherian, i.e., that there are no infinitely long strictly increasing chains $I_1 \subset I_2 \subset I_3 \subset \ldots$ of ideals in $\mathbb{Z}[x_1, \ldots, x_n]$. This implies that every ideal of $\mathbb{Z}[x_1, \ldots, x_n]$ is finitely generated.

It is crucial for our algorithm that we can compute effectively with ideals. While Hilbert's basis theorem ensures that we can represent every ideal of $\mathbb{Z}[x_1, \ldots, x_n]$ by a finite basis, it does not give effective procedures for basic questions like membership tests or equality tests of ideals represented in this way. Indeed, Hilbert's proof of the basis theorem was famous (and controversial) at its time for its non-constructive nature.

Fortunately, the theory of Gröbner bases and the Buchberger algorithm provide a solution for some of these problems. While a complete presentation of this theory is way beyond the scope of this monograph—the interested reader is pointed to the books mentioned above—a few sentences are in order here. A Gröbner basis is a basis for an ideal that has particularly nice properties. From any given finite basis of an ideal the Buchberger algorithm effectively computes a Gröbner basis. There is a natural notion of reduction of a polynomial with respect to a set of polynomials. Reduction of a polynomial p with respect to a Gröbner basis always terminates and yields a unique result. This result is the zero polynomial if and only if p belongs to the ideal represented by the Gröbner basis. Hence reduction with respect to a Gröbner basis yields an effective membership test, that in turn can be used to check equality and inclusion of ideals.

In the terminology of [55], $\mathbb{Z}[x_1, \ldots, x_n]$ is a *strongly computable ring*. This implies that the following operations are computable for ideals $I, I' \subseteq \mathbb{Z}[x_1, \ldots, x_n]$ given by finite bases B, B' and polynomials $p \in \mathbb{Z}[x_1, \ldots, x_n]$, cf. [55]:

Ideal membership: Given an ideal I and a polynomial p. Is $p \in I$?
Ideal inclusion: Given two ideals I, I'. Is $I \subseteq I'$?

Ideal equality: Given two ideals I, I'. Is $I = I'$?

Sum of ideals: Given two ideals I, I'. Compute a basis for $I + I' \overset{\text{def}}{=} \{p + p' \mid p \in I, p' \in I'\}$. As a matter of fact, $I + I' = \langle B \cup B' \rangle$.

Intersection of ideals: Given two ideals I, I'. Compute a basis for $I \cap I'$.

It is straightforward (and well-known) that $I + I'$ and $I \cap I'$ are again ideals if I and I' are. We can use the above operations as basic operations in our algorithms.

3.6 More About $\mathbb{Z}[x_1, \ldots, x_n]$

3.6.1 $\mathbb{Z}[x_1, \ldots, x_n]$ as a Complete Lattice

Interestingly, the ideals in $\mathbb{Z}[x_1, \ldots, x_n]$ form also a complete lattice under subset inclusion $\subseteq$. Suppose we are given a set $\mathcal{I}$ of ideals in $\mathbb{Z}[x_1, \ldots, x_n]$. Then the largest ideal contained in all ideals in $\mathcal{I}$ obviously is $\bigcap \mathcal{I}$, and the smallest ideal that contains all ideals in $\mathcal{I}$ is $\sum \mathcal{I} := \{r_1 \cdot a_1 + \ldots + r_k \cdot a_k \mid r_1, \ldots, r_k \in \mathbb{Z}[x_1, \ldots, x_n], a_1, \ldots, a_k \in \bigcup \mathcal{I}\}$. The least element of the lattice is the zero ideal $\{0\}$ that consists only of the zero polynomial and the largest element is $\mathbb{Z}[x_1, \ldots, x_n]$. While this lattice does not have finite height it is Noetherian by Hilbert's basis theorem such that we can effectively compute least fixpoints of monotonic functions on ideals of $\mathbb{Z}[x_1, \ldots, x_n]$ by standard fixpoint iteration.

3.6.2 Zeros

As mentioned, we represent assertions by the zeros of ideals in our algorithm. A state σ is called a *zero* of polynomial p if $p^\sigma = 0$; we denote the set of zeros of polynomial p by $\mathcal{Z}(p)$. More generally, for a subset $B \subseteq \mathbb{Z}[x_1, \ldots, x_n]$, $\mathcal{Z}(B) = \{\sigma \mid \forall p \in B : p^\sigma = 0\}$. For later use some facts concerning zeros are collected in the following lemma, in particular of the relationship of ideal operations with operations on their zeros.

Lemma 3.6.1. *Suppose B, B' are sets of polynomials, q is a polynomial, I, I' are ideals, and $\mathcal{I}$ is a set of ideals in $\mathbb{Z}[x_1, \ldots, x_n]$.*

1. *If $B \subseteq B'$ then $\mathcal{Z}(B) \supseteq \mathcal{Z}(B')$.*
2. *$\mathcal{Z}(B) = \mathcal{Z}(\langle B \rangle) = \bigcap_{p \in B} \mathcal{Z}(p)$. In particular, $\mathcal{Z}(q) = \mathcal{Z}(\langle q \rangle)$.*
3. *$\mathcal{Z}(\sum \mathcal{I}) = \bigcap \{\mathcal{Z}(I) \mid I \in \mathcal{I}\}$. In particular, $\mathcal{Z}(I + I') = \mathcal{Z}(I) \cap \mathcal{Z}(I')$.*
4. *$\mathcal{Z}(\bigcap \mathcal{I}) = \bigcup \{\mathcal{Z}(I) \mid I \in \mathcal{I}\}$, if $\mathcal{I}$ is finite. In particular, $\mathcal{Z}(I \cap I') = \mathcal{Z}(I) \cup \mathcal{Z}(I')$.*
5. *$\mathcal{Z}(\{0\}) = \Sigma$ and $\mathcal{Z}(\mathbb{Z}[x_1, \ldots, x_n]) = \emptyset$.*
6. *$\mathcal{Z}(I) = \Sigma$ if and only if $I = \{0\} = \langle 0 \rangle$.*

Proof. We only prove Property 4; the proof of the other properties is simpler and is left to the reader. So suppose $\mathcal{I} = \{I_1, \ldots, I_k\} \subseteq \mathbb{Z}[x_1, \ldots, x_n]$ is a finite set of ideals.

'$\supseteq$'. Suppose $\sigma \in \bigcup\{\mathcal{Z}(I) \mid I \in \mathcal{I}\}$. Then there is $j \in \{1,\ldots,k\}$ with $\sigma \in \mathcal{Z}(I_j)$. Then, by Property 1, we have $\sigma \in \mathcal{Z}(I_j) \subseteq \mathcal{Z}(\bigcap\mathcal{I})$ because $I_j \supseteq \bigcap\mathcal{I}$.

'$\subseteq$'. We use contraposition. So suppose $\sigma \notin \bigcup\{\mathcal{Z}(I) \mid I \in \mathcal{I}\}$. Then we can choose for each $j = 1,\ldots,k$ a polynomial $p_j \in I_j$ with $p_j^\sigma \neq 0$. For the product of these polynomials we have $\prod_{j=1}^{k} p_j \in \bigcap\mathcal{I}$ and $(\prod_{j=1}^{k} p_j)^\sigma = \prod_{j=1}^{k} p_j^\sigma \neq 0$. Hence, $\sigma \notin \mathcal{Z}(\bigcap\mathcal{I})$. $\qquad\square$

Note that the assumption that $\mathcal{I}$ is finite is essential in Property 4: if we choose, for instance, $\mathcal{I} = \{(\langle x^i \rangle \mid i > 1\}$ we have $\mathcal{Z}(\bigcap\mathcal{I}) = \mathcal{Z}(\{0\}) = \mathbb{Z}$ but $\bigcup\{\mathcal{Z}(I) \mid I \in \mathcal{I}\} = \{0\}$ because $\mathcal{Z}(\langle x^i \rangle) = \mathcal{Z}(x^i) = \{0\}$ for all $i > 0$.

3.6.3 Substitution

Suppose we are given a polynomial $p \in \mathbb{Z}[x_1,\ldots,x_n]$ and a variable $x \in X$. We can define a substitution operation on ideals I as follows: $I[p/x] = (\{q[p/x] \mid q \in I\})$, where the substitution of polynomial p for x in q, $q[p/x]$, is defined as usual. By definition, $I[p/x]$ is the smallest ideal that contains all polynomials $q[p/x]$ with $q \in I$. From a basis for I, a basis for $I[p/x]$ is obtained in the expected way: if $I = \langle B \rangle$, then $I[p/x] = \langle\{b[p/x] \mid b \in B\}\rangle$. Thus, we can easily obtain a finite basis for $I[p/x]$ from a finite basis for I: if $I = \langle b_1,\ldots,b_k\rangle$ then $I[p/x] = \langle b_1[p/x],\ldots,b_k[p/x]\rangle$. Hence we can add substitution to our list of computable operations.

The substitution operation on ideals defined in the previous paragraph mirrors precisely semantic substitution in assertions which has been defined in connection with $\mathsf{wp}(x := e)$.

Lemma 3.6.2. $\mathcal{Z}(I)[p/x] = \mathcal{Z}(I[p/x])$. $\qquad\square$

We leave the proof of this equation that involves the substitution lemma known from logic to the reader.

3.6.4 Projection

In this section we define projection operators $proj_i$, $i = 1,\ldots,n$, such that for each ideal I, $\mathcal{Z}(proj_i(I)) = \forall x_i(\mathcal{Z}(I))$. Semantic universal quantification over assertions has been defined in connection with $\mathsf{wp}(x :=?)$.

A polynomial $p \in \mathbb{Z}[x_1,\ldots,x_n]$ can uniquely be written as a polynomial in x_i with coefficients in $\mathbb{Z}[x_1,\ldots,x_{i-1},x_{i+1},x_n]$, i.e., in the form $p = c_k x_i^k + \ldots + c_0 x_i^0$, where $c_0,\ldots,c_k \in \mathbb{Z}[x_1,\ldots,x_{i-1},x_{i+1},x_n]$, and $c_k \neq 0$ if $k > 0$. We call $c_0,\ldots,c_k$ the coefficients of p with respect to x_i and let $\mathcal{C}_i(p) = \{c_0,\ldots,c_k\}$.

Lemma 3.6.3. $\forall x_i(\mathcal{Z}(p)) = \mathcal{Z}(\mathcal{C}_i(p))$.

Proof. Let $p = c_k x_i^k + \ldots + c_0 x_i^0$ with $\mathcal{C}_i(p) = \{c_0,\ldots,c_k\}$.

'$\supseteq$'. Let $\sigma \in \mathcal{Z}(\mathcal{C}_i(p))$. We have $c_j^{\sigma[x_i \mapsto d]} = c_j^\sigma = 0$ for all $d \in \mathbb{Z}$, $j = 0, \ldots, k$, because c_j is independent of x_i. Hence, $p^{\sigma[x_i \mapsto d]} = c_k^{\sigma[x_i \mapsto d]} d^k + \ldots + c_0^{\sigma[x_i \mapsto d]} d^0 = 0 d^k + \ldots + 0 d^0 = 0$ for all $d \in \mathbb{Z}$, i.e. $\sigma \in \forall x_i(\mathcal{Z}(p))$.

'$\subseteq$'. Let $\sigma \in \forall x_i(\mathcal{Z}(p))$. Again, we have $c_j^{\sigma[x_i \mapsto d]} = c_j^\sigma$ for all $d \in \mathbb{Z}$, $j = 0, \ldots, k$, because c_k is independent of x_i. Therefore, $c_k^\sigma d^k + \ldots + c_0^\sigma d^0 = c_k^{\sigma[x_i \mapsto d]} d^k + \ldots + c_0^{\sigma[x_i \mapsto d]} d^0 = p^{\sigma[x \mapsto d]} = 0$ for all $d \in \mathbb{Z}$ because of $\sigma \in \forall x_i(\mathcal{Z}(p))$. This means that the polynomial $c_k^\sigma x_i^k + \ldots + c_0^\sigma x_i^0$ vanishes for all values of x_i. Hence, it has more than k zeros which implies that it is the zero polynomial. Consequently, $c_j^\sigma = 0$ for all $j = 0, \ldots, k$, i.e., $\sigma \in \mathcal{Z}(\mathcal{C}_i(p))$. $\square$

Suppose $I \subseteq \mathbb{Z}[x_1, \ldots, x_n]$ is an ideal with basis B.

Lemma 3.6.4. $\forall x_i(\mathcal{Z}(I)) = \mathcal{Z}(\bigcup_{f \in B} \mathcal{C}_i(f))$.

Proof. The proof is by the following calculation: $\forall x_i(\mathcal{Z}(I)) = \forall x_i(\mathcal{Z}(B)) = \forall x_i(\bigcap_{p \in B} \mathcal{Z}(p)) = \bigcap_{p \in B} \forall x_i(\mathcal{Z}(p)) = \bigcap_{p \in B}(\mathcal{Z}(\mathcal{C}_i(p))) = \mathcal{Z}(\bigcup_{p \in B} \mathcal{C}_i(p))$. $\square$

In view of this formula, it is natural to define $proj_i(I) = (\bigcup_{p \in B} \mathcal{C}_i(p))$ where B is a basis of I. It is not hard but tedious to show that this definition is independent of the basis; we leave this proof to the reader. Obviously, $proj_i$ is effective: if I is given by a finite basis $\{b_1, \ldots, b_k\}$ then $proj_i(I)$ is given by the finite basis $\bigcup_{j=1}^{k} \mathcal{C}_i(b_j)$.

Corollary 3.6.1. $\forall x_i(\mathcal{Z}(I)) = \mathcal{Z}(proj_i(I))$.

Proof. $\forall x_i(\mathcal{Z}(I)) = \mathcal{Z}(\bigcup_{p \in B} \mathcal{C}_i(p)) = \mathcal{Z}((\bigcup_{p \in B} \mathcal{C}_i(p))) = \mathcal{Z}(proj_i(I))$. $\square$

3.7 Detection of Polynomial Constants

We represent assertions by ideals of the polynomial ring $\mathbb{Z}[x_1, \ldots, x_n]$ in the detection algorithm for polynomial constants. Thus, let $\mathbb{D}$ be the set of ideals of $\mathbb{Z}[x_1, \ldots, x_n])$ and $\sqsubseteq$ be $\supseteq$. The representation mapping is $\gamma(I) = \mathcal{Z}(I)$. Note that the order is *reverse* inclusion of ideals. This is because larger ideals have smaller sets of zeros. Thus, the *meet* operation is the *sum* operation of ideals and the top element is the ideal $\{0\} = \langle 0 \rangle$.

In a practical algorithm, ideals are represented by finite bases. For transparency, we suppress this further representation step but ensure that only operations that can effectively be computed on bases are used.

The lattice $(\mathbb{D}, \supseteq)$ satisfies requirements (a)–(g) of Section 3.3:

(a) $\mathbb{Z}[x_1, \ldots, x_n]$ is Noetherian.
(b) By the identity $\mathcal{Z}(\sum \mathcal{I}) = \bigcap \{\mathcal{Z}(I) \mid I \in \mathcal{I}\}$, $\mathcal{Z}$ is universally conjunctive.
(c) Suppose $x \in X$ and $c \in \mathbb{Z}$. Certainly, a state is a zero of the ideal generated by the polynomial $x - c$ if and only if it maps x to c. Hence, we choose $d_{x=c}$ as the ideal $\langle x - c \rangle$ generated by $x - c$.

(d) In Section 3.5 we have seen that the sum of two ideals can effectively be computed on bases.
(e) By Section 3.6.3, $(\cdot)[p/x]$ is an adequate, computable substitution operation.
(f) Again by Section 3.6.4, $proj_i$ is an adequate, computable projection operation.
(g) We know that $\mathcal{Z}(I) = \Sigma$ if and only if $I = \{0\}$. Moreover, the only basis of the ideal $\{0\}$ is $\{0\}$ itself. Hence, in order to decide whether an ideal I given by a basis B represents Σ, we only need to check whether $B = \{0\}$.

We can thus apply the generic algorithm from Section 3.3 for the detection of polynomial constants. In order to make this more specific, we put the pieces together, and describe the resulting algorithm in more detail.

Suppose we are given a variable $x \in X$ and a program point $w \in N$ in a flow graph $G = (N, E, A, \mathbf{s}, \mathbf{e})$. Then the following algorithm decides whether x is a polynomial constant at w or not:

Phase 1: Determine a candidate value $c \in \mathbb{Z}$ for x at w by executing an arbitrary (cycle-free) path from $\mathbf{s}$ to w.

Phase 2: Associate with each edge $(u, v) \in E$ a transfer function $f_{(u,v)} :$ $\mathbb{D} \to \mathbb{D}$ that represents $\mathsf{wp}(A_S(u, v))$:

$$
f_{(u,v)}(I) = \begin{cases}
I & \text{if } A(u, v) = \mathbf{skip} \\
I[p/x] & \text{if } A(u, v) = (x := p) \text{ with } p \in \mathbb{Z}[x_1, \ldots, x_n] \\
proj_x(I) & \text{if } A(u, v) = (x := t) \text{ with } t \notin \mathbb{Z}[x_1, \ldots, x_n] \\
proj_x(I) & \text{if } A(u, v) = (x :=?)
\end{cases}
$$

Set $A_0[w] = \langle x - c \rangle$ and $A_0[u] = \langle 0 \rangle$ for all $u \in N \setminus \{w\}$ and compute the largest solution (w.r.t. $\sqsubseteq = \supseteq$) of the equation system

$$
\mathbf{A}[u] = A_0[u] + \sum_{v \in Succ[u]} f_{(u,v)}(\mathbf{A}[v]) \quad \text{for each } u \in N .
$$

We can do this as follows. Starting from $A_0[u]$ we iteratively compute, simultaneously for all program points $u \in N$, the following sequences of ideals

$$
A_{i+1}[u] = A_i[u] + \sum_{v \in Succ[u]} f_{(u,v)}(\mathbf{A}_i[v]) .
$$

We stop upon stabilization, i.e., when we encounter an index i_s such that $A_{i_s+1}[u] = A_{i_s}[u]$ for all $u \in N$. Obviously, $A_0[u] \subseteq A_1[u] \subseteq A_2[u] \subseteq \ldots$, such that computation must terminate eventually because $\mathbb{Z}[x_1, \ldots, x_n]$ is Noetherian. In this computation we represent ideals by finite bases and perform Gröbner-basis computations in order to check whether $A_{i+1}[u] = A_i[u]$.[3]

---

[3] As $A_{i+1}[u] \supseteq A_i[u]$ by construction, it suffices to check $A_{i+1}[u] \subseteq A_i[u]$.

Phase 3: Check if the ideal computed for the start node, $A_{i_s}[\mathbf{s}]$, is $\langle 0 \rangle$. If so, x is a polynomial constant of value v at w; otherwise, x is not a polynomial constant at w.

Phase 2 can be seen as a backwards dataflow analysis in a framework in which ideals of $\mathbb{Z}[x_1, \ldots, x_n]$ constitute dataflow facts, the transfer functions are the functions $f_{(u,v)}$ specified above, and the start value is A_0. Of course, we can use any evaluation strategy instead of naive iteration.

These considerations prove:

Theorem 3.7.1. *Polynomial constants are decidable.* □

We do not know any complexity bound for our algorithm. Our termination proof relies on Hilbert's basis theorem and its standard proof is non-constructive and does not provide an upper bound for the maximal length of strictly increasing chains of ideals. Therefore, we cannot bound the number of iterations performed by our algorithm.

3.8 Conclusion

In this chapter we have shown that Presburger constants can be detected in polynomial time and that polynomial constants are decidable. These classes are interesting from a practical point of view because the sets of operators $+, -$ and $+, -, *$, respectively, are very frequently used, e.g., for computing memory addresses of array components. The algorithm for Presburger constants has first been sketched in [60] while the algorithm for polynomial constants has been presented at the Static Analysis Symposium 2002 [62].

The polynomial-constant detection algorithm can easily be extended to handle conditions of the form $p \neq 0$ with $p \in \mathbb{Z}[x_1, \ldots, x_n]$. The weakest precondition is $\mathsf{wp}(p \neq 0)(\phi) = (p \neq 0 \Rightarrow \phi) = (p = 0 \lor \phi)$ and if ϕ is represented by an ideal I, the assertion $p = 0 \lor \phi$ is represented by the ideal $I \cap \langle p \rangle$ according to Lemma 3.6.1. This observation can be used to handle such conditions in our algorithm. We can extend this easily to an arbitrary mixture of disjunctions and conjunctions of conditions of the form $p \neq 0$. Of course, we cannot handle the dual form of conditions, $p = 0$: with both types of conditions we can obviously simulate two-counter machines. In contrast, the Presburger constant detection algorithm cannot easily be extended to conditions as affine spaces are not closed under union.

The detection algorithms of this chapter use an indirect three phase approach; the main work is done in the second phase. In the first phase a candidate value is computed that is verified in the second and third phase by means of a symbolic weakest precondition computation. We have analyzed the demands for making this general algorithmic idea effective which results in a generic framework for the construction of S-constant-propagation algorithms. Assertions are represented by affine subspaces of $\mathbb{Q}^n$ for Presburger constants and by ideals in the polynomial ring $\mathbb{Z}[x_1, \ldots, x_n]$ for polynomial constants.

We have exploited the idea of effective weakest precondition computations also in recent related work on interprocedural computation of affine invariants [65, 66] and in work on intra- and interprocedural analysis relative to Herbrand interpretation [67, 68]. Related to Presburger constant detection is also recent work by Gulwani and Necula on likely affine invariants [27, 28]. Computable ring theory has been used in recent related program analysis research by Colón, Manna, Sankaranarayanan and Sipma, e.g., [11, 84, 10], Rodríguez-Carbonell, and Kapur, e.g., [82, 81], and ourselves [63]. However, up to our knowledge, our conference paper [62] that originally proposed the algorithm for detection of polynomial constants described in this chapter preceeded all this work.

Standard constant propagation relies on forward propagation while we use backwards propagation of assertions here. Interestingly, Presburger constants can also be detected by forward propagation of affine spaces. In a seminal paper, Karr [39] describes such an algorithm. His algorithms computes valid affine relationships by forward propagation of affine spaces. It can be used for constant detection and can be shown to find all Presburger constants. While Karr discusses in his paper neither completeness issues nor means for controlling growth of number representations, we proposed in [64] a version of Karr's algorithm that avoids exponential growth of numbers, improves upon the asymptotic running time of his original algorithm, and has a completeness guarantee that ensures that all Presburger constants are found.

In forward propagation of affine spaces we effectively compute strongest postconditions rather than weakest preconditions. This computation involves union of assertions rather than intersection. Because affine spaces are not closed under union, Karr defines a (complicated) union operator of affine spaces that over-approximates their actual union by an affine space. One is tempted to consider forward propagation of ideals of $\mathbb{Z}[x_1, \ldots, x_n]$. At first glance, this idea looks promising, because ideals are closed under intersection and intersection of ideals corresponds to union of their sets of zeros, such that we can even precisely represent the union of assertions. There is, however, another problem: $\mathbb{Z}[x_1, \ldots, x_n]$ is not 'co-Noetherian', i.e., there are infinitely long strictly *decreasing* chains of ideals, e.g., $\langle x \rangle \supset \langle x^2 \rangle \supset \langle x^3 \rangle \supset \ldots$. Therefore, strongest postcondition computations with ideals cannot be guaranteed to stabilize in general and widening must be used to enforce termination.

Our approach to compute weakest preconditions symbolically with effective representations is closely related to abstract interpretation [14, 15]. Requirement (b) of the generic algorithm – the representation mapping $\gamma : \mathbb{D} \to 2^\Sigma$ is universal conjunctive – implies that γ has a lower adjoint, i.e., that there is a monotonic mapping $\alpha : 2^\Sigma \to \mathbb{D}$ such that (α, γ) is a Galois connection [52]. In the standard abstract interpretation framework, we are interested in computation of least fixpoints and the lower adjoint, α, is the

Table 3.1. Complexity of constant detection: final summary.

		Must-Constants	May-Constants	
			single value	multiple value
acyclic control flow	Copy Constants			
	Linear Constants			
	Presburger Constants			NP complete
	+,-,* Constants	Co-NP compl.	NP complete	
	Full Constants			
unrestricted control flow	Copy Constants			PSPACE-compl.
	Linear Constants		NP-hard	
	Presburger Constants			
	+,-,* Constants	PSPACE-hard decidable	undecidable	
	Full Constants			

abstraction mapping. Here, we are in the dual situation: we are interested in computation of greatest fixpoints. Thus, the role of the abstraction is played by the upper adjoint, $\gamma : \mathbb{D} \to 2^{\Sigma}$. Funnily, this means that in a technical sense the members of $\mathbb{D}$ provide more concrete information than the members of 2^{Σ} and that we compute on the concrete side of the abstract interpretation. Thus, we interpret the lattice $\mathbb{D}$ as an *exact partial representation* rather than an abstract interpretation. The representation via $\mathbb{D}$ is *partial* because it does not represent all assertions exactly; this is indispensable due to countability reasons because we cannot represent all assertions effectively. It is an *exact representation* because it allows us to infer the weakest preconditions arising in the S-constant algorithms precisely, which is achieved by ensuring that the initial value of the fixpoint computation is represented exactly and that the occurring operations on representations mirror the corresponding operations on assertions precisely.

By the very nature of Galois connections, the representation mapping γ and its lower adjoint α satisfy the two inequalities $\alpha \circ \gamma \sqsubseteq \mathsf{Id}_{\mathbb{D}}$ and $\mathsf{Id}_{2^{\Sigma}} \subseteq \gamma \circ \alpha$, where $\mathsf{Id}_{\mathbb{D}}$ and $\mathsf{Id}_{2^{\Sigma}}$ are the identities on $\mathbb{D}$ and 2^{Σ}, respectively. Interestingly, none of these inequalities degenerates to an equality when we represent assertions by ideals of $\mathbb{Z}[x_1, \ldots, x_n]$ as in our algorithm for detection of polynomial constants. On the one hand, $\gamma \circ \alpha \neq \mathsf{Id}_{2^{\Sigma}}$ because the representation is necessarily partial. On the other hand, $\alpha \circ \gamma \neq \mathsf{Id}_\mathbb{D}$ because the representation of assertions is not unique. For example, if $p \in \mathbb{Z}[x_1, \ldots, x_n]$ does not have a zero in the integers, we have $\mathcal{Z}(\langle p \rangle) = \emptyset$ such that $\mathcal{Z}(\langle p \rangle) = \mathcal{Z}(\langle 1 \rangle) = \mathcal{Z}(\mathbb{Z}[x_1, \ldots, x_n])$. But by undecidability of Hilbert's tenth problem, we cannot decide whether we are faced with such a polynomial p and thus cannot effectively identify $\langle p \rangle$ and $\langle 1 \rangle$. This forces us to work with a non-unique representation. While we cannot decide whether the set of zeros of an ideal I given by a basis B is empty, we can decide whether it equals Σ because this only holds for $I = \langle 0 \rangle$. Fortunately, this is the only question that needs to be answered for the weakest precondition.

As a consequence of non-uniqueness, the weakest precondition computation on ideals does not necessarily stop once it has found a collection of ideals that represents the largest fixpoint on assertions but may proceed to larger ideals that represent the same assertions. Fortunately, we can still prove termination by arguing on ideals directly.

The decidability and complexity results of this and the previous chapter are summarized in Table 3.1. We almost completely succeeded in filling the white fields of Table 2.1. As apparent, only two questions are unsolved so far. Firstly, there is a gap between the lower bound (PSPACE-hardness) and the upper bound (decidability) for polynomial must-constants. Secondly, we miss an upper bound for linear may-constants. To attack these problems opens up opportunities for future research. The table shows that detection of may-constants is significantly harder than detecting their must-counterparts.

4. Limits of Parallel Flow Analysis

Automatic analysis of parallel programs is known as a notoriously hard problem. A well-known obstacle is the so-called *state-explosion problem*: the number of (control) states of a parallel program grows exponentially with the number of parallel components. Therefore, most practical flow analysis algorithms of concurrent programs conservatively approximate the effects arising from interference of different threads in order to achieve efficiency. A recent survey on practical research towards analysis of concurrent programs with many references is provided by Rinard [80]. In contrast to this research, we are interested in analyses of parallel programs that are *exact (or precise)* except for the common abstraction of guarded branching to non-deterministic branching that is well-known from analysis of sequential programs.

Surprisingly, certain basic but important dataflow analysis problems can still be solved precisely and efficiently for programs with a fork/join kind of parallelism. Results of this kind have been obtained by extending fixpoint computation techniques common in classic dataflow analysis to parallel programs [44, 41, 85] and by automata-theoretic techniques [18, 19]. The most general result so far shown by Seidl and Steffen [85] is that all *gen/kill problems*[1] can be solved interprocedurally in fork/join parallel programs efficiently and precisely. This comprises the important class of *bit-vector analyses*, e.g., live/dead variable analysis, available expression analysis, and reaching definitions analysis [56]

In this chapter, we consider the question whether these results can be generalized to richer classes of dataflow problems. For this purpose we investigate the complexity of copy-constant detection [20]. Copy-constant detection may be seen as a canonic representative of the next level of difficulty beyond gen/kill problems. In the sequential setting it gives rise to a *distributive* dataflow framework on a lattices with a small chain height and can thus—by the classic result of Kildall [40, 56]—completely and efficiently be solved by a fixpoint computation.

Specifically, we show by means of a reduction from the halting problem for two-counter machines that copy-constant detection is undecidable in par-

---

[1] Gen/kill problems are characterized by the fact that all transfer functions are of the form $(\lambda x : (x \wedge a) \vee b)$, where a, b are constants from the underlying lattice of dataflow facts.

allel programs with procedures (parallel interprocedural analysis). We refine this result by proving copy-constant detection to be PSPACE-complete in case that there are no procedure calls (parallel intraprocedural analysis), and co-NP-complete if also loops are abandoned (parallel acyclic analysis). The latter results are shown by means of reductions from the intersection problem for regular and star-free regular expressions, respectively. These reductions have first been presented at the ACM Symposium on Theory of Computing (STOC 2001) [61]. They render the possibility of complete and efficient dataflow algorithms for parallel programs for more extensive classes of analyses unlikely even for loop-free programs, as it is generally believed that the inclusions $P \subseteq \text{co-NP} \subseteq \text{PSPACE}$ are proper.

The prototypic framework in which these results are obtained poses only weak requirements such that the results apply to many concurrent programming languages. In particular the results are independent of synchronization operations which distinguishes them from previous intractability and undecidability results for *synchronization-sensitive flow analysis* in parallel languages [91, 77]. They should also be compared to undecidability of LTL model-checking for parallel languages as proved by Bouajjani and Habermehl [6]. While Bouajjani and Habermehl also consider a parallel language without explicit synchronization operations, they use the LTL formula to synchronize the runs of two parallel threads that simulate a two-counter machine. Thus, our results point to a more fundamental limitation for flow analysis of parallel programs as they exploit no synchronization properties.

One remark concerning the parallel composition operator is in order here. It is inherent in the definition of parallel composition that $\pi_1 \parallel \pi_2$ terminates if and when both threads π_1 and π_2 terminate (like, for instance, in OCCAM [33]). This means that there is an implicit synchronization between π_1 and π_2 at the termination point. However, as explained in Section 4.6, the hardness results remain valid without this assumption. Therefore, they also apply to languages like JAVA in which spawned threads run and terminate independently of the spawning thread.

In order to perform our reductions without relying on synchronization we use a subtle technique involving re-initialization of variables. In all reductions programs are constructed in such a way that certain *well-behaved runs* simulate some intended behavior, e.g., the execution sequences of the given two-counter machine in the undecidability proof. But we cannot avoid that the constructed programs have also certain runs that bear no correspondence to the behavior to be simulated. Let us call such runs *spurious runs*. One would typically use synchronization to exclude spurious runs but in the absence of synchronization primitives this is not possible. In order to solve this problem, we ensure by well-directed re-initialization of variables that the spurious runs do not contribute to the information that is to be determined by the analysis. In order to verify this crucial property in the reductions, we present formal program proofs in the style of Owicki and Gries [71, 21, 3] for

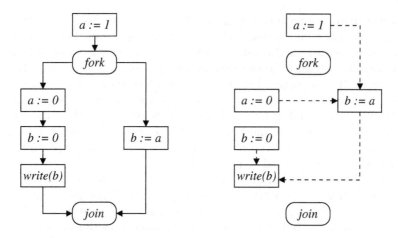

(a) CFG–like representation   (b) Def/use relationships

Fig. 4.1. An illustrative example.

the programs constructed in the reductions. Intuitively, one may interpret the
well-directed re-initialization of variables as a kind of "internal synchronization". However, in contrast to synchronization well-directed re-initialization
does not prohibit execution of spurious runs from happening; it only ensures
that spurious runs do not influence the analysis result.

In this chapter we assume that each basic statement executes as an atomic
step, a standard assumption in verification and analysis of concurrent programs. Although we use only basic statements of a very simple form, we will
see in the remaining chapters that this assumption is not as innocent as it
may seem: interprocedural copy-constant detection becomes indeed decidable in parallel programs if this assumption is abandoned as we will see in
Chapter 8.

4.1 A Motivating Example

Before we turn to the technical results, let us discuss a small example that
illustrates the subtlety of copy-constant detection in parallel programs and
the crucial re-initialization technique in our reductions. Consider the program

$$a := 1; [(a := 0; b := 0; \textbf{write}(b)) \parallel b := a].$$

In Fig. 4.1 (a) a control flow graph-like representation of the program is
shown and in (b) the *def/use relationships* between the basic statements.
There is a def/use relationship from a statement S to a statement T if there
is a program execution in which S updates a variable that is later referenced
by T without another update of this variable in between.

Although there is a path in the graph of def/use edges from the initialization $a := 1$ to the instruction **write**(b), b is a (copy) constant of value 0 at the write instruction. In order to see this, consider the following. In any execution, $b := 0$ must be executed either after or before $b := a$ in the parallel thread. If it is executed after $b := a$ then b certainly holds 0 at the write statement because 0 is assigned to b in the last executed assignment, $b := 0$. On the other hand, if $b := 0$ is executed before $b := a$ then also the re-initialization of a, $a := 0$, must have been executed before $b := a$ such that $b := a$ also loads the value 0 to b. Note that this reasoning exploits the causality inherent in sequential composition.

From this example we learn two things. Firstly, a thread can prohibit a parallel thread from propagating an 'interesting' value via a copying assignment $b := a$ by re-initializing first a and then b with an 'uninteresting' value. This is exploited in the reductions. Secondly, transitive relationships in the graph of def/use edges do not necessarily correspond to indirect dependences that can be realized in executions, in contrast to the (intraprocedural) sequential case. Following transitive relationships in the def/use graph is thus an incomplete (albeit sound) approach for dependency analysis in parallel program. Thus, while we can efficiently determine the def/use relationships in a parallel program—this is a bit-vector problem—this information is not as useful as in a sequential program.

4.2 Parallel Programs

We consider a prototypic language with shared memory, atomic assignments and fork/join parallelism. A *procedural parallel program* comprises a finite set Proc of *procedure names* containing a distinguished name *Main*. Each procedure name P is associated with a statement π_P, the corresponding *procedure body*, constructed according to the following grammar, in which Q ranges over Proc $\setminus \{Main\}$ and x over some given finite set of variables:

$$
\begin{aligned}
e &::= c \mid x \\
\pi &::= x := e \mid \textbf{write}(e) \mid \textbf{skip} \mid Q \mid \pi_1 ; \pi_2 \mid \\
&\quad \pi_1 \parallel \pi_2 \mid \pi_1 \sqcap \pi_2 \mid \textbf{loop } \pi \textbf{ end}.
\end{aligned}
$$

We use the syntax **procedure** $P; \pi_P$ **end** to indicate the association of procedure bodies to procedure names. Note that procedures do not have parameters.

The specific nature of constants and the domain in which they are interpreted is immaterial; we only need that 0 and 1 are two constants representing different values, which—by abuse of notation—are denoted by 0 and 1, too. In other words we only need Boolean variables. The atomic statements of the language are assignment statements $x := e$ that assign the current value of e to variable x, the do-nothing statement **skip**, and write statements.

In our programs we use a write statement **write**(x) to mark the program point where we are interested in constancy of a variable x; this is the only purpose of write instructions. A statement of the form Q denotes a call of procedure Q. The operator ; denotes sequential composition and $\parallel$ parallel composition. The operator $\sqcap$ represents non-deterministic branching and **loop** π **end** stands for a loop that iterates π an indefinite number of times. Such constructs are chosen in accordance with the abstraction of guarded branching to non-deterministic branching discussed in the introduction. We apply the non-deterministic choice operator also to finite sets of statements; $\sqcap\{\pi_1,\ldots,\pi_n\}$ denotes $\pi_1 \sqcap \cdots \sqcap \pi_n$. The ambiguity inherent in this notation is harmless because $\sqcap$ is commutative, associative, and idempotent semantically.

Note that there are no synchronization operations in the language. The synchronization of start and termination inherent in fork- and join-parallelism is also not essential for our results; see Section 4.6.

Parallelism is understood in an interleaving fashion; assignments and write statements are assumed to be atomic. A *run* of a program is a maximal sequence of atomic statements that may be executed in this order in an execution of the program. The program $(x := 1 \,; x := y) \parallel y := x$, for example, has the three runs $\langle x := 1, x := y, y := x \rangle$, $\langle x := 1, y := x, x := y \rangle$, and $\langle y := x, x := 1, x := y \rangle$. We denote the set of runs of program π by $\mathsf{Runs}(\pi)$.

Note that the prototypic language has only assignments of a very simple form: $x := k$ where k is either a constant or a variable. These are just the assignments that are interpreted in copy-constant detection. Consequently, for the prototypic language, constants and copy constants coincide. Hardness results for constant detection in programs of this prototypic language can immediately be interpreted as hardness results for copy-constant detection in more general parallel languages. This justifies to identify for the purpose of this chapter the copy-constant detection problem in parallel programs with the detection problem of constants in programs of the prototypic language.

4.3 Interprocedural Copy-Constant Detection

The goal of this section is to prove the following theorem.

Theorem 4.3.1. *Parallel interprocedural copy-constant detection is undecidable.*

It is well-known that the termination problem for two-counter machines is undecidable [54]. In the remainder of this section, we reduce this problem to an interprocedural copy-constant detection problem thereby proving Theorem 4.3.1.

4.3.1 Two-Counter Machines

A two-counter machine has two counter variables c_0 and c_1 that can be incremented, decremented, and tested against zero. It is common to use a combined decrement- and test-instruction in order to avoid complications with decrementing a zero counter. The basic idea of our reduction is to represent the values of the counters by the stack height of two threads of procedures running in parallel. Incrementing a counter is represented by calling another procedure in the corresponding thread, decrementing by returning from the current procedure, and the test against zero by using different procedures at the first and the other stack levels that represent the possible moves for zero and non-zero counters, respectively. It simplifies the argumentation if computation steps involving the two counters alternate. This can always be enforced by adding skip-instructions that do nothing except of transferring control.

Formally, we use the following model. A *two-counter machine* M comprises a finite set of (control) states S. S is partitioned into two sets $P = \{p_1, \ldots, p_n\}$ and $Q = \{q_1, \ldots, q_m\}$; moves involving counter c_0 start from P and moves involving counter c_1 from Q. Execution commences at a distinguished *start state* which, without loss of generality, is p_1. There is also a distinguished *final state*, without loss of generality p_n, at which execution terminates. Each state $s \in S$ except of the final state p_n is associated with an instruction $I(s)$ taken from the following selection:

- $c_i := c_i + 1; \textbf{goto } s'$ (increment),
- **if** $c_i = 0$ **then goto** s' **else** $c_i := c_i - 1;$ **goto** s'' (test-decrement), or
- **goto** s' (skip),

where $i = 0$ and $s', s'' \in Q$ if $s \in P$, and $i = 1$ and $s', s'' \in P$ if $s \in Q$. Note that this condition captures that moves alternate.

Execution of a two-counter machine M is represented by a transition relation $\to_M$ on configurations $\langle s, x_0, x_1 \rangle$ that consist of a current state $s \in S$ and current values $x_0 \geq 0$ and $x_1 \geq 0$ of the counters. Configurations with $s = p_n$ are called *final configurations*. We have $\langle s, x_0, x_1 \rangle \to_M \langle s', x'_0, x'_1 \rangle$ if and only if one of the following conditions is valid for $i = 0, 1$:

- $I(s) = c_i := c_i + 1; \textbf{goto } s'$, $x'_i = x_i + 1$, and $x'_{1-i} = x_{1-i}$.
- $I(s) = \textbf{if } c_i = 0 \textbf{ then goto } s' \textbf{ else } c_i := c_i - 1;$ **goto** s'', $x_i = 0$, $x'_i = x_i$, and $x'_{1-i} = x_{1-i}$.
- $I(s) = \textbf{if } c_i = 0 \textbf{ then goto } s'' \textbf{ else } c_i := c_i - 1;$ **goto** s', $x_i \neq 0$, $x'_i = x_i - 1$, and $x'_{1-i} = x_{1-i}$.
- $I(s) = \textbf{goto } s'$, $x'_i = x_i$, and $x'_{1-i} = x_{1-i}$.

Thus, each non-final configuration has a unique successor configuration. We denote the reflexive transitive closure of $\to_M$ by $\to_M^*$ and omit the subscript M if it is clear from the context.

procedure P_0;
loop
   $\sqcap \{p := x_k \,; \mathsf{KillAll}_P \,; y_l := p \,; P_{\neq 0} \mid$
      $I(p_k) \;=\; c_0 := c_0 + 1; \mathbf{goto}\ q_l\} \sqcap$
   $\sqcap \{p := x_k \,; \mathsf{KillAll}_P \,; y_l := p \mid$
      $I(p_k) \;=\; \mathbf{if}\ c_0 = 0\ \mathbf{then\ goto}\ q_l\ \mathbf{else} \ldots\} \sqcap$
   $\sqcap \{p := x_k \,; \mathsf{KillAll}_P \,; y_l := p \mid I(p_k) \;=\; \mathbf{goto}\ q_l\}$
end
end

procedure $P_{\neq 0}$;
loop
   $\sqcap \{p := x_k \,; \mathsf{KillAll}_P \,; y_l := p \,; P_{\neq 0} \mid$
      $I(p_k) \;=\; c_0 := c_0 + 1; \mathbf{goto}\ q_l\} \sqcap$
   $\sqcap \{p := x_k \,; \mathsf{KillAll}_P \,; y_l := p \mid I(p_k) \;=\; \mathbf{goto}\ q_l\}$
end ;
$\sqcap \{p := x_k \,; \mathsf{KillAll}_P \,; y_l := p \mid$
      $I(p_k) \;=\; \mathbf{if}\ c_0 = 0\ \mathbf{then} \ldots \mathbf{else} \ldots \mathbf{goto}\ q_l\}$
end

procedure $\mathsf{KillAll}_P$;
$y_1 := 0 \,; \ldots \,; y_m := 0 \,; q := 0 \,; x_1 := 0 \,; \ldots \,; x_n := 0$
end

Fig. 4.2. Definition of P_0 and $P_{\neq 0}$.

Execution of a two-counter machine commences at the start state with the counters initialized by zero, i.e. in the configuration $\langle p_1, 0, 0 \rangle$. The two-counter machine *terminates* if it ever reaches the final state, i.e. if $\langle p_1, 0, 0 \rangle \rightarrow^*$ $\langle p_n, x_0, x_1 \rangle$ for some x_0, x_1. As far as the halting behavior is concerned, we can assume without loss of generality that both counters are zero upon termination. This can be ensured by adding two loops at the final state that iteratively decrement the counters until they become zero. Obviously, this modification preserves the termination behavior of the two-counter machine. Note that for the modified machine the conditions "$\langle p_1, 0, 0 \rangle \rightarrow^* \langle p_n, x_0, x_1 \rangle$ for some x_0, x_1" and "$\langle p_1, 0, 0 \rangle \rightarrow^* \langle p_n, 0, 0 \rangle$" are equivalent. We assume in the following that such loops have been added to the given machine.

4.3.2 Constructing a Program

From a two-counter machine we construct a parallel program, π_M. For each state $p_k \in P$ the program uses a variable x_k and for each state $q_l \in Q$ a variable y_l. Intuitively, x_k holds the value 1 in an execution of the program iff this execution corresponds to a run of the two-counter machine reaching state p_k, and similarly for the y_l.

```
procedure Q₀;
loop
    ⊓ {q := y_k ; KillAll_Q ; x_l := q ; Q_≠0 |
        I(q_k) = c_1 := c_1 + 1; goto p_l} ⊓
    ⊓ {q := y_k ; KillAll_Q ; x_l := q |
        I(q_k) = if c_1 = 0 then goto p_l else ...} ⊓
    ⊓ {q := y_k ; KillAll_Q ; x_l := q | I(q_k) = goto p_l}
end
end

procedure Q_≠0;
loop
    ⊓ {q := y_k ; KillAll_Q ; x_l := q ; Q_≠0 |
        I(q_k) = c_1 := c_1 + 1; goto p_l} ⊓
    ⊓ {q := y_k ; KillAll_Q ; x_l := q | I(q_k) = goto p_l}
end ;
    ⊓ {q := y_k ; KillAll_Q ; x_l := q |
        I(q_k) = if c_1 = 0 then ... else ... goto p_l}
end

procedure KillAll_Q;
x_1 := 0 ; ... ; x_n := 0 ; p := 0 ; y_1 := 0 ; ... ; y_m := 0
end
```

Fig. 4.3. Definition of Q_0 and $Q_{\neq 0}$.

The main procedure of π_M reads as follows:

```
procedure Main;
x_1 := 1 ; Init ;
(P_0 ∥ Q_0) ;
(x_n := 0 ⊓ skip) ; write(x_n)
end
```

```
procedure Init;
x_2 := 0 ; ... ; x_n := 0 ;
y_1 := 0 ; ... ; y_m := 0
end
```

The threads P_0 and Q_0 are constructed such that M terminates if and only if x_n is not a constant at the write instruction. Note that this implies Theorem 4.3.1.

The initialization $x_1 := 1$ is the only occurrence of the constant 1 in the program; all other variables are initialized by 0. Moreover, all other assignment statements only copy values or re-initialize variables by 0. Thus, x_n can hold only the values 0 or 1 at the write statement. Clearly, x_n may hold 0 due to the statement $(x_n := 0 \sqcap \mathbf{skip})$ immediately before the write statement. Thus x_n can only be a constant of value 0, and, obviously, this is the case if and only if x_n cannot hold value 1 at the write instruction. Thus, we can reformulate the goal of the construction as follows:

M terminates if and only if x_n may hold 1 at the write statement.

(4.1)

The initialization of all variables except x_1 by 0 reflects that p_1 is the initial state. For each of the two counters the program uses two procedures, P_0

and $P_{\neq 0}$ for counter c_0 and Q_0 and $Q_{\neq 0}$ for counter c_1. They are defined in Fig. 4.2 and 4.3. We describe P_0 and $P_{\neq 0}$ in detail in the following, Q_0 and $Q_{\neq 0}$ are completely analogous.

Intuitively, P_0 and $P_{\neq 0}$ mirror transitions of M induced by counter c_0 being $=0$ and $\neq 0$, respectively, hence their name. Each procedure non-deterministically guesses the next transition. Such a transition involves two things: firstly, a state change and, secondly, an effect on the counter value. The state change from some p_k to some q_l is represented by copying x_k to y_l via an auxiliary variable p and re-initializing x_k by zero as part of KillAll$_P$. The effect on the counter value is represented by how we proceed:

- For transitions that do not change the counter we jump back to the beginning of the procedure such that other transitions with the same counter value can be simulated subsequently. This applies to skip-transitions and test-decrement transitions for a zero counter, i.e. test-decrement transitions simulated in P_0.
- For incrementing transitions we call another instance of $P_{\neq 0}$ that simulates the transitions induced by the incremented counter. A return from this new instance of $P_{\neq 0}$ means that the counter is decremented, i.e. has the old value. We therefore jump back to the beginning of the procedure after the return from $P_{\neq 0}$.
- For test-decrement transitions simulated in $P_{\neq 0}$, we leave the current procedure.

This behavior is described in a structured way by means of loops and sequential and non-deterministic composition and is consistent with the representation of the counter value by the number of instances of $P_{\neq 0}$ on the stack.

The problem with achieving (4.1) is that an execution may try to 'cheat': it may execute the code representing a transition from p_i to q_j although x_i does not hold the value 1. If this is a decrementing or incrementing transition the coincidence between counter values and stack heights may then be destroyed and the value 1 may subsequently be propagated erroneously. Cheating may thus invalidate the 'if' direction.

This problem is solved as follows. We ensure by appropriate re-initialization that all variables are set to 0 in any cheating executions. Thus, cheating executions cannot contribute to the propagation of the value 1. But re-initializing a set of variables safely is not trivial in a concurrent environment. We have only atomic assignments to single variables available; a variable just set to 0 may well be set to another value by instructions executed by instances of the procedures Q_0 and $Q_{\neq 0}$ running in parallel while we are initializing the other variables. Here our assumption that moves involving the counters alternate comes into play. Due to this assumption all copying assignments in Q_0 and $Q_{\neq 0}$ are of the form $q := y_i$ or $x_j := q$ (q is the analog of the auxiliary variable p). Thus, we can safely assign 0 to the y_i in P_0 and $P_{\neq 0}$ as they are not the target of a copy instruction in Q_0 or $Q_{\neq 0}$. After this, we can safely assign 0 to q; a copy instruction $q := y_i$ executed by the parallel thread cannot destroy the value 0 as all y_i contain 0 already. After that we can safely assign 0 to the x_i by a similar argument. This explains the definition of $\mathsf{KillAll}_P$.

4.3.3 Correctness of the Reduction

From the intuition underlying the definition of π_M, the 'only if' direction of (4.1) is rather obvious: If M terminates, i.e., if it has transitions leading from $\langle p_1, 0, 0 \rangle$ to $\langle p_n, 0, 0 \rangle$, we can simulate these transitions by a propagating run of π_M. By explaining the definition of $\mathsf{KillAll}_P$, we justified the 'if' direction as well. A formal proof can be given along the lines of the classic Owicki/Gries method for proving partial correctness of parallel programs [71, 21, 3]. Although this method is usually presented for programs without procedures it is sound also for procedural programs. In the Owicki/Gries method, programs are annotated with assertions that represent properties valid for any execution reaching the program point at which the assertion is written down. This annotation is subject to certain rules that guarantee soundness of the method.

Specifically, we prove that just before the write instruction in π_M the following assertion is valid:

$$x_n = 1 \;\Rightarrow\; \langle p_1, 0, 0 \rangle \rightarrow^* \langle p_n, 0, 0 \rangle \,.$$

Validity of this assertion implies the 'if' direction of (4.1). The details of this proof are deferred to Section 4.8 in order to increase readability of this chapter.

Our proof should be compared to undecidability of reachability in presence of synchronization as proved by Ramalingam [77], and undecidability of LTL model-checking for parallel languages (even without synchronization) as proved by Bouajjani and Habermehl [6]. Both proofs employ two sequential threads running in parallel. Ramalingam uses the two recursion stacks of the threads to simulate context-free grammar derivations of two words whose equality is enforced by the synchronization facilities of the programming language. Bouajjani and Habermehl use the two recursion stacks to simulate two counters (as we do) whose joint operation then is synchronized through the LTL formula. Thus, both proofs rely on some kind of "external synchronization" of the two threads – which is not available in our scenario. Instead, our undecidability proof works with "internal synchronization" which is provided implicitly by killing the circulating value 1 as soon as one thread deviates from the intended synchronous behavior.

4.4 Intraprocedural Copy-Constant Detection

The undecidability result just presented means that we cannot expect to detect all copy constants in parallel programs. Therefore, we must lower our expectation. In dataflow analysis one often investigates also *intraprocedural* problems. These can be viewed as problems for programs without procedure calls. Here, we find:

Theorem 4.4.1. *Copy-constant detection is PSPACE-complete for parallel programs intraprocedurally.*

We can construct a non-deterministic algorithm that determines non-constancy by guessing two runs witnessing different values for the variable in question at the program point of interest. This algorithm can be implemented in polynomial space: In a fork/join parallel program without procedures, the number of threads potentially running in parallel is bounded by the size of the program. Therefore, every run of the program can be simulated by a Turing machine using just a polynomial amount of space. Moreover, as no arithmetic is involved, only values present in the program have to be represented during the computation of the runs. We conclude that the intraprocedural copy-constant detection problem is in NPSPACE=PSPACE.

It remains to show that PSPACE is also a lower bound on the complexity of copy-constant detection, i.e. PSPACE-hardness. This is done by a reduction from the REGULAR EXPRESSION INTERSECTION problem. This problem is chosen in favor of the better known intersection problem for finite automata as we are heading for structured programs and not for flow graphs.

An instance of REGULAR EXPRESSION INTERSECTION is given by a sequence $r_1, \ldots, r_n$ of regular expressions over some finite alphabet A. The problem is to decide whether $L(r_1) \cap \ldots \cap L(r_n)$ is non-empty.

Proposition 4.4.1. *The* REGULAR EXPRESSION INTERSECTION *problem is PSPACE-complete.* □

PSPACE-hardness of the REGULAR EXPRESSION INTERSECTION problem follows by a reduction from the acceptance problem for linear space bounded Turing machines along the lines of the corresponding proof for finite automata [45]. The problem remains PSPACE-complete if we consider expressions without ∅.

Suppose now that $A = \{a_1, \ldots, a_k\}$, and we are given n regular expressions $r_1, \ldots, r_n$. In our reduction we construct a parallel program that starts $n + 1$ threads $\pi_0, \ldots, \pi_n$ after some initialization of the variables used in the program:

> **procedure** *Main*;
> KillXY$_0$; . . . ; KillXY$_n$; $x_{n,a_1} := 1$;
> $[\pi_0 \parallel \pi_1 \parallel \cdots \parallel \pi_n]$;
> $(x_{0,a_1} := 0 \sqcap \textbf{skip})$; $\textbf{write}(x_{0,a_1})$
> **end**

The threads refer to variables $x_{i,a}$ and y_i ($i \in \{0, \ldots, n\}$, $a \in A$). Thread π_0 is defined as follows.

$$\pi_0 = \textbf{loop}$$
$$\sqcap \{y_0 := x_{n,a} \,; \mathsf{KillAll}_0 \,; x_{0,b} := y_0 \mid a, b \in A\}$$
$$\textbf{end}$$

The statement $\mathsf{KillAll}_0$ that is defined below ensures that all variables except y_0 are re-initialized by 0 irrespective of the behavior of the other threads as shown below.

For $i = 1, \ldots, n$, the thread π_i is induced by the regular expression r_i. It is given by $\pi_i = \pi_i(r_i)$, where $\pi_i(r)$ is defined by induction on r as follows.

$$
\begin{aligned}
\pi_i(\varepsilon) &= \textbf{skip} \\
\pi_i(a) &= y_i := x_{i-1,a} \,; \mathsf{KillAll}_i \,; x_{i,a} := y_i \\
\pi_i(r_1 \cdot r_2) &= \pi_i(r_1) \,; \pi_i(r_2) \\
\pi_i(r_1 + r_2) &= \pi_i(r_1) \sqcap \pi_i(r_2) \\
\pi_i(r^*) &= \textbf{loop}\ \pi_i(r)\ \textbf{end}
\end{aligned}
$$

The statement $\mathsf{KillAll}_i$ re-initializes all variables except y_i. This statement as well as statements KillX_j and KillXY_j on which its definition is based, are defined as follows.

$$
\begin{aligned}
\mathsf{KillX}_j &= x_{j,a_1} := 0; \ldots; x_{j,a_k} := 0 \\
\mathsf{KillXY}_j &= y_j := 0; \mathsf{KillX}_j \\
\mathsf{KillAll}_i &= \mathsf{KillX}_i; \mathsf{KillXY}_{i+1}; \ldots; \mathsf{KillXY}_n; \\
&\quad\ \mathsf{KillXY}_0; \ldots; \mathsf{KillXY}_{i-1}
\end{aligned}
$$

Again it is not obvious that thread π_i can safely re-initialize the variables because the other threads may arbitrarily interleave. But by exploiting that only copy instructions of the form $y_j := x_{j-1,a}$ and $x_{j,a} := y_j$ with $j \neq i$ are present in the other threads this can be done by performing the re-initializations in the order specified above.[2] Two crucial properties are exploited for this. First, whenever $a := b$ is a copying assignments in a parallel thread, variable b is re-initialized before a. Therefore, execution of $a := b$ after the re-initialization of b just copies the value 0 from b to a but cannot destroy the re-initialization of a. Secondly, in all constant assignments $a := k$ in parallel threads k equals 0 such that no other values can be generated.

Altogether, the threads are constructed in such a way that the following is valid.

$$L(r_1) \cap \ldots \cap L(r_n) \neq \emptyset \text{ if and only if} \tag{4.2}$$
$$x_{0,a_1} \text{ is not a constant (of value 0) at the write statement.}$$

Again, the latter is the case if and only if there is a run that propagates the value 1 by which x_{n,a_1} is initialized to the **write**-instruction. In the following,

---

[2] Here and in the following, addition and subtraction in subscripts of variables and processes is understood modulo $n + 1$.

we describe the intuition underlying the construction and at the same time prove (4.2).

The threads can be considered to form a ring of processes in which process π_i has processes π_{i-1} as left neighbor and π_{i+1} as right neighbor. Each thread π_i $(i = 1, \ldots, n)$ guesses a word in $L(r_i)$; thread π_0 guesses some word in A^*. The special form of the threads ensures that they can propagate the initialization value 1 for x_{n,a_1} if and only if all of them agree on the guessed word and interleave the corresponding runs in a disciplined fashion. Obviously, the latter is possible iff $L(r_1) \cap \ldots \cap L(r_n) \neq \emptyset$.

Let $w = c_1 \cdot \ldots \cdot c_l$ be a word in $L(r_1) \cap \ldots \cap L(r_n)$ and let $c_0 = a_1$, the first letter in alphabet A. In the run induced by w that successfully propagates the value 1, the threads circulate the value 1 around the ring of processes in the variables x_{i,c_i} for each letter c_i of w. We call this the *propagation game* in the following. At the beginning of the j-th round, $j = 1, \ldots, l$, process π_0 'proposes' the letter c_j by copying the value 1 from the variable $x_{n,c_{j-1}}$ to x_{0,c_j} in which it was left by the previous round or by the initialization, respectively. For technical reasons this copying is done via the 'local' variable[3] y_0. Afterwards the processes π_i $(i = 1, \ldots, n)$ successively copy the value from x_{i-1,c_j} to x_{i,c_j} via their 'local' variables y_i. From x_{n,c_j} it is copied by π_0 in the next round to $x_{0,c_{j+1}}$ and so on. After the last round $(j = l)$ π_0 finally copies the value 1 from x_{n,c_l} to x_{0,a_1} and all processes terminate. Writing— by a little abuse of notation—$\pi_i(a)$ for the single run of $\pi_i(a)$ and $\pi_0(a, b)$ for the single run of $y_0 := x_{n,a}$; $\mathsf{KillAll}_0$; $x_{0,b} := y_0$, we can summarize above discussion by saying that

$$\pi_0(a_1, c_1) \cdot \pi_1(c_1) \cdot \ldots \cdot \pi_n(c_1) \cdot$$
$$\pi_0(c_1, c_2) \cdot \pi_1(c_2) \cdot \ldots \cdot \pi_n(c_2) \cdot$$
$$\vdots$$
$$\pi_0(c_{l-1}, c_l) \cdot \pi_1(c_l) \cdot \ldots \cdot \pi_n(c_l) \cdot$$
$$\pi_0(c_l, a_1)$$

is a run of $\pi_0 \parallel \ldots \parallel \pi_n$ that witnesses that x_{0,a_1} may hold the value 1 finally, and is thus not a constant at the write statement. This implies the 'only if' direction of (4.2).

Next we show that the construction of the threads ensures that runs not following the propagation game cannot propagate the value 1 to the write instruction. In particular, if $L(r_1) \cap \ldots \cap L(r_n) = \emptyset$, no propagating run exists, which implies the 'if' direction of (4.2).

Note first that all runs of π_i are composed of pieces of the form $\pi_i(a)$ and all runs of π_0 of pieces of the form $\pi_0(a, b)$ which is easily shown by induction. A run can now deviate from the propagation game in two ways. First, it can follow the rules but terminate in the middle of a round:

---

[3] Variable y_i is not local to π_i in a strict sense. But the other threads do not use it as target or source of a copying assignment; they only re-initialize it.

$$\pi_0(a_1, c_1) \cdot \pi_1(c_1) \cdot \ldots \cdot \pi_i(c_1) \cdot \ldots \cdot \pi_n(c_1) \cdot$$
$$\pi_0(c_1, c_2) \cdot \pi_1(c_2) \cdot \ldots \cdot \pi_i(c_2) \cdot \ldots \cdot \pi_n(c_2) \cdot$$
$$\vdots$$
$$\pi_0(c_{m-1}, c_m) \cdot \pi_1(c_m) \cdot \ldots \cdot \pi_i(c_m)$$

Such a run does not propagate the value 1 to the write instruction as $\mathsf{KillAll}_i$ in $\pi_i(c_m)$ re-initializes x_{0,a_1}.

Secondly, a run might cease following the rules of the propagation game after some initial (possibly empty) part. Consider then the first code piece $\pi_i(a)$ or $\pi_0(a, b)$ that is started in ignorance of the propagation game rules. It is not hard to see that the first statement in this code piece, $y_i := x_{i-1,a}$ or $y_0 := x_{n,a}$, respectively, then sets the local variable y_i or y_0 to zero. The reason is that the propagation game ensures that variable $x_{i-1,a}$ or $x_{n,a}$ holds 0 unless the next statement to be executed according to the rules of the propagation game comes from $\pi_i(a)$ or some $\pi_0(a, b)$, respectively. The subsequent statement $\mathsf{KillAll}_i$ or $\mathsf{KillAll}_0$ then irrevocably re-initializes all the other variables irrespective of the behavior of the other threads as we have shown above. Thus, such a run also cannot propagate the value 1 to the write instruction.

An Owicki/Gries style proof that confirms the crucial 'if' direction of (4.2) can be found in Section 4.9.

4.5 Copy-Constant Detection in Loop-Free Programs

We may lower our expectation even more, and ban not only procedures but also loops from the programs. But even then, copy-constant detection remains intractable, unless P=NP.

Theorem 4.5.1. *The parallel intraprocedural copy-constant detection problem in loop-free programs is co-NP-complete.*

That the problem is in co-NP is easy to see. If a variable x is not a constant at a certain program point p, we can guess two runs of the program that witness different values for x at p. Each of these runs can involve each statement in the program at most once as the program is loop-free. Hence its length is linear in the size of the given program. As no arithmetic is involved in copy-constant detection, only values present in the input program have to be represented such that the time necessary for guessing the runs is polynomial in the size of the input program.

Co-NP-hardness can be proved by specializing the construction from Section 4.4 to star-free regular expressions. The intersection problem for such expressions is NP-complete.

An alternative reduction from the well-known SAT problem is presented in Chapter 9. In contrast to the construction of the current chapter, the reduction there relies only on propagation along copying assignments but not on "quasi-synchronization" through well-directed re-initialization of variables. However, this technique does not seem to generalize to the general intraprocedural and the interprocedural case.

4.6 Beyond Fork/Join Parallelism

A weak form of synchronization is inherent in the fork/join parallelism assumed in this chapter, as start and termination of threads is synchronized. The hardness results of this chapter, however, are not restricted to such settings but can also be shown without assuming synchronous start and termination. Therefore, they also apply to languages like JAVA.

The PSPACE-hardness proof in Section 4.4, for instance, can be modified as follows. Let c, d be two new distinct letters and $B = A \cup \{c, d\}$. Now π_i is defined as $\pi_i(c \cdot r_i \cdot d)$ and the initialization and the final write instruction is moved to thread π_0. More specifically, π_0 is redefined as follows:

$$\pi_0 = \mathsf{KillAll}_0 \, ; x_{0,c} := 1 \, ;$$
$$\quad \mathbf{loop}$$
$$\quad\quad \sqcap \{ y_0 := x_{n,a} \, ; \mathsf{KillAll}_0 \, ; x_{0,b} := y_0 \mid a, b \in B \}$$
$$\quad \mathbf{end} \, ;$$
$$\quad (x_{n,d} := 0 \sqcap \mathbf{skip}) \, ; \mathbf{write}(x_{n,d})$$

(Of course the statements KillX_i have to re-initialize also the new variables $x_{i,c}$ and $x_{i,d}$.) Essentially this modification amounts to requiring that the propagation game is played with a first round for letter c—this ensures a quasi-synchronous start of the threads—and a final round for letter d—this ensures a quasi-synchronous termination. Thus,

$L(r_1) \cap \ldots \cap L(r_n) \neq \emptyset$ if and only if
$x_{n,d}$ is not a constant (of value 0) at the write statement.

Similar modifications work for the reductions in Section 4.3 and 4.5.

4.7 Owicki/Gries-Style Program Proofs

Reasoning about parallel programs is known as a notoriously error-prone activity. The actions of different threads can interleave in many different ways and far too easily certain interleavings are overlooked that invalidate an informal argument for subtle reasons. In order to safeguard against error in our reasoning, we perform formal program proofs in the style of Owicki and Gries' classic method [71, 21, 3] that confirm the critical parts of the reasoning in the reductions. In the remainder of this section we briefly recall the Owicki/Gries method and in the following two sections we present the proofs for the critical directions in the undecidability proof of Section 4.3 and the PSPACE-hardness proof of Section 4.4. These sections may safely be skipped on first reading.

The Owicki/Gries method relies on *proof outlines* which are programs annotated with assertions. Assertions are formulas that represent properties valid for any execution that reaches the program point where the assertion is written down. As usual we write assertions in braces. The annotation is subject to the rules well-known from sequential program proofs. For example if an assignment statement $x := e$ is preceded by an assertion $\{\phi\}$ and followed by an assertion $\{\psi\}$, then ϕ must imply $\psi[e/x]$, where $\psi[e/x]$ denotes the assertion obtained by substituting e for x in ψ. We assume that the reader is familiar with this style of program proofs (for details see e.g. [71, 21, 3]).

The rule for parallel programs looks as follows [3, Rule 19]:

$$\frac{\text{The standard proof outlines } \{p_i\}S_i^*\{q_i\},\ i \in \{1, \ldots, n\},\ \text{are interference free}}{\{\bigwedge_{i=1}^n p_i\}[S_1 \parallel \ldots \parallel S_n]\{\bigwedge_{i=1}^n q_i\}}$$

In this rule S_i^* stands for an annotated version of parallel component S_i and the requirement that the proof outlines for the component programs are 'standard' means in our context that every atomic statement is surrounded by assertions.

The crucial additional premise for parallel programs is *interference freedom*. The following must be true in an interference-free proof outline for a parallel program: Suppose $\{\phi\}$ is an assertion in one parallel component and S is an atomic statement in another parallel component that is preceded by the assertion $pre(S)$. Then $\{\phi \wedge pre(S)\}S\{\phi\}$ must be valid in the usual sense of partial correctness. Intuitively, inference freedom guarantees that validity of an assertion is not destroyed by instructions of threads running in parallel.

4.8 Correctness of the Reduction in Section 4.3

Let us now formally prove the 'if' direction of (4.1). We assume all notations and definitions of Section 4.3. As mentioned, we prove that just before the write instruction in π_M the following assertion is valid in the sense of partial correctness, i.e., that any execution reaching this program point satisfies the property:

$$x_n = 1 \;\Rightarrow\; \langle p_0, 0, 0 \rangle \rightarrow^* \langle p_n, 0, 0 \rangle. \tag{4.3}$$

Validity of this assertion corresponds directly to the 'if' direction of (4.1).

4.8.1 Enriching the Program

Before we discuss proof outlines, we enrich the program π_M by two variables c_0 and c_1 that reflect the values of the counters. Initialization statements

$c_0 := 0$ and $c_1 := 0$ are added to the *Init* procedure. Furthermore, c_0 and c_1 are incremented and decremented at appropriate places in P_0, $P_{\neq 0}$, Q_0, and $Q_{\neq 0}$. (For the purpose of performing the proof we allow more general expressions in assignment statements.) Specifically, the code pieces of the form

$$p := x_k \,; \mathsf{KillAll}_P \,; y_l := p \,; P_{\neq 0}$$

that represent incrementing transitions in P_0 and $P_{\neq 0}$ are replaced by

$$p := x_k \,; \mathsf{KillAll}_P \,; c_0 := c_0 + 1 \,; y_l := p \,; P_{\neq 0}$$

and the code pieces after the loop in $P_{\neq 0}$ that represent decrementing transitions are replaced by

$$p := x_k \,; \mathsf{KillAll}_P \,; c_0 := c_0 - 1 \,; y_l := p \,.$$

Analogous modifications are made in Q_0 and $Q_{\neq 0}$ for counter c_1. It is obvious that Assertion (4.3) holds in the modified program if and only if it holds in the original program as c_0 and c_1 are only used in assignments to themselves. (c_0 and c_1 are *auxiliary variables* in the formal sense of the term used in connection with the Owicki/Gries method. It is well-known that the Owicki/Gries method is incomplete without auxiliary variables [21].)

4.8.2 The Proof Outlines

The assertions in the proof ensure that certain configurations are reachable in M if a certain variable in π_M holds value 1. We introduce an abbreviation for the formula expressing this fact:

$$\mathsf{OK}(x, s, c_0, c_1) \quad :\Leftrightarrow \quad x = 1 \;\Rightarrow\; \langle p_1, 0, 0 \rangle \to^* \langle s, c_0, c_1 \rangle$$

Here x is a variable of the constructed program, s is a state of the two-counter machine and c_0, c_1 are expressions involving the auxiliary variables from above. Note that Assertion (4.3) is simply $\mathsf{OK}(x_n, p_n, 0, 0)$.

The proof outline for the body of procedure *Main* looks as follows. For clarity, we use a comma to denote conjunction in assertions.

[1]   {true}
[2] $x_1 := 1$;
[3] $\{x_1 = 1\}$
[4]   *Init*
[5] $\{x_1 = 1,\ c_0 = 0,\ c_1 = 0,\ \bigwedge_{i=2}^{n} x_i = 0,\ \bigwedge_{i=1}^{m} y_i = 0\}$
[6] $\{c_0 = 0,\ c_1 = 0,\ \bigwedge_{i=1}^{n} \mathsf{OK}(x_i, p_i, c_0, c_1),\ \bigwedge_{i=1}^{m} \mathsf{OK}(y_i, q_i, c_0, c_1)\}$
[7] $(P_0 \parallel Q_0)$;
[8] $\{c_0 = 0,\ c_1 = 0,\ \bigwedge_{i=1}^{n} \mathsf{OK}(x_i, p_i, c_0, c_1),\ \bigwedge_{i=1}^{m} \mathsf{OK}(y_i, q_i, c_0, c_1)\}$
[9] $(x_n := 0 \sqcap \mathbf{skip})$;
[10] $\{\mathsf{OK}(x_n, p_n, 0, 0)\}$
[11]   **write**(x_n)

The obvious proof outline for *Init* is omitted. It is easy to see that line [5] implies the assertion in line [6] as $OK(x, s, 0, 0)$ trivially holds if x holds 0 or if s is p_1. Also statement [9] is partially correct with respect to the surrounding assertions: $x_n := 0$ establishes Assertion [10] for trivial reasons; and validity for **skip** follows from the fact that the Assertion [8] implies the Assertion [10] which is obvious.

It remains to show that the statement in line [7], $P_0 \parallel Q_0$, is partially correct with respect to the surrounding assertions. For this purpose we show—by interference free proof outlines—that P_0 and Q_0 satisfy the following specifications and apply the parallel rule of the Owicki/Gries method:

$$\{c_0 = 0, \bigwedge_{i=1}^{n} OK(x_i, p_i, c_0, c_1)\} \qquad \{c_1 = 0, \bigwedge_{i=1}^{m} OK(y_i, q_i, c_0, c_1)\}$$
$$P_0 \qquad\qquad\qquad\qquad Q_0$$
$$\{c_0 = 0, \bigwedge_{i=1}^{n} OK(x_i, p_i, c_0, c_1)\} \qquad \{c_1 = 0, \bigwedge_{i=1}^{m} OK(y_i, p_i, c_0, c_1)\}$$

Simultaneously, we prove similar specifications for $P_{\neq 0}$ and $Q_{\neq 0}$ that are parameterized by a constant $k > 0$:

$$\{c_0 = k, \bigwedge_{i=1}^{n} OK(x_i, p_i, c_0, c_1)\} \qquad \{c_1 = k, \bigwedge_{i=1}^{m} OK(y_i, q_i, c_0, c_1)\}$$
$$P_{\neq 0} \qquad\qquad\qquad\qquad Q_{\neq 0}$$
$$\{c_0 = k-1, \bigwedge_{i=1}^{n} OK(x_i, p_i, c_0, c_1)\} \qquad \{c_1 = k-1, \bigwedge_{i=1}^{m} OK(y_i, q_i, c_0, c_1)\}$$

As we are concerned with partial correctness, it suffices to show that the body of the procedures satisfy these specification, under the assumption that recursive calls do.

In the following we present the proof outlines for P_0 and $P_{\neq 0}$ in detail; the proofs for Q_0 and $Q_{\neq 0}$ are completely analogous. Afterwards we show interference freedom, a proof that reflects crucial properties of our construction.

The first goal is to show that the precondition of each procedure is an invariant of the loop in the body of that procedure. This amounts to proving that each path through the loop preserves the precondition. Let $k = 0$ for the proof in P_0 and $k > 0$ for the proof in $P_{\neq 0}$.

This is the proof for the paths induced by skip-transitions in both procedures or test-decrement transitions in P_0 :

[11] $\{c_0 = k, \ \bigwedge_{i=1}^{n} OK(x_i, p_i, c_0, c_1)\}$
[12] $p := x_k$;
[13] $\{c_0 = k, \ OK(p, p_k, c_0, c_1)\}$
[14] $KillAll_P$
[15] $\{c_0 = k, \ OK(p, p_k, c_0, c_1), \bigwedge_{i=1}^{m} y_i = 0, \ q = 0, \ \bigwedge_{i=1}^{n} x_i = 0\}$
[16] $y_l := p$
[17] $\{c_0 = k, \ \bigwedge_{i=1}^{n} OK(x_i, p_i, c_0, c_1)\}$

Instruction [16] leaves all variables x_i untouched. Hence, it establishes its postcondition [17], because all x_i are ensured to be zero in [15] and, if $x_i =$

0, $OK(x_i, p_i, c_0, c_1)$ holds trivially. It may be surprising that the conjunct $OK(p, p_k, c_0, c_1)$ is not needed in this proof because, intuitively, it captures a crucial property of the construction. The reason is that the proofs of P_0 and $P_{\neq 0}$ establish only a property about the x_i. The conjunct $OK(p, p_k, c_0, c_1)$ is, however, important to ensure interference freedom of [16] with the proof outlines for Q_0 and $Q_{\neq 0}$ that concern the variables y_i.

The specification of $KillAll_P$, viz. $\{[13]\}\ KillAll_P\ \{[15]\}$, is again parameterized by a constant $k \geq 0$ and is also used in the proof outlines that follow. It is straightforward to construct a proof outline witnessing this specification: the variables that have already been re-initialized are collected in an increasingly larger conjunction.

The proof outline for the paths through the loop bodies induced by incrementing transitions is similar but has to reflect the change of the counter. It also applies the assumption about recursive calls of $P_{\neq 0}$ (for $k_{new} = k + 1$):

[18] $\{c_0 = k,\ \bigwedge_{i=1}^{n} OK(x_i, p_i, c_0, c_1)\}$
[19] $p := x_k\,;$
[20] $\{c_0 = k,\ OK(p, p_k, c_0, c_1)\}$
[21] $KillAll_P$
[22] $\{c_0 = k,\ OK(p, p_k, c_0, c_1),\ \bigwedge_{i=1}^{m} y_i = 0,\ q = 0,\ \bigwedge_{i=1}^{n} x_i = 0\}$
[23] $c_0 := c_0 + 1$
[24] $\{c_0 = k + 1,\ OK(p, p_k, c_0 - 1, c_1),\ \bigwedge_{i=1}^{m} y_i = 0,\ q = 0,\ \bigwedge_{i=1}^{n} x_i = 0\}$
[25] $y_l := p$
[26] $\{c_0 = k + 1,\ \bigwedge_{i=1}^{n} OK(x_i, p_i, c_0, c_1)\}$
[27] $P_{\neq 0}$
[28] $\{c_0 = k,\ \bigwedge_{i=1}^{n} OK(x_i, p_i, c_0, c_1)\}$

This completes the proof that the preconditions of P_0 and $P_{\neq 0}$ are loop invariants and also finishes the proof outline for P_0, as its pre- and postcondition coincide and its body just consists of the loop.

It remains to show that the paths from the loop exit to the procedure exit in $P_{\neq 0}$ induced by decrementing transitions establish the postcondition from the loop invariant, i.e. the precondition of $P_{\neq 0}$:

[29] $\{c_0 = k,\ \bigwedge_{i=1}^{n} OK(x_i, p_i, c_0, c_1)\}$
[30] $p := x_k\,;$
[31] $\{c_0 = k,\ OK(p, p_k, c_0, c_1)\}$
[32] $KillAll_P$
[33] $\{c_0 = k,\ OK(p, p_k, c_0, c_1),\ \bigwedge_{i=1}^{m} y_i = 0,\ q = 0,\ \bigwedge_{i=1}^{n} x_i = 0\}$
[34] $c_0 := c_0 - 1\,;$
[35] $\{c_0 = k - 1,\ OK(p, p_k, c_0 + 1, c_1),\ \bigwedge_{i=1}^{m} y_i = 0,\ q = 0,\ \bigwedge_{i=1}^{n} x_i = 0\}$
[36] $y_l := p$
[37] $\{c_0 = k - 1,\ \bigwedge_{i=1}^{n} OK(x_i, p_i, c_0, c_1)\}$

4.8.3 Interference Freedom

Let us now check interference freedom. We look at each type of assignment found in Q_0 and $Q_{\neq 0}$. It is clear that an assignment to a variable z cannot invalidate conjuncts in assertions that do not mention z. Therefore, we only need to consider conjuncts in assertions mentioning the variable to which the statement in question assigns.

- $x_i := 0$, $y_i := 0$, $p := 0$: these re-initializing assignment statements cannot invalidate any assertion in the proof outlines because all conjuncts that mention the left-hand-side variable trivially hold if the variable is zero. This holds in particular for conjuncts of the form $OK(x, s, c_0, c_1)$.
- $c_1 := c_1 + 1$ and $c_1 := c_1 - 1$: all conjuncts of the form $OK(p, p_k, c_0, c_1)$ or $OK(x_i, p_i, c_0, c_1)$ could potentially be invalidated by these statements. All incrementations and decrementations of c_1 are however—in analogy to [22] and [33]—guarded by a precondition that ensures that p as well as all variables x_i hold zero, which make $OK(p, p_k, c_0, c_1)$ or $OK(x_i, p_i, c_0, c_1)$ true for trivial reasons.

  Note that this argument exploits that the variables are re-initialized in order to avoid 'cheating'.
- $q := y_k$: such a statement could potentially invalidate a conjunct of the form $q = 0$. However, the conjunct $q = 0$ appears in assertions only together with the conjunct $\bigwedge_{i=1}^{m} y_i = 0$. In particular this holds in the (omitted) proof outline for $\mathsf{KillAll}_p$ because the variables y_i are re-initialized before q. Therefore, $q := y_k$ cannot destroy validity of the assertion.

  Note that it is essential for this argument that the re-initializations in $\mathsf{KillAll}_P$ are done in the correct order as discussed in Section 4.3.2.
- $x_l := q$: such a statement could potentially invalidate conjuncts of the form $x_l = 0$ or $OK(x_l, p_l, c_0, c_1)$.

  All assertions that contain $x_l = 0$ also contain a conjunct $q = 0$. Thus, we can argue as for instructions of the form $q := y_k$.

  For conjuncts of the form $OK(x_l, p_l, c_0, c_1)$ the argument is more subtle. Similarly to [15], [24], and [35], $x_l := q$ is preceded by an assertion that ensures in particular that $OK(q, q_k, c_0, c_1 + \iota)$ holds, where $\iota \in \{-1, 0, 1\}$. By the construction of π_M, $\iota = -1$, 1, or 0 iff there is a transition from q_k to p_l that increments, decrements, or leaves the counter c_1 unchanged, respectively. Now suppose that x_l is assigned the value 1 by $x_l := q$, otherwise $OK(x_l, p_l, c_0, c_1)$ holds trivially. Then clearly $q = 1$ which implies $\langle p_1, 0, 0 \rangle \to^* \langle q_k, c_0, c_1 + x \rangle$ by $OK(q, q_k, c_0, c_1 + x)$. By the transition from q_k to p_l, this transition sequence can now be extended to a sequence $\langle p_1, 0, 0 \rangle \to^* \langle p_l, c_0, c_1 \rangle$. Hence, $OK(x_l, p_l, c_0, c_1)$ holds.

It is interesting to observe that the crucial properties of the construction are reflected in the interference freedom proof rather than the local proofs. Note, however, that the interference freedom proof exploits the preconditions of the interleaving statements that are established by the local proofs.

4.9 Correctness of the Reduction in Section 4.4

In this section we provide a formal proof of the 'if' direction of (4.2). As in Section 4.8 we present an Owicki/Gries-style program proof. Specifically, we show that the assertion

$$x_{0,a_1} = 1 \quad \Rightarrow \quad L(r_1) \cap \ldots \cap L(r_n) \neq \emptyset \tag{4.4}$$

is valid in the sense of partial correctness just before the write instruction in *Main*. This suffices to establish the 'if' direction of (4.2) because x_{0,a_1} can hold only the values 0 and 1.

4.9.1 Enriching the Program

In order to perform the proof of (4.4), the threads are enriched by auxiliary variables w_i, $i = 0, \ldots, n$, that take values in A^* and record the words guessed by the threads π_i. For this purpose the definition of π_0 and $\pi_i(a)$ is modified as follows:

$$
\begin{aligned}
\pi_0 \quad = \quad & \mathbf{loop} \\
& \quad \sqcap \{ y_0 := x_{n,a} \,;\, \mathsf{KillAll}_0 \,; \\
& \qquad\quad w_0 := w_0 \cdot b \,;\, x_{0,b} := y_0 \mid a, b \in A \} \\
& \mathbf{end} \\
\pi_i(a) \quad = \quad & y_i := x_{i-1,a} \,;\, \mathsf{KillAll}_i \,;\, w_i := w_i \cdot a \,;\, x_{i,a} := y_i \,.
\end{aligned}
$$

The other clauses for π_i are left unchanged. The auxiliary variables w_i are initialized with the empty word ε in the *Main* procedure:

```
procedure Main;
KillXY₀ ; . . . ; KillXYₙ ; xₙ,ₐ₁ := 1 ;
w₀ := ε ; . . . ; wₙ := ε ;
[π₀ ‖ π₁ ‖ · · · ‖ πₙ] ;
(x₀,ₐ₁ := 0 ⊓ skip) ;
write(x₀,ₐ₁)
end
```

Obviously, adding the variables w_i does not affect validity of Assertion (4.4).

4.9.2 An Auxiliary Predicate

A crucial property of the constructed program is the following: the fact that a certain variable holds the value 1 at a certain point in the program means that the propagation game has been played correctly up to this point in the execution and is in a certain stage. In the formal proof we try to capture the essence of this by an assertion on the words w_i guessed by the parallel threads so far. To allow a concise statement of the corresponding assertions in the proof of thread π_i, we introduce a predicate $\mathsf{OK}(x, i, c)$ as an abbreviation, where x is a variable, $i \in \{1, \ldots, n+1\}$ is a thread number ($n+1$ stands for thread π_0) and $c \in A$ is a letter.

Intuitively, $\mathsf{OK}(x, i, c)$ expresses the following: if variable x holds value 1 then all threads $j < i$ have guessed the same word—as a reference we use word w_0—and all threads $j \geq i$ have guessed the word obtained from w_0 by removing the last letter; moreover, c is this last letter. Formally, we define:

$$\mathsf{OK}(x, i, c) \quad :\Leftrightarrow \quad x = 1 \Rightarrow \left(\bigwedge_{0 \leq j < i} w_0 = w_j \wedge \bigwedge_{i \leq j < n+1} w_0 = w_j \cdot c \right).$$

Note that the OK-predicate refers to all the variables w_i but does not list them explicitly in the argument list.

In the following we discuss first the specification of thread π_0 and then a generic specification for the threads π_i, $i = 1, \ldots, n$, and give corresponding proof outlines. Afterwards we present the proof outline for the *Main* procedure and discuss interference freedom. Only validity of non-trivial local proof obligations is discussed in detail.

4.9.3 Proof Outline for π_0

The specification for π_0 reads as follows:

$$\{ \textstyle\bigwedge_{c \in A} \mathsf{OK}(x_{n,c}, n+1, c) \} \quad \pi_0 \quad \{ \textstyle\bigwedge_{c \in A} \mathsf{OK}(x_{n,c}, n+1, c) \}$$

Note that pre- and postcondition coincide. The specification is shown to be valid by proving that the precondition is an invariant of the loop that constitutes π_0:

[1] $\{ \bigwedge_{c \in A} \mathsf{OK}(x_{n,c}, n+1, c) \}$
[2] $y_0 := x_{n,a}$;
[3] $\{ \mathsf{OK}(y_0, n+1, a) \}$
[4] $\mathsf{KillAll}_0$;
[5] $\{ \mathsf{OK}(y_0, n+1, a), \ \bigwedge_{j=0}^{n} \bigwedge_{c \in A} x_{j,c} = 0, \ \bigwedge_{j=1}^{n} y_j = 0 \}$
[6] $w_0 := w_0 \cdot b$;
[7] $\{ \mathsf{OK}(y_0, 0, b), \ \bigwedge_{j=0}^{n} \bigwedge_{c \in A} x_{j,c} = 0, \ \bigwedge_{j=1}^{n} y_j = 0 \}$
[8] $x_{0,b} := y_0$
[9] $\{ \bigwedge_{c \in A} \mathsf{OK}(x_{n,c}, n+1, c) \}$

In the step from Assertion [5] to [7], only the OK-predicates are of interest. To see the validity of this step note that $\mathsf{OK}(y_0, n+1, a)$ simplifies to

$$y_0 = 1 \quad \Rightarrow \quad \bigwedge_{0 \leq j < n+1} w_0 = w_j$$

and $\mathsf{OK}(y_0, 0, b)$ to

$$y_0 = 1 \;\Rightarrow\; \bigwedge_{0 \le j < n+1} w_0 = w_j \cdot b .$$

The step from Assertion [7] to [9] exploits that $\mathsf{OK}(x, i, c)$ holds trivially if $x = 0$. Interestingly, the conjunct $\mathsf{OK}(y_0, 0, b)$ is not needed for proving the postcondition [9]. But it is crucial for showing interference freedom of $x_{0,b} := y_0$ with the assertion $\mathsf{OK}(x_{0,b}, 1, b)$ that occurs in the proof outline for π_1. To be complete, we should also state a proof outline for $\mathsf{KillAll}_0$. But this proof outline is straightforward: we simply collect the variables that have already been set to 0 in an increasingly larger conjunction.

4.9.4 Proof Outline for $\pi_i(r)$

The specification of thread π_i, for $i = 0, \ldots, n$, reads as follows.

$$\{w_i = \varepsilon, \; \bigwedge_{c \in A} \mathsf{OK}(x_{i-1,c}, i, c)\}$$
$$\pi_i \tag{4.5}$$
$$\{w_i \in L(r), \; \bigwedge_{c \in A} \mathsf{OK}(x_{i-1,c}, i, c)\}$$

Thread $\pi_i = \pi_i(r_i)$ is defined by induction on the structure of the regular expression r_i. In order to show validity of (4.5) we show a generalized specification for $\pi_i(r)$ also by induction on r:

$$\{w_i \in L, \; \bigwedge_{c \in A} \mathsf{OK}(x_{i-1,c}, i, c)\}$$
$$\pi_i(r)$$
$$\{w_i \in L \cdot L(r), \; \bigwedge_{c \in A} \mathsf{OK}(x_{i-1,c}, i, c)\}$$

for any language $L \subseteq A^*$ and regular expression r. Specification (4.5) then follows by instantiating L by $\{\varepsilon\}$ and r by r_i.

Now we discuss the proof outlines in the structural induction on r. The proof outline for $\pi_i(a)$ is similar to the one of π_0. We therefore omit a detailed justification of the local steps.

[10] $\{w_i \in L, \; \bigwedge_{c \in A} \mathsf{OK}(x_{i-1,c}, i, c)\}$
[11] $y_i := x_{i-1,a}$;
[12] $\{w_i \in L, \; \mathsf{OK}(y_i, i, a)\}$
[13] $\mathsf{KillAll}_i$;
[14] $\{w_i \in L, \; \mathsf{OK}(y_i, i, a), \; \bigwedge_{j=0}^{n} \bigwedge_{c \in A} x_{j,c} = 0, \; \bigwedge_{j \ne i} y_j = 0\}$
[15] $w_i := w_i \cdot a$;
[16] $\{w_i \in L \cdot L(a), \; \mathsf{OK}(y_i, i+1, a), \; \bigwedge_{j=0}^{n} \bigwedge_{c \in A} x_{j,c} = 0, \; \bigwedge_{j \ne i} y_j = 0\}$
[17] $x_{i,a} := y_i$
[18] $\{w_i \in L \cdot L(a), \; \bigwedge_{c \in A} \mathsf{OK}(x_{i-1,c}, i, c)\}$

The proof for KillAll$_i$ is just as straightforward as the proof for KillAll$_0$ mentioned above.

The proof outline for $\pi_i(r_1 \cdot r_2)$ is very simple, given that we can apply the induction hypothesis for $\pi_i(r_1)$ and $\pi_i(r_2)$:

$$
\begin{array}{ll}
[19] & \{w_i \in L, \bigwedge_{c \in A} \mathsf{OK}(x_{i-1,c}, i, c)\} \\
[20] & \pi_i(r_1) \\
[21] & \{w_i \in L \cdot L(r_1), \bigwedge_{c \in A} \mathsf{OK}(x_{i-1,c}, i, c)\} \\
[22] & \pi_i(r_2) \\
[23] & \{w_i \in L \cdot L(r_1) \cdot L(r_2), \bigwedge_{c \in A} \mathsf{OK}(x_{i-1,c}, i, c)\} \\
[24] & \{w_i \in L \cdot L(r_1 \cdot r_2), \bigwedge_{c \in A} \mathsf{OK}(x_{i-1,c}, i, c)\}
\end{array}
$$

In the proof for $\pi_i(r_1 + r_2)$, we have to show that every component in the non-deterministic choice comprising $\pi_i(r_1 + r_2)$ satisfies the specification. Using the induction hypothesis this is again quite easy. Suppose $l \in \{1, 2\}$. Then

$$
\begin{array}{ll}
[25] & \{w_i \in L, \bigwedge_{c \in A} \mathsf{OK}(x_{i-1,c}, i, c)\} \\
[26] & \pi_i(r_l) \\
[27] & \{w_i \in L \cdot L(r_l), \bigwedge_{c \in A} \mathsf{OK}(x_{i-1,c}, i, c)\} \\
[28] & \{w_i \in L \cdot L(r_1 + r_2), \bigwedge_{c \in A} \mathsf{OK}(x_{i-1,c}, i, c)\}
\end{array}
$$

Assertion [27] implies [28], as $L(r_l) \subseteq L(r_1 + r_2)$.

For $\pi_i(r^*)$ we have to show validity of

$$
\{w_i \in L, \bigwedge_{c \in A} \mathsf{OK}(x_{i-1,c}, i, c)\}
$$
loop $\pi_i(r)$ **end**
$$
\{w_i \in L \cdot L(r)^*, \bigwedge_{c \in A} \mathsf{OK}(x_{i-1,c}, i, c)\}
$$

We prove that the postcondition is a loop invariant. First of all, it follows from the precondition because $\varepsilon \in L(r)^*$. Secondly, it is preserved by the loop body, which follows easily from the induction hypothesis and the inclusion $L(r)^* \cdot L(r) \subseteq L(r)^*$:

$$
\begin{array}{ll}
[29] & \{w_i \in L \cdot L(r)^*, \bigwedge_{c \in A} \mathsf{OK}(x_{i-1,c}, i, c)\} \\
[30] & \pi_i(r) \\
[31] & \{w_i \in L \cdot L(r)^* \cdot L(r), \bigwedge_{c \in A} \mathsf{OK}(x_{i-1,c}, i, c)\} \\
[32] & \{w_i \in L \cdot L(r)^*, \bigwedge_{c \in A} \mathsf{OK}(x_{i-1,c}, i, c)\}
\end{array}
$$

4.9.5 Proof Outline for *Main*

Now we are ready to give the proof for the *Main* procedure that relies on the specifications for the π_i proved above. Note that this proof yields that (4.4) is indeed valid just before the write instruction.

[33] $\{\mathbf{true}\}$
[34] $\mathsf{KillXY}_0\,;\dots;\mathsf{KillXY}_n\,;x_{n,a_1}:=1\,;$
[35] $w_0:=\varepsilon\,;\dots;w_n:=\varepsilon\,;$
[36] $\{x_{n,a_1}=1,\ \bigwedge_{(j,c)\neq(n,a_1)}x_{j,c}=0,\ \bigwedge_{j=0}^n y_j=0,\ \bigwedge_{j=0}^n w_j=\varepsilon\}$
[37] $[\pi_0\ \|\ \pi_1\ \|\ \cdots\ \|\ \pi_n]\,;$
[38] $\{\mathsf{OK}(x_{0,a_1},1,a_1),\ \bigwedge_{j=1}^n w_j\in L(r_j)\}$
[39] $(x_{0,a_1}:=0\sqcap\mathbf{skip})\,;$
[40] $\{x_{0,a_1}=1\ \Rightarrow\ L(r_1)\cap\dots\cap L(r_n)\neq\emptyset\}$
[41] $\mathbf{write}(x_{0,a_1})$

It is obvious that Assertion [36] is established by the initialization. It is also easy to see that [36] implies all the preconditions of the parallel threads: the conjuncts $w_i=\varepsilon$ in the preconditions of the π_i, $i=1,\dots,n$, are also present in [36]. All the other conjuncts found in the preconditions have the form $\mathsf{OK}(x_{j-1,c},j,c)$ for some $j=1,\dots,n+1$ and $c\in A$. Of these, the predicate $\mathsf{OK}(x_{n,a_1},n+1,a_1)$, which is present in the precondition of π_0, holds, because all the variables w_j are guaranteed by [36] to hold the same word ε; and all the other $\mathsf{OK}(x_{j-1},j,c)$-predicates are trivially valid as the corresponding variable $x_{j-1,c}$ is guaranteed by [36] to hold the value 0.

All the conjuncts in Assertion [38] are found in the postconditions of the parallel threads: $\mathsf{OK}(x_{0,a_1},1,a_1)$ is a conjunct in the postcondition of π_1 and, for $j=1,\dots,n$, $w_j\in L(r_j)$ is a conjunct in the postcondition of π_j. In the following section we show that the proof outlines for the threads π_i are interference-free. We can thus conclude by the parallel rule of the Owicki/Gries method that the step from Assertion [36] to [38] is valid.

Let us now consider the step from Assertion [38] to [40]. First of all, $x_{0,a_1}:=0$ establishes Assertion [40] for trivial reasons. Correctness of this step for **skip** holds, because Assertion [40] is implied by Assertion [38]: as a consequence of $\mathsf{OK}(x_{0,a_1},1,a_1)$, $x_{0,a_1}=1$ implies $w_0=w_j\cdot a_1$ for $j=1,\dots,n$ which in turn implies that all the variables $w_1,\dots,w_n$ contain the same word. By $\bigwedge_{j=1}^n w_j\in L(r_j)$, this word lies in $L(r_1)\cap\dots\cap L(r_n)$, which consequently is non-empty.

4.9.6 Interference Freedom

We now check interference freedom of the local proof outlines for the threads π_i, $i=0,\dots,n$. As in Section 4.8 we look at each type of assignment found in one of the threads and check that it cannot invalidate conjuncts in assertions in other threads that refer to the left hand side variable of that assignment. Throughout this discussion, we suppose $i,j\in\{0,\dots,n\}$ and use i as the subscript of the thread in which the assignment in question appears. Subscripts of variables and threads are understood modulo $n+1$.

– $w_i:=w_i\cdot a$ in π_i: none of the assertions in a thread different from π_i mentions the variable w_i.

- $y_i := x_{i-1,a}$ in π_i: in other threads π_j, $j \neq i$, variable y_i is mentioned only in conjuncts of the form $y_i = 0$. However, these conjuncts always appear together with a conjunct $x_{i-1,a} = 0$, which ensures that $y_i := x_{i-1,a}$ does not destroy validity of the assertion. This in particular holds in the omitted straightforward proofs for KillAll due to the order in which the re-initializations are performed. The re-initialization order ensures that variable $x_{i-1,a}$ is re-initialized before y_i.

- $x_{i,a} := y_i$ in π_i: there are two different conjuncts in other threads in which variable $x_{i,a}$ is mentioned. Firstly, it is mentioned in conjuncts of the form $x_{i,a} = 0$. These, however, appear only together with the assertion $y_i = 0$. We can thus argue similar to the case of assignment statements of the form $y_i := x_{i-1,a}$.

  Secondly, variable $x_{i,a}$ appears in conjuncts of the form $\mathsf{OK}(x_{i,a}, i+1, a)$ in assertions in π_{i+1}. Here the precondition of $x_{i,a} := y_i$, viz $\mathsf{OK}(y_i, i+1, a)$, ensures that $\mathsf{OK}(x_{i,a}, i+1, a)$ remains valid.

- $y_j := 0$, or $x_{j,c} := 0$ in KillAll$_i$: the left hand side variable of these re-initialization statements appears only in conjuncts of the form $z = 0$ or $\mathsf{OK}(z, k, c)$. Both of them are made true by the re-initialization statement for trivial reasons.

4.10 Conclusion

In this chapter we have studied the complexity of copy-constant detection in parallel programs, in order to pinpoint limitations of synchronization-independent program analysis. By means of a reduction from the halting problem for two-counter machines, we have shown that the interprocedural problem is undecidable. If we consider programs without procedure calls (intraprocedural problem) copy-constant detection becomes decidable but is still intractable. More specifically, we have shown it to be PSPACE-hard by means of a reduction from the intersection problem for regular expressions. Finally, even if we restrict attention to parallel programs without loops, the problem remains NP-hard. These lower bounds are tight because matching upper bounds are easy to establish.

It is interesting to contrast the results of this chapter with the detection problem for *strong* copy constants. Strong copy constants differ from (full) copy constants in that only constant assignments are taken into account by the analysis. In particular, each variable that is a strong copy constant at a program point p is also a copy constant but not vice versa. The detection of strong copy constants turns out to be a much simpler problem as it can be solved in polynomial time [41, 85].

Previous complexity and undecidability results for dataflow problems for concurrent languages [91, 77] exploit in an essential way synchronization primitives of the considered languages. In contrast our results hold independently of any synchronization. They only exploit interleaving of atomic statements and are thus applicable to a much wider class of concurrent languages. Our results rely, however, on the assumption that basic statements execute atomically. We can show that this assumption is indeed crucial for the undecidability result: in Chapter 8 we show that the interprocedural copy-constants detection problem in parallel programs can indeed be solved (in exponential time) if this assumption is abandoned.

The techniques used here can be used to obtain similar results also for other optimal program analysis problems, in particular, the detection of *truly live variables* and the computation of *optimal slices*. In fact, the reductions have been presented for slicing originally [61]. True liveness of variables is a refinement of the more well-known notion of live variables that gives rise to a stronger form of dead code elimination known as *faint-code elimination* [25]. Program slicing [94] is an established program-reduction technique that has applications in program understanding, debugging, and testing [92]. It has also been proposed as a technique for ameliorating the state-explosion problem when formally verifying software or hardware [35, 29, 8, 53].

5. Parallel Flow Graphs

In Chapter 4 we have seen that copy-constant detection is undecidable for parallel programs with procedures *if we assume that assignments execute atomically*, a quite common idealization. However, in many execution scenarios for concurrent programs this assumption is hardly realistic (see Chapter 6). Thus, it is interesting to investigate whether these results still hold without the assumption of atomic execution.

Surprisingly, copy-constant detection becomes decidable, if assignments execute non-atomically. Specifically, we develop an EXPTIME-algorithm for this problem as well as for the elimination of faint code. The crucial new idea is to abstract sets of runs to *antichains of short dependence traces*, an abstraction that turns out to be precise relative to a semantics capturing non-atomic execution of assignments. Based on the information in these antichains that can effectively be computed in exponential time, the two program analysis problems mentioned above can be answered easily [59]. It is somewhat involved to set up the technical framework for these results. Therefore, the presentation which largely follows [59] is spread over a number of chapters.[1] In the following we briefly outline the contents of these chapters.

In the current chapter we introduce a flow graph model for parallel programs (cf. [85, 44, 26]). Edges in the flow graph are annotated with a base statement, a call of a single procedure, or a parallel call of two procedures. As base statements we allow assignment statements and the do-nothing statement **skip**. We assume that branching is non-deterministic, a common abstraction in flow analysis. We define a symbolic operational semantics for parallel flow graphs that captures possible sequences of atomic actions. A sequence of atomic actions is called a *run*. The symbolic operational semantics is taken as a basis for defining a number of run sets of interest, *reaching runs*, *terminating runs*, and *bridging runs*. We then develop constraint systems that characterize these run sets as the smallest solution of systems of subset constraints. Setting up these constraint systems correctly is easier if we assume atomic execution of base statements. Therefore, in this chapter we still adopt this idealization.

---

[1] Updated material from Reference [59], Theoretical Computer Science, Volume 311, Markus Müller-Olm, Precise interprocedural dependence analysis of parallel programs, pp. 325–388, © 2003, reprinted with permission from Elsevier.

By redefining the operators used in the constraint systems appropriately, we can capture *non-atomic* execution of base statements. In Chapter 6 we discuss why non-atomic execution is a more realistic assumption and develop a corresponding interpretation of the operators in the constraint systems. This results in a reference semantics that can be used to measure the precision of flow analyzers relative to non-atomic execution of base statements.

We can perform program analysis by solving the constraint systems over an abstract lattice with finite chain height by fixpoint iteration (Appendix A). In Chapter 7 we develop such a lattice, the most important component of which is given by the antichains of dependence traces mentioned above. We define abstract interpretations for the operators in the constraint systems on this lattice and show that these abstract operations are precise abstractions of the operations in the non-atomic execution semantics. By solving the constraint systems developed in the current chapter over this abstract lattice, we can thus do *exact interprocedural dependence analysis in parallel programs* relative to non-atomic execution. This in turn can be used for exact interprocedural copy-constant propagation and complete faint-code elimination in parallel programs. Corresponding EXPTIME-algorithms are developed in Chapter 8.

Although we have not yet been able to fully characterize the complexity of these two problems in the non-atomic execution scenario, we have made some progress into that direction (Chapter 9). We show that—as in the atomic execution scenario—the loop-free intraprocedural problem is NP-complete. While this implies that also the general intra- and interprocedural problem are intractable it gives no upper bound for their complexity. As a step into that direction we indicate that the general interprocedural problem is unlikely to be in NP, by showing that there are dependences exhibited only by exponentially long runs.

5.1 Parallel Flow Graphs

There are two reasons for using a flow graph model instead of syntactic programs as in Chapter 4. First of all, it is technically more convenient. The nodes of a flow graph directly correspond to program points. Thus, they provide a natural entity to associate dataflow information with. In contrast, in a syntactic program model there is no entity that directly corresponds to a program point and some way to work around this deficiency has to be found. Nielson, Nielson, and Hankin, for instance, require in their book [70] that each basic statement and condition in a program is annotated with a unique label. In the analyses covered in their book [70] these labels are associated with dataflow information. Using unique labels identifying base-statement instances as a substitute for program points is an elegant albeit non-standard approach.

The second reason for using a flow-graph model in this part of the monograph is that such a model is slightly more general than a syntactic program model. It also covers programs with unstructured control flow. This makes the positive results shown in this part (decidability of various analysis problems) slightly more general.

It is not hard to describe a translation of syntactic parallel programs as used in Chapter 4 to parallel flow graphs. Because such a translation is tedious to specify and does not give any new insight it is omitted from this monograph.

Let X be a finite set of (global) *program variables* and Expr a set of expressions (or terms) over X. The precise nature of expressions is immaterial; we only need that each variable $x \in X$ is also an expression: $X \subseteq$ Expr, and that we can determine for an expression $t \in$ Expr the set of variables occurring in t, $\mathsf{var}(t) \subseteq X$. Let $\mathsf{Stmt} := \{x := t \mid x \in X, t \in \mathsf{Expr}\} \cup \{\mathbf{skip}\}$ be the set of *base statements*. We use *stmt* to range over base statements.

Formally, a *parallel flow graph* comprises a finite set Proc of *procedure names* that contains a distinguished procedure *Main*. Intuitively, *Main* is the procedure with which execution starts. For simplicity, we assume that all procedures work on the same set X of global program variables and do not have local variables. Each procedure name $p \in$ Proc is associated with a control flow graph $G_p = (N_p, E_p, A_p, e_p, r_p)$ that consists of:

- a set N_p of *program points*;
- a set of edges $E_p \subseteq N_p \times N_p$;
- a mapping $A_p : E_p \to \mathsf{Stmt} \cup \mathsf{Proc} \cup \mathsf{Proc}^2$ that annotates each edge with a base statement, a call of a single procedure, or a parallel call of two procedures; and
- a special *entry (or start) point* $e_p \in N_p$ and a special *return point* $r_p \in N_p$.

We assume that the program points of different procedures are disjoint: $N_p \cap N_q = \emptyset$ for $p \neq q$. This can always be enforced by renaming program points. We write N for $\bigcup_{p \in \mathsf{Proc}} N_p$, E for $\bigcup_{p \in \mathsf{Proc}} E_p$, and A for $\bigcup_{p \in \mathsf{Proc}} A_p$. We also agree that $\mathsf{Base} = \{e \mid A(e) \in \mathsf{Stmt}\}$ is the set of base edges, $\mathsf{Call}_p = \{e \mid A(e) = p\}$ is the set of edges that call procedure p, and $\mathsf{Pcall}_{p,q} = \{e \mid A(e) = (p,q)\}$ is the set of edges that call procedure p and q in parallel. Moreover, we write Call for $\bigcup_{p \in \mathsf{Proc}} \mathsf{Call}_p$ and Pcall for $\bigcup_{p,q \in \mathsf{Proc}} \mathsf{Pcall}_{p,q}$.

Example 5.1.1. Figure 5.1 shows an example parallel flow graph with three procedures, *Main*, p, and q. The entry state of each procedure is marked by an arrow and the return state is indicated by a doubly circled state. The edge annotation **skip** is suppressed for clarity.

The main procedure of the example flow graph sequentially starts procedures p and q. Procedure p sets variable y to an arbitrary non-negative value and initializes x by 0. Procedure q has a choice: it can execute either the upper path, where it starts two new instances of q in parallel, or the lower path, where it increments x by 2. Note that arbitrarily many instances of q

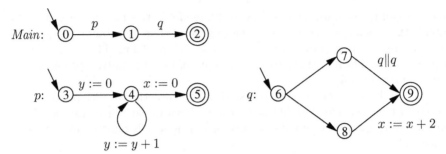

Fig. 5.1. Example of a parallel flow graph.

can run in parallel. Upon termination y can hold an arbitrary non-negative number and x can hold an arbitrary even positive number.   □

The purpose of the remainder of this chapter is to set up a number of constraint systems, the solutions of which capture certain sets of program executions. In the next section we define an operational semantics that is useful as a reference point for setting up these constraint systems correctly.

5.2 Operational Semantics

We define a symbolic operational semantics of parallel flow graphs that specifies possible sequences of atomic actions. The evaluation of base statements is not described in this semantics. Thus, the configurations of the operational semantic represent control information only. In a sequential flow graph control information is simply given by a single flow-graph node. In a sequential program with procedures configurations would consist of sequences of flow-graph nodes. Such a sequence would model a stack of return addresses (or rather return nodes). In parallel flow graphs procedures can also be called in parallel. We model this by generalizing configurations from sequences to trees. Each node of the tree is labeled by a flow-graph node. Each inner node of the tree has either degree one—such nodes correspond to return addresses from simple calls or to return addresses from parallel calls where one of the parallel threads has terminated already—or degree two—such nodes correspond to return addresses from parallel calls. The active control points are given by the leaves of the tree. Correspondingly, transitions are induced by the leaves. Transitions are labeled by base edges e, procedure names p, pairs of procedure names $p_0 \| p_1$, or the symbol ret. There are four transition rules:

Base Step Rule: $c \xrightarrow{e} c'$, if $e = (u, v) \in$ Base and c' results from c by replacing a leaf labeled u by a leaf labeled v.

Simple Call Rule: $c \xrightarrow{p} c'$, if there is an edge $e = (u, v) \in \mathsf{Call}_p$ such that c' results from c by replacing a leaf labeled u by a tree consisting of two nodes, a root labeled v and a successor node of the root labeled e_p.

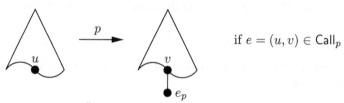

Parallel Call Rule: $c \xrightarrow{p_0 \| p_1} c'$, if there is an edge $e = (u, v) \in \mathsf{Call}_{p_0, p_1}$ such that c' results from c by replacing a leaf labeled u by a tree consisting of three nodes, a root labeled v with two successor nodes labeled e_{p_0} and e_{p_1}.

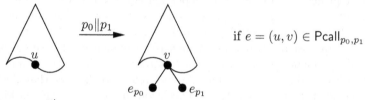

Return Rule: $c \xrightarrow{\mathsf{ret}} c'$, if c' results from c by removing a leaf labeled by r_p for some $p \in \mathsf{Proc}$.

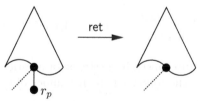

Note that the father of the node labeled r_p may become a leaf after application of this rule and may thus become active again. This models a return to the stacked return address. Just as well, however, the father of the node labeled r_p may still have a child if it has degree two in c as indicated by the dotted line in the picture. In this case the father becomes active only after the second leaf also vanishes. This models synchronized termination of threads started by a parallel call.

Note also that the application of this rule to a tree consisting of just a root results in the empty tree. Such a step models overall termination.

Let Conf be the set of configurations, i.e., trees the degree of which is bounded by two and in which each node is annotated by a program point $u \in N$. We identify each program point $u \in N$ with the tree consisting of just a root labeled with u. We also write nil for the empty tree. A program point $u \in N$ is *active* in a configuration c, if it labels one of the leaves of c. The predicate $At_u(c)$ is true if u is active in c and false otherwise.

Let Label = Base $\cup$ Proc $\cup$ Proc$^2 \cup \{$ret$\}$ be the set of transition labels and $\longrightarrow \subseteq$ Conf $\times$ Label $\times$ Conf be the transition relation defined by the rules above. We define the transitive generalization $\Longrightarrow \subseteq$ Conf $\times$ Label$^* \times$ Conf of $\longrightarrow$, by

$$\stackrel{\varepsilon}{\Longrightarrow} = \text{Id} \qquad\qquad \stackrel{r \cdot \langle l \rangle}{\Longrightarrow} = \stackrel{r}{\Longrightarrow}; \stackrel{l}{\longrightarrow},$$

where 'ε' denotes the empty sequence and ';' denotes relational composition. We write $\Longrightarrow$ for $\bigcup_{r \in \text{Label}^*} \stackrel{r}{\Longrightarrow}$.

5.3 Atomic Runs

As procedures do not have local variables, only the base edge labels in a transition sequence are of interest for dependence analysis and constant propagation. The other labels (calls, parallel calls, and returns) that appear between these labels can be ignored without losing interesting information. Therefore, we can abstract transition sequences to sequences of base edges safely. We call a sequence of base edges an *(atomic) run*; the set of atomic runs is Runs = Base*. The classification 'atomic' refers to the fact that flow graph edges constitute atomic entities of execution; in Section 6 we consider 'non-atomic runs'. We define for a label sequence l, $\hat{l}$ to be the run obtained from l by retaining just the base edges and removing everything else:

$$\hat{\varepsilon} = \varepsilon \quad \text{and} \quad \widehat{r \cdot \langle l \rangle} = \begin{cases} \hat{r} \cdot \langle l \rangle & \text{if } l \in \text{Base} \\ \hat{r} & \text{otherwise} \end{cases} \quad \text{for } r \in \text{Label}^*, l \in \text{Label}.$$

In the following we are going to set up constraint systems for a variety of run sets. These constraint systems use the following small number of operators and constants on run sets.

Semantics of base edges: $[\![e]\!] = \{\langle e \rangle\}$ for $e \in$ Base. This characterizes the run induced by a base edge in isolation.

Sequential composition operator: $R ; S = \{r \cdot s \mid r \in R, s \in S\}$. This characterizes the sequential composition of run sets.

Interleaving operator: In order to define the interleaving (or parallel composition) operator some notation is needed. Let $r = \langle e_1, \ldots, e_n \rangle$ be a sequence and $I = \{i_1, \ldots, i_k\}$ a subset of positions in r such that $1 \leq i_1 < i_2 < \cdots < i_k \leq n$. Then $r|I$ is the sequence $\langle e_{i_1}, \ldots, e_{i_k} \rangle$. We write $|r|$ for the length of r, viz. n.

Then the interleaving of R and S is defined by

$$R \otimes S \;=\; \{r \mid \exists I_R, I_S : \; I_R \cup I_S = \{1, \ldots, |r|\}, I_R \cap I_S = \emptyset,$$
$$r|I_R \in R, r|I_S \in S\}.$$

Prefix operator: $pre(R) = \{r \mid \exists s : r \cdot s \in R\}$. This captures prefixes of the runs in R.

Postfix operator: $post(R) = \{r \mid \exists s : s \cdot r \in R\}$. This captures postfixes of the runs in R.

Alternatively, atomic runs may be defined as sequences of base statements instead of base edges. For this we only need to re-define Runs as Stmt^* instead of Base^* and $[\![e]\!]$ by $[\![e]\!] = \{\langle A(e)\rangle\}$. In this setting we should also re-define the hat-operator to incorporate the transition from base edges to base statements:

$$\hat{\varepsilon} = \varepsilon \quad \text{and} \quad \widehat{r \cdot \langle l \rangle} = \begin{cases} \hat{r} \cdot \langle A(l) \rangle & \text{if } l \in \mathsf{Base} \\ \hat{r} & \text{otherwise} \end{cases} \quad \text{for } r \in \mathsf{Label}^*, l \in \mathsf{Label}.$$

The remainder of this chapter can be read with both interpretations.

By re-defining the operators on run sets, we can obtain non-standard semantics. On the one hand, this is used in Chapter 6 for defining a semantics for parallel flow graphs in which execution of base edges is no longer assumed to be atomic. On the other hand, we can re-define these operators on an abstract domain with a finite chain height. Over such a domain we can effectively solve the constraint systems to be introduced soon. If we can show that all operators are correct or even precise abstractions of the concrete operators on atomic or non-atomic run sets, standard abstraction theorems from abstract interpretation ensure that the solution we get is a correct or even precise abstraction of the run sets characterized by the constraint systems. This is the idea of constraint-based program analysis.

5.4 The Run Sets of Ultimate Interest

We are ultimately interested in setting up constraint systems that characterize for each $u \in N$ the following sets of runs:

Reaching runs: $\mathsf{R}(u) = \{\hat{r} \mid e_{Main} \overset{r}{\Longrightarrow} c, At_u(c)\}$.

Terminating runs: $\mathsf{T}(u) = \{\hat{r} \mid e_{Main} \Longrightarrow c \overset{r}{\Longrightarrow} \mathsf{nil}, At_u(c)\}$.

One distinguishes between *forward-* and *backward*-analyses. Forward-analyses calculate abstractions of the reaching runs and backward-analyses abstractions of the terminating runs.

We are also interested for all program points $u, v \in N$ in the set of those runs that potentially transfer information from u to v. We call these the *bridging runs from u to v*.

Bridging runs: $B_v(u) = \{\hat{r} \mid e_{Main} \Longrightarrow c_u \overset{r}{\Longrightarrow} c_v, At_u(c_u), At_v(c_v)\}.$

In the sections that follow, we present constraint systems that characterize the above run sets. That is: the smallest solution of these constraint systems consists of the run sets defined above. In addition to the above run sets, auxiliary run sets are necessary in order to formulate these constraint systems. These auxiliary run sets are introduced stepwise. We always explain the underlying intuition and outline the correctness proof but leave the details of the proof to the reader. The constraint systems for same-level, reaching and terminating runs are essentially taken from [85] where, however, they are not justified with reference to an explicitly given underlying operational semantics. The constraint system for bridging runs is new.

5.5 The Constraint Systems

5.5.1 Same-Level Runs

First of all, we characterize so-called *same-level runs*. Same-level runs of procedures capture complete runs of procedures in isolation.

Same-level runs of procedures: $S(q) = \{\hat{r} \mid e_q \overset{r}{\Longrightarrow} \text{nil}\}$ for $q \in \text{Proc}$.

As auxiliary sets we consider same-level runs to program nodes.

Same-level runs to program nodes: $S(u) = \{\hat{r} \mid e_q \overset{r}{\Longrightarrow} u\}$ for $u \in N_q$, $q \in \text{Proc}$.

Same-level runs of procedures form an important building block for the other constraint systems. They play a similar role as summary edges in interprocedural program analysis:[2] the same-level runs of procedure q summarize the complete effect of call edges $e \in \text{Call}_p$. Also the complete effect of a parallel call edge $e \in \text{Pcall}_{p_0,p_1}$ is obtained easily from the same-level runs of procedures p_0 and p_1: it is given by $S(p_0) \otimes S(p_1)$.

The same-level runs of procedures and program nodes are the smallest solution of the following constraint system:

$$
\begin{array}{lll}
[\text{S1}] & S(q) \supseteq S(r_q) \\
[\text{S2}] & S(e_q) \supseteq \{\varepsilon\} \\
[\text{S3}] & S(v) \supseteq S(u)\,;[\![e]\!]\,, & \text{if } e = (u,v) \in \text{Base} \\
[\text{S4}] & S(v) \supseteq S(u)\,;S(p)\,, & \text{if } e = (u,v) \in \text{Call}_p \\
[\text{S5}] & S(v) \supseteq S(u)\,;[S(p_0) \otimes S(p_1)]\,, & \text{if } e = (u,v) \in \text{Pcall}_{p_0,p_1}
\end{array}
$$

---

[2] Indeed, the information associated with a summary edge for p usually is an abstraction of the same-level runs of p.

It is easy to see that the same-level runs satisfy all constraints:

[S1]: A same-level run of the return point of procedure q gives rise to a same-level run of q by the Return Rule.

[S2]: It follows trivially from the definition that ε is a same-level run of the entry point of a procedure.

[S3]: If $e = (u, v)$ is a base edge, we get a same-level run to v by extending a same-level run to u with e by the Base Steps Rule.

[S4]: If $e = (u, v)$ is an edge that calls p, we get a same-level run to v if we extend a same-level run to u by a same-level run of p: we follow the execution underlying the same-level run to v and call p according to the Simple Call Rule; we then follow the execution underlying the same-level run of p (with v waiting on the stack to become active) and return to v according to the Return Rule.

[S5]: Similarly, if $e = (u, v)$ is an edge that calls p_0 and p_1 in parallel, we can—after seeing a same-level run to u—follow this edge; then p_0 and p_1 are performed to completion in parallel, which results in an interleaving of a same-level run of p_0 and p_1; after that, execution returns to v. We thus obtain a same-level run to v by extending a same-level run of u with an interleaving of same-level runs of p_0 and p_1.

On the other hand, we can easily prove by induction on the length of the transition sequences inducing same-level runs, that each same-level run lies in any solution of the constraint system, in particular in the smallest one: in the base case we consider the empty execution ε. It can only give rise to the same-level run ε to e_q for some procedure q. But ε is enforced to lie in any solution of $S(r_p)$ explicitly by constraint [S2].

In the induction step, we consider longer executions leading to same-level runs. The execution underlying a same-level run of a procedure q necessarily involves a final return from r_q after an execution that gives rise to a same-level run of r_q. The latter execution is one step shorter and thus the same-level run of r_q is contained in any solution of $S(r_q)$ by the induction hypothesis. Now, the constraint [S1] ensures that it is also contained in the set assigned to $S(q)$ in a solution.

The last step of a non-empty execution r inducing a same-level run $\hat{r}$ to a program point v must be induced either by the Base Rule or the Return Rule because the Simple and Parallel Call Rule never lead to a configuration which consists of just a single state. If the last step is induced by the Base Rule, the previous configuration is a program point u. Then $\hat{r}$ is composed of a same-level run to u and the base edge $e = (u, v)$. The same-level run to u is induced by a shorter execution and hence contained in the set associated with $S(u)$ in any solution by the induction hypothesis. Thus, $\hat{r}$ is in $S(v)$ by the constraint [S3]. If the last step is induced by the Return Rule, then there must be a simple or parallel call from which this step returns. The constraints for simple and parallel call edges ([S4] and [S5]) together with the induction hypothesis then ensure that $\hat{r}$ is contained in $S(v)$.

5.5.2 Inverse Same-Level Runs

We also consider a kind of dual to same-level runs of program points: runs from a program point to the return point of the corresponding procedure. We call these *inverse same-level runs of program point*. They are needed in order to capture terminating runs.

Inverse same-level runs of program points:
$$S^i(u) = \{\hat{r} \mid u \stackrel{r}{\Longrightarrow} \text{nil}\} \text{ for } u \in N.$$

Inverse same-level runs of procedures and program nodes are obtained by backwards accumulation as the smallest solution of the following system of constraints:

[SI1] $S^i(r_q) \supseteq \{\varepsilon\}$

[SI2] $S^i(u) \supseteq [\![e]\!] ; S^i(v),$ if $e = (u,v) \in \mathsf{Base}$

[SI3] $S^i(u) \supseteq S(p) ; S^i(v),$ if $e = (u,v) \in \mathsf{Call}_p$

[SI4] $S^i(u) \supseteq [S(p_0) \otimes S(p_1)] ; S^i(v),$ if $e = (u,v) \in \mathsf{Pcall}_{p_0,p_1}$

The last two constraints refer to same-level runs of procedures. Therefore, it appears that we need to calculate same-level runs before we can calculate inverse same-level runs by the above constraint system. However, by adding for each procedure $q \in \mathsf{Proc}$ the constraint

$$[\text{SI5}] \quad S(q) \supseteq S^i(e_q)$$

we can calculate same-level runs of procedures simultaneously with inverse same-level runs. Thus, we can also calculate inverse same-level runs in isolation.

It is easy to see that the sets of inverse same-level runs satisfy all constraints:

[SI1]: By the Return rule, ε clearly is an inverse same-level run of the return point r_q of a procedure.

[SI2]: If $e = (u,v)$ is a base edge, we get an inverse same-level run of u by prefixing a same-level run of v with e.

[SI3]: If $e = (u,v)$ is an edge that calls p, we can follow this edge in an execution from u; then p is performed until termination, which results in a same-level run of p; after that execution proceeds at v. We thus obtain an inverse same-level run of u by prefixing an inverse same-level run of v by a same-level run of p.

[SI4]: Similarly, if $e = (u,v)$ is an edge that calls p_0 and p_1 in parallel, we can follow this edge in an execution from u; then p_0 and p_1 are performed to completion in parallel, which results in an interleaving of a same-level run of p_0 and p_1; after that execution returns to v. We thus obtain an inverse same-level run of u by prefixing an inverse same-level run of v with an interleaving of same-level runs of p_0 and p_1.

On the other hand, we can easily prove by induction on the length of the transition sequences inducing inverse same-level runs, i.e. those that lead to nil, that each inverse same-level run is in the smallest solution of the constraint system: in the base case we consider the shortest executions that lead to same-level runs. These are executions of the form $r_p \xrightarrow{\text{ret}} \text{nil}$ for some procedure p. They witness that $\varepsilon \in S(r_p)$. But ε is enforced to be in a solution of $S(r_p)$ explicitly by constraint [SI1].

In the induction step, we consider longer executions leading to same-level runs. These necessarily start with a transition induced by a base edge, a simple, or a parallel call edge. The resulting run is then composed from shorter runs as specified in the constraints for base edges ([SI2]), simple calls ([SI3]), and parallel calls ([SI4]), respectively.

5.5.3 Two Assumptions and a Simple Analysis

The following two assumptions simplify the constraint systems that follow:

ASS1: every program point $u \in N_q$ in a procedure q can be reached by a same-level run from the entry point e_q of q:

$$\forall q \in \mathsf{Proc}, u \in N_q : S(u) \neq \emptyset.$$

ASS2: from every program point $u \in N_q$ the return point r_q can be reached by a same-level run:

$$\forall q \in \mathsf{Proc}, u \in N_q : S^{\mathsf{i}}(u) \neq \emptyset.$$

These assumptions are not as innocent as they may seem at first glance. In particular it does *not* suffice to require that there are paths from e_q to u and from u to r_q in the flow graph G_q for q. The paradigmatic counter-example is a procedure that calls itself and has no bypassing terminating branch:

Although there is a path from e_q to r_q in the flow graph, no execution can reach r_q from e_q, as there is no terminating bypass of the recursive call of q. Hence both $S(r_q)$ and $S^{\mathsf{i}}(e_q)$ are empty. Examples like this show that we cannot assume without loss of generality that practical flow graphs satisfy ASS1 and ASS2.

While assumptions ASS1 and ASS2 simplify the presentation and justification of the constraint systems in the remainder of this chapter, they are not strictly necessary. We can well design constraint systems that work in the general case, but they are more complex and therefore harder to explain. In order to avoid overloading the presentation we first present and justify the simpler constraint systems that work if ASS1 and ASS2 are satisfied. Afterwards we explain the changes for the general case, cf. Section 5.5.7.

In order to compute the information needed to decide ASS1 and ASS2, we design a simple analysis procedure. It is based on an abstract interpretation of the operators and constants used in the constraint systems. We work with a two point domain $(\mathbb{D} = \{\bot, \top\}, \leq)$ ordered as $\bot \leq \top$. The idea is that $\bot$ represents definite emptiness and $\top$ potential non-emptiness of a run set. Correspondingly, we define the abstraction mapping $\alpha : 2^{\mathsf{Runs}} \to \mathbb{D}$ by $\alpha(\emptyset) = \bot$ and $\alpha(R) = \top$ for $R \neq \emptyset$. The fact that the abstract interpretation developed below is precise guarantees that it computes indeed $\bot$ for all empty run sets and $\top$ just for non-empty run sets. Obviously, α is universally disjunctive. We define the abstract interpretation of the operators by

$$x;^{\#} y = x \otimes^{\#} y = x \wedge y, \quad pre^{\#}(x) = post^{\#}(x) = x, \quad [\![e]\!]^{\#} = \{\varepsilon\}^{\#} = \top$$

for $x, y \in \mathbb{D}$, $e \in E$. It is easy to see that the abstract operators are precise abstractions of the corresponding operators on run sets: a sequential or parallel composition of two run sets is non-empty iff both arguments are non-empty; the set of prefixes and the set of postfixes of a run set R are non-empty iff R is; and each base edge gives rise to a non-empty run set. In other words, α is a strong homomorphism in the sense of Appendix A. Therefore, by computing the least solution of the constraint systems for same-level and inverse same-level runs over the above abstract interpretation we get precise information about the emptiness of the sets of same-level and inverse same-level runs of program points.

This analysis is cheap: as $(\mathbb{D}, \leq)$ has chain height two, the information for each constraint variable can change at most once in the fixpoint iteration. By standard work-list techniques, we can organize the computation of the least solution such that each operator in the constraint system is evaluated at most once. Thus, the computation can be done in time $\mathcal{O}(|E| + |\mathsf{Proc}|)$, the number of operators in the constraint systems. As in all practical flow graphs out-degrees of program nodes are bounded, typically by 2, and $|\mathsf{Proc}|$ is trivially bounded by $|N|$ as each procedure has a distinguished entry node, this is typically $\mathcal{O}(|N|)$. In the following we assume that this analysis has been done such that for each program node u and procedure q the information whether $\mathsf{S}(u)$, $\mathsf{S}^{\mathrm{i}}(u)$, $\mathsf{S}(q)$, or $\mathsf{S}^{\mathrm{i}}(q)$ is empty or not is readily available.

Another analysis that can determine information about reachability of program points in parallel flow graphs has been described by Seidl and Steffen [85] as an instance of their generic analysis framework for solving gen/kill dataflow problems for parallel programs.

5.5.4 Reaching Runs

As auxiliary sets for characterizing the runs that reach a program point u, we consider the runs that reach u from a call to procedure q.

Reaching runs from procedures: $R(u,q) = \{\hat{r} \mid e_q \overset{r}{\Longrightarrow} c, At_u(c)\}$ for $u \in N$, $q \in \mathsf{Proc}$.

With this definition, we obviously have $R(u) = R(u, Main)$. Hence we are done with characterizing reaching runs if we succeed in characterizing reaching runs from procedures. The latter can be done by the following constraint system:

[R1] $R(u,q) \supseteq S(u)$,   if $u \in N_q$
[R2] $R(u,q) \supseteq S(v)\,;R(u,p)$,   if $(v,\_) \in E_q \cap \mathsf{Call}_p$
[R3] $R(u,q) \supseteq S(v)\,;[R(u,p_i) \otimes pre(S(p_{1-i}))]$, if $(v,\_) \in E_q \cap \mathsf{Pcall}_{p_0,p_1}$

The last clause is meant to specify two constraint for $i = 0$ and $i = 1$.

The reaching runs satisfy the constraints:

[R1]: Firstly, each same-level run of u clearly is also a reaching run of u.
[R2]: Secondly, if we have a program point v in q that has an outgoing edge calling p—the situation described in the second constraint—we obtain a run that reaches u from q when we extend a same-level run $\hat{r}$ to v with a run $\hat{r}'$ that reaches u from p (where r and r' are the underlying executions).
[R3]: Thirdly, consider a program point v in q that has an outgoing edge calling p_0 and p_1 in parallel, the situation described in the third constraint. Similar to the second case, we get a run reaching u by extending a same-level run of v with a run that reaches u in the parallel call. The latter can happen either in p_0 or p_1 hence the two cases with $i = 0, 1$. Now until p_i has reached u in p_i the other procedure p_{1-i} can perform a prefix of a same-level run.

On the other hand, the constraint system captures all the ways how u may be reached from e_q. There are just three possibilities: either u is on the same-level, in a simple call, or in a parallel call. These cases are completely covered by the constraints.

Note that assumption ASS2 is crucial for making the constraint for parallel calls sufficiently rich. If it is violated, the partial run exhibited by p_{1-i} while p_i is in the process of reaching u need not be a prefix of a same-level run. For example, the following procedure q might execute $x := e$ arbitrarily often, although $S(q)$ and hence $pre(S(q))$ is empty.

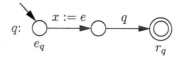

A possible remedy is described in Section 5.5.7.

5.5.5 Terminating Runs

The approach for capturing terminating runs is dual to the one for reaching runs. As auxiliary sets we consider terminating runs of u in a call to procedure q.

Terminating runs in procedures: $T(u, q) = \{\hat{r} \mid e_q \Longrightarrow c \overset{r}{\Longrightarrow} \text{nil}, At_u(c)\}$
for $u \in N$, $q \in \text{Proc}$.

Obviously, we have $T(u) = T(u, Main)$ such that it suffices to capture terminating runs in procedures in the constraint system. The constraint system is dual to the one for reaching runs:

[T1] $T(u, q) \supseteq S^i(u)$,   if $u \in N_q$

[T2] $T(u, q) \supseteq T(u, p) \,; S^i(w)$,   if $(\_, w) \in E_q \cap \text{Call}_p$

[T3] $T(u, q) \supseteq [T(u, p_i) \otimes post(S(p_{1-i}))] \,; S^i(w)$, if $(\_, w) \in E_q \cap \text{Pcall}_{p_0, p_1}$

Again, $i = 0, 1$ in the last constraint. The justification of this constraint system is similar to reaching runs; therefore, the details are left to the reader. We should mention, however, that assumption ASS1 is crucial here, like ASS2 in the case of reaching runs, but for a quite different reason. The difference is the requirement that the configuration c with $At_u(c)$ is reachable ($e_q \Longrightarrow c$) in terminating runs, a requirement that has no parallel for reaching runs. As a consequence, $post(S(p_{1-i}))$ is now sufficient to capture the interleaving potential in the constraint for parallel calls even in the general case, in contrast to $pre(R(p_{1-i}))$ in the corresponding constraint for reaching runs.

However, the reachability requirement for configuration c, implies that some of the constraints are not satisfied by the sets $T(u, q)$ in the general case. For example, an inverse same-level run r from a program point $u \in N_q$ is not always a terminating run. Being an inverse same-level run just means that $u \overset{r}{\Longrightarrow} \text{nil}$ holds, but for a terminating run we additionally need $e_q \Longrightarrow u$. This is implied by ASS1 but can be wrong in the general case. Similarly, we need that the start node of the edge e in the second and third constraint can be reached for making the constraints valid for the operationally defined sets. A possible remedy is to remove the constraints induced by non-reachable program points. This is detailed in Section 5.5.7.

5.5.6 Bridging Runs

Let $v \in N$ be a fixed program point. We want to determine the bridging runs $B_v(u)$ for each $u \in N$ as defined in Section 5.4. As a first step we capture for each program points u the runs that reach v, when execution is started directly with u. We call these the *simple bridging runs* of u w.r.t. v.

Simple bridging runs: $B_v^s(u) = \{\hat{r} \mid u \overset{r}{\Longrightarrow} c, At_v(c)\}$ for $u \in N$.

The simple bridging runs can be characterized as the smallest solution of the following constraint system:

[BS1] $B_v^s(v) \supseteq \{\varepsilon\}$

[BS2] $B_v^s(u) \supseteq [\![e]\!]\,; B_v^s(w)\,,$ if $e = (u, w) \in \mathsf{Base}$

[BS3] $B_v^s(u) \supseteq S(p)\,; B_v^s(w)\,,$ if $e = (u, w) \in \mathsf{Call}_p$

[BS4] $B_v^s(u) \supseteq B_v^s(e_p)\,,$ if $e = (u, \_) \in \mathsf{Call}_p$

[BS5] $B_v^s(u) \supseteq [S(p_0) \otimes S(p_1)]\,; B_v^s(w)\,,$ if $e = (u, w) \in \mathsf{Pcall}_{p_0, p_1}$

[BS6] $B_v^s(u) \supseteq B_v^s(e_{p_i}) \otimes pre(S(p_{1-i}))\,,$ if $e = (u, \_) \in \mathsf{Pcall}_{p_0, p_1}$

The last constraint is again included for $i = 0, 1$.

Let us explain why these constraints cover all the ways how v can be reached from u. If $u = v$ then there is the trivial way to reach v from u: by the empty execution; this is covered by Constraint [BS1]. Otherwise, we must proceed via an outgoing edge (u, w) of u. If this is a base edge $e = (u, w)$, we first see e and then a run that reaches v from w; this is covered by Constraint [BS2]. If e is an edge that calls a procedure p, we distinguish two cases: either v is reached after p has terminated—this case is covered by Constraint [BS3]—or v is reached during the execution of p—this case is covered by [BS4]. Similarly, if e is a parallel call of two procedures p_0 and p_1, we can reach v either after both procedures have terminated, which is covered by [BS5]. Or we can reach v in one of the called procedures p_i. In this case we see a run from e_{p_i} that reaches v interleaved with a prefix of a same-level run of procedure p_{1-i}. If assumption ASS2 is violated we must again reckon with procedure p_{1-i} providing runs that are not prefixes of same-level runs, as was the case for reaching runs. We can solve this problem as for reaching runs, cf. Section 5.5.7.

The reader should face no difficulties in persuading himself, that the $B_v^s(u)$ sets indeed solve all constraints.

As a second step we determine the bridging runs in a call to a procedure:

Bridging runs in procedure calls:
$B_v(u, q) = \{\hat{r} \mid e_q \Longrightarrow c_u \overset{r}{\Longrightarrow} c_v, At_u(c), At_v(c)\}$ for $u \in N$.

Clearly, we have $B_v(u) = B_v(u, Main)$ such that we are done, when we have successfully captured $B_v(u, q)$ for all u, q.

Basically, there are two ways how a bridging run may occur in a call to q. One possibility is that both u and v are reached in the same simple or parallel call in q. This case is captured by the following three types of constraints:

[B1] $B_v(u, q) \supseteq B_v(u, p)\,,$ if $e \in E_q \cap \mathsf{Call}_p$

[B2] $B_v(u, q) \supseteq B_v(u, p_i) \otimes post(pre(S(p_{1-i})))\,,$ if $e \in E_q \cap \mathsf{Pcall}_{p_0, p_1}$

[B3] $B_v(u, q) \supseteq pre(T(u, p_i)) \otimes post(R(v, p_{1-i}))\,,$ if $e \in E_q \cap \mathsf{Pcall}_{p_0, p_1}$

[B2] and [B3] apply for $i = 0, 1$.

Constraint [B1] captures the case that u and v are reached in the same simple call. Constraint [B2] is concerned with the case that u and v are reached in the same procedure p_i of a parallel call. Before u is reached in p_i the other procedure can already perform certain actions and it need not run to completion until v is reached. Therefore, p_{1-i} contributes a middle piece of a same-level run. Potential middle pieces can be characterized by $pre(post(S(p_{1-i}))$ as captured by the second constraint. Constraint [B3] captures the case that u is reached in procedure p_i and v in procedure p_{1-i}. After p_i has reached u it can further proceed; specifically p_i contributes a prefix of a run from $T(u)$ until v is reached in p_{1-i}. In order to reach v, p_{1-i} must execute a run from $R(v, p_{1-i})$. It can execute a prefix of this run before p_i leaves u. Therefore, we see a postfix of a run from $R(v, p_{1-i})$ as part of the bridging run.

The second possibility is that u and v are not reached in the same simple or parallel call. This gives rise to the following constraints:

[B4] $B_v(u, q) \supseteq B_v^s(u)$,   if $u \in N_q$

[B5] $B_v(u, q) \supseteq T(u, p) \, ; B_v^s(w)$,   if $(\_, w) \in E_q \cap \mathsf{Call}_p$

[B6] $B_v(u, q) \supseteq [T(u, p_i) \otimes post(S(p_{1-i}))] \, ; B_v^s(w)$, if $(\_, w) \in E_q \cap \mathsf{Pcall}_{p_0, p_1}$

where $i = 0, 1$ in the last constraint.

The first case is that u is reached on same-level, i.e. in the current instance of q. Then we see a simple bridging run of u (Constraint [B4]). The second case is that u is reached in a procedure p called by a simple call edge $e = (\_, v) \in E_q$. Then we see a run from $T(u, p)$ followed by a simple bridging run from w (Constraint [B5]). The third case is that u is reached in a procedure p_i called by a parallel call edge $e = (\_, v) \in E_q$. Then we see a run from $T(u, p_i) \otimes post(S(p_{1-i}))$ followed by a simple bridging run from w (Constraint [B6]).

5.5.7 The General Case

In this section we describe the changes that are necessary in the general case, i.e., if assumptions ASS1 and ASS2 are potentially violated.

As explained in connection with constraint [R3] one of the problems is that in the general case $pre(S(q))$ does not capture all partial runs of procedure q. Thus, interleaving $R(u, p_i)$ with $pre(S(p_{1-i}))$ does not capture all possible run that reach u in a parallel call. This problem also arises in constraints [BS6] and [B2]. A possible remedy is to introduce new variables $P(q)$, $q \in \mathsf{Proc}$, that characterize finite prefixes of (finite or infinite) runs, i.e. $P(q) = \{\hat{r} \mid e_q \overset{r}{\Longrightarrow} c\}$, and to use $P(p_{1-i})$ instead of $pre(S(p_{1-i}))$ in [R3], [BS6], and [B2]. A simple way to calculate $P(q)$ is to add a constraint of the following form for each procedure q and program point u to the constraint system for reaching runs:[3]

---

[3] If we are working with a non-atomic interpretation of assignments we must use the following constraint instead of [P]:

[P1] $P(q) \supseteq P(e_q)$

[P2] $P(u) \supseteq \{\varepsilon\}$

[P3] $P(u) \supseteq [\![e]\!] ; P(v) ,$ if $e = (u, v) \in \mathsf{Base}$

[P4] $P(u) \supseteq P(p) ,$ if $(u, \_) \in \mathsf{Call}_p$

[P5] $P(u) \supseteq S(p) ; P(v) ,$ if $(u, v) \in \mathsf{Call}_p$

[P6] $P(u) \supseteq [P(p_0) \otimes P(p_1)] ,$ if $(u, v) \in \mathsf{Pcall}_{p_0, p_1}$

[P7] $P(u) \supseteq [S(p_0) \otimes S(p_1)] ; P(v) ,$ if $(u, v) \in \mathsf{Pcall}_{p_0, p_1}$

Fig. 5.2. A constraint system characterizing finite prefixes.

$$[\mathrm{P}] \quad P(q) \supseteq R(u, q) .$$

While this way of calculating $P(q)$ is easy to specify it has the disadvantage of introducing $|N| \cdot |\mathsf{Proc}|$ new constraints, i.e. quadratically many. Although this does not spoil the overall asymptotic complexity—already the constraint system for reaching runs has $\mathcal{O}(|N| \cdot |\mathsf{Proc}|)$ constraints—we should mention that $P(q)$ can be calculated also by $\mathcal{O}(|N|)$ constraints. A corresponding constraint system is given in Fig. 5.2. It determines as auxiliary information finite prefixes of (finite or infinite) runs from program points, defined by $P(u) = \{\hat{r} \mid u \stackrel{r}{\Longrightarrow} c\}$ by backwards accumulation and is similar to the constraint system for simple bridging runs.

A similar problem arises in constraint [B3]: if assumption ASS2 is violated, $pre(T(u, p_i))$ does not necessarily capture all partial runs exhibited by p_i after reaching u because u could be reached at a configuration from which termination is impossible. The information needed in place of $pre(T(u, p_i))$ is $Q(u, p_i)$ where $Q(u, q) = \{\hat{r} \mid e_q \Longrightarrow c \stackrel{r}{\Longrightarrow} c', At_u(c)\}$ for $u \in N$, $q \in \mathsf{Proc}$. These sets can be characterized by the constraint system in Fig. 5.3

The above changes ensure that the run sets characterized by the constraint systems are sufficiently large. They are necessary to make flow analysis based on abstract interpretation of the constraint systems sound. The changes described now ensure that the run sets do not become too large. Thus, they are necessary to make analyses based on a precise abstract interpretation complete.

As explained in connection with terminating runs, constraints induced by unreachable program points are not satisfied by the run sets (defined from the

$$[\mathrm{P}'] \quad P(q) \supseteq pre(R(u, q)) .$$

In the atomic interpretation, any configuration c satisfies $At_u(c)$ for at least one program point u. Therefore, the simpler constraint [P] without the pre-operator is sufficient. In the non-atomic interpretation, however, there are (implicitly) *transient* configurations that correspond to intermediate stages of executions in which no program point is active. Fortunately, from all transient configurations c a configuration c' with some active program point is reachable. Therefore, we can capture the runs to transient configurations by means of the pre-operator.

[Q1] $Q(u, q) \supseteq P(u)$,   if $u \in S_q$
[Q2] $Q(u, q) \supseteq Q(u, p)$,   if $(v, \_) \in E_q \cap \mathsf{Call}_p$
[Q3] $Q(u, q) \supseteq T(u, p) \, ; P(w)$,   if $(v, w) \in E_q \cap \mathsf{Call}_p$
[Q4] $Q(u, q) \supseteq Q(u, p_i) \otimes post(P(p_{1-i}))$,   if $(v, \_) \in E_q \cap \mathsf{Call}_{p_0, p_1}$
[Q5] $Q(u, q) \supseteq [T(u, p_i) \otimes post(S(p_{1-i}))] \, ; P(w)$,   if $(v, w) \in E_q \cap \mathsf{Call}_{p_0, p_1}$

Fig. 5.3. A constraint system for partial runs that can be exhibited in a procedure after a given program point has been reached. All constraints [Q1]-[Q5] are only for program points v with $S(v) \neq \emptyset$. In [Q4] and [Q5], $i = 0, 1$.

operational semantics) that we intend to characterize. As these constraints pose unnecessary additional requirements they make the solutions larger than necessary. Fortunately, such constraints are also unnecessary for soundness and can simply be removed. Specifically, we must include the constraints [T1], [B1], and [B4] only for program points u with $S(u) \neq \emptyset$, and the constraints [T2], [T3], [B2], [B3], [B5], and [B6] only for edges $e = (v, w)$ with $S(v) \neq \emptyset$. We have seen in Section 5.5.3, that we can determine this information with a very simple and cheap analysis.

With the changes described in this section we obtain constraint systems that are both sound and complete in the general case.

5.6 Discussion

In this chapter we have introduced parallel flow graphs. After that we defined a symbolic operational semantics. It works on configurations that take the form of a tree, the nodes of which are annotated by program points. Such a tree models a generalization of a run time stack that may branch to parallel stacks in addition to the common stack operations. Branching is crucial to model parallel calls. We have described the transitions of the operational semantics by rules that work directly on configurations of this form.

There are obvious alternatives to this way of describing the operational semantics. We can, for instance, use the approach of Esparza, Knoop, and Podelski in their work on flow analysis of parallel programs [18, 19]. They map a parallel flow graph to a PA-processes; PA is a class of process models with both a sequential and a concurrent composition operator [5, 47]. Execution of PA-processes in turn is described by a structured operational semantics (SOS) [73]. This allows them to apply results about model-checking of PA-processes to flow analysis. For our purposes the approach chosen here is sufficient and produces less notational overhead.

Based on the operational semantics we have defined a number of run sets of particular interest and have then developed constraint systems that characterize these run sets. The constraint systems for same-level runs and reaching runs are essentially the ones used by Seidl and Steffen [85]. Also the constraint systems for inverse same-level runs and terminating runs are indicated in their work. The constraint system for bridging runs, however, is new. Seidl and Steffen *postulate* their constraint systems, while we use an operational semantics as a reference point. While this might be considered a minor or even trivial difference, in our opinion an operational justification of the constraint systems increases our understanding of what exactly is specified by the constraint systems.

Many reasonable variants of the run sets in question may be considered. For example, one could define reaching runs by

$$\mathsf{R}'(u) = \{\hat{r} \mid e_{Main} \overset{r}{\Longrightarrow} c \Longrightarrow \varepsilon, At_u(c)\} \,.$$

This definition deviates from our previous definition in that it considers only configurations c from which termination is possible, i.e., it characterizes the runs that both reach u and can be completed to a terminating run. In general, if assumption ASS2 is violated, this definition gives rise to smaller run sets. Similarly, many reasonable variants of the other run sets are conceivable and by techniques similar to the ones of Section 5.5.7 sound and complete constraint systems for these variants can be constructed. Operational specifications of the run sets in question allow us distinguish these variants much more clearly than implicit specifications by means of constraint systems.

Validating constraint systems with respect to an operational semantics has another advantage: it helps to uncover subtle bugs. In the absence of an operational semantics, Seidl and Steffen, for instance, fail to notice that constraint [R3] in the constraint system for reaching runs is not rich enough to characterize all reaching runs in a parallel composition if assumption ASS2 does not hold. We detected this error while trying to justify the soundness of the constraint system. As a consequence their constraint system for reaching runs is unsound in the general case. To be fair, we should note that this does not affect the soundness of their analysis procedure that is not directly based on the constraint system for reaching runs. We should also say that they solve the problems that arise when assumption ASS1 is violated correctly. Here they validly propose to remove edges leaving unreachable program points before the analysis. This has essentially the same effect as the side conditions of the form $S(u) \neq \emptyset$ added to the various constraints in Section 5.5.7.

6. Non-atomic Execution

The idealization that assignments execute atomically is quite common in the literature on program verification as well as in the theoretical literature on flow analysis of parallel programs. However, in a multi-processor environment where a number of concurrently executing processors share a common memory this assumption is hardly realistic. In such an environment two threads of control may well interfere while each of them is in the process of executing an assignment. The reason is that assignments are broken into smaller instructions before execution.

As a simple example, consider a program in which a shared variable x is incremented by two threads in parallel:

$$x := x + 1 \parallel x := x + 1.$$

Let us assume that x holds 0 initially. If assignments execute atomically, this program clearly will increment x twice and so terminate in a state in which variable x holds 2. However, in a multi-processor environment this program may well set x to 1. For example, the following execution may happen: first, one of the processors accesses the memory in order to get the value of x. While it is in the process of incrementing this value, but before it has written back the result, the second processors may access the memory, too, in order to get the value of x. In such a run, both processors read the initial value 0 for x, both will increment just this value, and both will write back 1 for x. Consequently, the program will terminate in a state where x holds 1 instead of 2.

In order to be more specific, let us assume that the processors are stack machines. Then a compiler might generate the following piece of code for the assignment $x := x + 1$:

```
1    PUSH x
2    PUSH 1
3    ADD
4    POP x
```

Using unprimed numbers for the statements of the first processor and primed numbers for the statements of the second one, the two processors may then, e.g., execute their instructions in the following order:

$$1, 2, 1', 2', 3', 4', 3, 4.$$

We leave it to the reader to check that this execution increments x just by 1.

The moral of this discussion is that, in the real world of multi-processor execution, we cannot assume atomic execution of assignments. What we typically *may* safely assume, however, is that single reads of variables and single writes of variables are atomic, because the access to the memory is usually synchronized, e.g., through a common bus.

This said, we should mention that there are indeed execution scenarios for concurrent programs that guarantee atomic execution of assignments. In particular in a time-shared multi-tasking environment, where concurrent execution of threads is simulated by a single processor that switches between execution of code pieces implementing the different threads, assuming atomic execution of assignments may be safe, if context switches happen only between assignments, but not in the process of executing the code implementing a single assignment. The built-in scheduler of the Transputer, for instance, performs context switches only after certain types of instructions that typically end execution of assignment code [34].[1]

Note how non-atomic execution of assignments was modeled in the above example: first each assignment NR was broken into the smaller instructions of the stack machine; each of these instructions may be considered as an atomic unit of execution. Then the two threads $1, 2, 3, 4$ and $1', 2', 3', 4'$ of more fine-grained stack machine instructions was interleaved. This example tells us that we can develop an interleaving semantics for parallel programs that adequately models non-atomic execution of assignments by means of breaking assignments into more fine-grained atomic actions, an observation that is exploited in a moment.

The purpose of this chapter is to provide parallel flow graphs with an interleaving semantics that models non-atomic execution of assignments adequately. For this purpose we define a domain NR of sets of (non-atomic) runs and provide adequate definitions for the constants and operators used in the constraint systems in Section 5.5. Specifically, we provide

- an interpretation $[\![e]\!] \in$ NR for the non-atomic runs of a base edge; and
- interpretations for the operators ;, $\otimes$, *pre*, and *post* used in the constraint systems.

Solving the constraint systems from Section 5.5 over this new interpretation immediately gives us adequate definitions for the reaching, terminating,

---

[1] The Transputer designers chose this strategy in order to make context switches cheap and fast. In typical code, the contents of certain registers used for expression evaluation is no longer needed after such instructions. Therefore, these registers are not stored during context switches, which makes context switches fast. Actually, it is the compiler writer's task to ensure that the generated code does not rely on the registers keeping their contents after such instructions. Atomic execution of assignments in typical code is a neat side-effect of this design.

and bridging runs of a parallel flow graph when assignments execute non-atomically.

6.1 Modeling Non-atomic Execution by Virtual Variables

Suppose given a parallel flow graph and let X be the set of *program variables* which the statements of the flow graph refer to. In order to explain the meaning of non-atomic statements appropriately suppose furthermore given an infinite set V of *virtual (or internal) variables* disjoint from X. Intuitively, virtual variables are used to store intermediate results that are private to the threads. The parallel composition (or interleaving) operator defined later ensures that parallel threads do not interfere on virtual variables. We use the letters x, y to range over X, u, v to range over V, and the letters a, b to range over $X \cup V$.

For the purpose of the semantics, assignments are split into atomic operations. As an example consider an assignment statement $x := e(y_1, \dots, y_k)$ in the program where $y_1, \dots, y_k$ refer to the occurrences of (program) variables in expression e. There are many sensible atomicity assumptions. For example, we could work with the rather pessimistic assumption that just reads and writes of variables are atomic and that variables appearing more than once in e are re-read for every occurrences. Then $x := e(y_1, \dots, y_k)$ is replaced by a sequence of assignments

$$\langle v_{\pi(1)} := y_{\pi(1)}, \dots, v_{\pi(k)} := y_{\pi(k)}, x := e(v_1, \dots, v_k) \rangle \,,$$

where $v_1, \dots, v_k$ are arbitrary distinct virtual variables and π is a permutation of $\{1, \dots, k\}$. The idea is that the other threads can execute atomic operations between these assignments.

More coarse-granular atomicity assumptions can be captured in a similar way. If we assume, for instance, that evaluation of right-hand-side expressions is atomic then we would replace $x := e(y_1, \dots, y_k)$ by

$$v := e(y_1, \dots, y_k) \,; x := v \,.$$

The important observation is the following: whatever the specific atomicity assumption may be, if we assume that the execution of all assignments is non-atomic, then all assignments in a run that refer to a *program variable* on the left hand side have only *virtual variables* on the right hand side. Thus, all assignments belong to the set

$$\mathsf{Asg} \;\; = \;\; \{ a := e(b_1, \dots, b_k) \mid a \in X \Rightarrow b_1, \dots, b_k \in V \} \,.$$

One way to define a semantics for non-atomically executing assignments is to transform the assignments in the program prior to semantic interpretation.

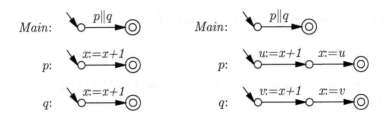

a) Original program.   b) Transformed Program.

Fig. 6.1. Introduction of virtual variables.

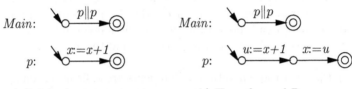

a) Original program.   b) Transformed Program.

Fig. 6.2. Confusion of virtual variables.

As an example consider the program in Fig. 6.1(a) which corresponds to the example discussed in the introduction. We could transform it to the program in Fig. 6.1(b) and then apply the standard interpretation. The problem with this approach is that we must be careful not to confuse virtual variables of different threads. This is simple if only instances of different procedures run in parallel: then we can simply use different names for the virtual variables in different procedures. However, it becomes problematic if different instances of the same procedure may run in parallel like in the program in Fig. 6.2. Then we must model the virtual variables by local variables of the procedures which is not supported by the flow-graph model developed up to now. Therefore, we use a different approach. Instead of transforming flow graphs we incorporate the transformation implicitly into the semantic interpretation of assignments.

Before we turn to the technical details of the new semantic interpretation we revisit the example from Section 4.1 in order to show that the answer to a constant detection problem may depend on the atomicity assumption for base statements. This example illustrates also that the main mechanism underlying the undecidability proof of interprocedural parallel constant detection from Chapter 4 does not carry over to the non-atomic case.

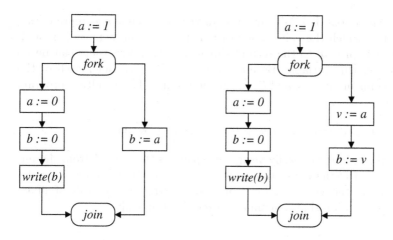

(a) Original program   (b) A virtual variable has been introduced

Fig. 6.3. Introduction of a virtual variable.

6.2 A Motivating Example

Consider again the following program for which a control flow graph-like representation is shown in Figure 6.3 (a):

$$a := 1; [(a := 0; b := 0; \mathbf{write}(b)) \parallel b := a].$$

Assume first that assignment statements execute atomically. From Section 4.1 we know that under this assumption variable b is a (copy) constant of value 0 at the write instruction. Let us briefly recall the underlying reasoning. In any execution $b := 0$ must be executed either after or before $b := a$ in the parallel thread. If it is executed after $b := a$ then b holds 0 at the write statement because 0 is assigned to b in the last executed assignment, $b := 0$. On the other hand, if $b := 0$ is executed before $b := a$ then also the re-initialization of a, $a := 0$, is executed before $b := a$ such that $b := a$ also loads the value 0 to b.

The situation is dramatically different if assignment statements may execute non-atomically. If, in particular, the assignment $b := a$ in the second thread executes non-atomically, the first thread may execute the two statements $a := 0$ and $b := 0$ that kill a and b after a is loaded from the shared memory but before the loaded value is stored to b. This results in a run of the program that propagates the value 1 from the initialization $a := 1$ to the final write-statement.

As explained in the previous section, we may model the two stage non-atomic execution of $b := a$ by splitting it into two assignments $v := a$ and $b := v$, where v is a new *virtual variable* that cannot be accessed by the first thread (cf. Figure 6.3 (b)). We can think of virtual variable v as representing the register in which the value loaded from the common memory is stored. This register is private to the second thread and therefore there can be no interference on this variable. Because of this, we can consider each of the virtual assignments $v := a$ and $b := v$ to be atomic. The resulting program has the run

$$r = \langle a := 1, v := a, a := 0, b := 0, b := v, \mathbf{write}(b) \rangle .$$

which—as the reader can easily verify—propagates the value 1 from the initialization $a := 1$ to the write-statement. Thus, run r witnesses that b is *not* a copy constant at the write statement, in sharp contrast to the state of affairs under the assumption that assignments execute atomically.

6.3 The Domain of Non-atomic Run Sets

A *(non-atomic) run* r is a sequence of assignments from the set Asg defined above: Runs $=$ Asg*. We write virtual(r) for the set of virtual variables appearing in run r. As the specific choice of virtual variables is immaterial, we assume that all considered sets of runs are closed under bounded renaming of virtual variables. This allows a simple and adequate definition of the composition operators. In order to allow a technically clean treatment of this assumption, let $\equiv$ $\subseteq$ Runs $\times$ Runs be the equality of runs up to bounded renaming of virtual variables, i.e. $r \equiv r'$ hold if and only if r' can be obtained from r by bounded renaming of virtual variables.

Proposition 6.3.1. $\equiv$ *is an equivalence.*   □

For a set of runs $R \subseteq$ Runs we write $R^\equiv$ for the closure of R w.r.t. $\equiv$:

$$R^\equiv = \{ r \in \text{Runs} \mid \exists r' \in R : r \equiv r' \} .$$

Obviously, this defines a closure operator.

Proposition 6.3.2.

1. $R \subseteq R^\equiv$.
2. $(R^\equiv)^\equiv = R^\equiv$.
3. $R \subseteq S$ *implies* $R^\equiv \subseteq S^\equiv$.   □

The domain NR is given by the sets of runs that are closed under $\equiv$:

$$\text{NR} = \{ R \subseteq \text{Runs} \mid R = R^\equiv \} .$$

The members of NR model sets of runs in a scenario where assignments execute non-atomically.

Lemma 6.3.1. $(\mathsf{NR}, \subseteq)$ *is a complete lattice with least element* $\bot_{\mathsf{NR}} = \emptyset$ *and greatest element* $\top_{\mathsf{NR}} = \mathsf{Runs}$.

Proof. $(\mathsf{NR}, \subseteq)$ is a sub-lattice of the power set lattice $(2^{\mathsf{Runs}}, \subseteq)$. To show this, we have to check, that NR is closed under arbitrary intersections and unions.

Here is the proof for intersection. Suppose $\mathcal{R} \subseteq \mathsf{NR}$ and $r, r' \in \mathsf{Runs}$ with $r \equiv r'$. We have to show that $r \in \bigcap \mathcal{R}$ if and only if $r' \in \bigcap \mathcal{R}$ which is simple:

$$r \in \bigcap \mathcal{R}$$

iff   [Definition of $\bigcap \mathcal{R}$]
$$\forall R \in \mathcal{R} : r \in R$$

iff   [$\mathcal{R} \subseteq \mathsf{NR}$, hence all $R \in \mathcal{R}$ are closed under $\equiv$]
$$\forall R \in \mathcal{R} : r' \in R$$

iff   [Definition of $\bigcap \mathcal{R}$]
$$r' \in \bigcap \mathcal{R} .$$

The proof for unions is just as simple and, therefore, omitted.

The least and greatest element of $(2^{\mathsf{Runs}}, \subseteq)$ are $\emptyset$ and Runs, respectively. It is obvious that both of them are closed under $\equiv$ and hence are also the least and greatest elements, respectively, of $(\mathsf{NR}, \subseteq)$. $\qquad\square$

In the sections that follow we provide definitions for the operators and constants appearing in the constraint systems and show that they are well-defined.

6.3.1 Base Statements

We can work with various atomicity assumptions as discussed above. The most natural and conservative one is that just single reads and writes of variables are atomic and that variables appearing more than once in an expression are re-read for every occurrence. This is captured by defining the semantics of an assignment statement, $[\![x := e(y_1, \ldots, y_k)]\!] \in \mathsf{NR}$, where $y_1, \ldots, y_k$ refer to the variable occurrences in e, as the set of runs of the form

$$\langle v_{\pi(1)} := y_{\pi(1)}, \ldots, v_{\pi(k)} := y_{\pi(k)}, x := e(v_1, \ldots, v_k) \rangle ,$$

where π is a permutation of $\{1, \ldots, k\}$ and $v_1, \ldots, v_k$ are arbitrary distinct virtual variables. It is readily verified that $[\![x := e(y_1, \ldots, y_k)]\!]$ is well-defined, i.e., that it is a member of NR. We have to show that $[\![x := e(y_1, \ldots, y_k)]\!]$ is closed under $\equiv$ which is obvious as we admitted an arbitrary choice of virtual variables.

We may also work with more coarse-grained semantics of assignments. For our purposes the choice is arbitrary, because the dependence trace abstraction of an assignment will be precise with respect to any of these definitions.

Obviously, the only non-atomic run of statement **skip** is the empty run. Hence, $[\![\textbf{skip}]\!] = \{\varepsilon\}$. Obviously, $[\![\textbf{skip}]\!] \in \mathsf{NR}$.

The non-atomic runs induced by a base edge $e \in \mathsf{Base}$ are the non-atomic runs of the statement associated with e: $[\![e]\!] = [\![A(e)]\!]$, where $A(e)$ is the base statement associated with base edge e in the underlying flow graph.

6.3.2 Sequential Composition

The *sequential composition operator*, $\cdot\,;\cdot\, : \mathsf{NR} \times \mathsf{NR} \to \mathsf{NR}$, which is written as an infix operator, is defined by

$$R\,;S = \{r \cdot s \mid r \in R, s \in S, \mathsf{virtual}(r) \cap \mathsf{virtual}(s) = \emptyset\}^{\equiv} .$$

The condition about the local variables ensures that runs composed sequentially do not interact on local variables. It could be replaced by a condition that in a run all local variables are initialized before they are used. However, the latter condition would not be preserved by the post-operator and, therefore, we prefer the chosen solution. The outer closure operator ensures that ; is well-defined

6.3.3 Interleaving Operator

In order to define the interleaving (or parallel composition) operator we recall some notation from Chapter 5. Let $r = \langle e_1, \ldots, e_n \rangle$ be a sequence and $I = \{i_1, \ldots, i_k\}$ a subset of positions in r such that $1 \le i_1 < i_2 < \cdots < i_k \le n$. Then $r|I$ is the sequence $\langle e_{i_1}, \ldots, e_{i_k} \rangle$. We write $|r|$ for the length of r, viz. n. The *interleaving operator*, $\otimes : \mathsf{NR} \times \mathsf{NR} \to \mathsf{NR}$, which we write in an infix form, is defined by

$$R \otimes S \;=\; \{r \mid \exists I_R, I_S : \; I_R \cup I_S = \{1, \ldots, |r|\}, I_R \cap I_S = \emptyset,$$
$$r|I_R \in R, r|I_S \in S, \mathsf{virtual}(r|I_R) \cap \mathsf{virtual}(r|I_S) = \emptyset\}^{\equiv} .$$

The condition about the local variables in $r|I_R$ and $r|I_S$ ensures that parallel threads do not exchange values via local variables. The application of the closure operator $(\cdot)^{\equiv}$ guarantees well-definedness: $R \otimes S \in \mathsf{NR}$ for $R, S \in \mathsf{NR}$.

Suppose $r, s, t \in \mathsf{Runs}$ with $\mathsf{virtual}(r) \cap \mathsf{virtual}(s) = \emptyset$. We call t an *interleaving of r and s* if

$$\exists I_r, I_s : I_r \cup I_s = \{1, \ldots, |r|\}, I_r \cap I_s = \emptyset, t|I_r = r, t|I_s = s$$

and denote the set of interleavings of r and s by $r \otimes s$.

6.3.4 Pre-operator

The pre-operator, $pre : \mathsf{NR} \to \mathsf{NR}$ is defined as follows:

$$pre(R) \;=\; \{r \in \mathsf{Runs} \mid \exists r' \in \mathsf{Runs} : r \cdot r' \in R\}\,.$$

Lemma 6.3.2. *pre is well-defined.*

Proof. We have to show that, for any $R \in \mathsf{NR}$, $pre(R)$ is closed under $\equiv$. So suppose given $r, s \in \mathsf{Runs}$ with $s \equiv r \in pre(R)$. Then there is $r' \in \mathsf{Runs}$ with $r \cdot r' \in R$. By bounded renaming of local variables in r' we can construct a run s' such that $s \cdot s' \equiv r \cdot r'$. As R is closed under $\equiv$, $s \cdot s' \in R$ and hence $s \in pre(R)$. □

6.3.5 Post-operator

Analogously to the pre-operator, the post operator $post : \mathsf{NR} \to \mathsf{NR}$ is defined as follows:

$$post(R) \;=\; \{r \in \mathsf{Runs} \mid \exists r' \in \mathsf{Runs} : r' \cdot r \in R\}\,.$$

Lemma 6.3.3. *post is well-defined.* □

6.4 Conclusion

We have defined a complete lattice $(\mathsf{NR}, \subseteq)$ the members of which model sets of runs in a scenario in which assignment statements execute non-atomically. In order to enable an interleaving semantics to adequately capture the effect of non-atomic execution of assignments, we resorted to *virtual variables* that model storage locations that are private to threads. The members of NR are those sets of runs that are bounded under renaming of virtual variables. We have provided definitions for the operators and constants appearing in the constraint systems that capture reaching, terminating, and bridging runs in a parallel flow graph. The (smallest) solution of these constraint systems over this new interpretation induces a semantics of parallel flow graphs that captures non-atomic execution of assignments. Thus, it provides another reference point for assessing flow analyses. We will put this idea to advantage in Chapter 7 where we show that the dependence trace interpretation developed there is a precise abstraction of the non-atomic interpretation of parallel flow graphs.

7. Dependence Traces

We can indirectly detect copy constants and eliminate faint code on the basis of the following information: given a program point u and a variable x of interest; when control is at another program point v, which variables y may influence the value of x at u? Clearly, this information can be derived from the set of bridging runs from u to v and we have a constraint system characterizing this set (cf. Chapter 5.5). We would like to compute the above information by means of a precise and effective abstract interpretation. Before we start with the technical development we give a brief overview.

We call a pair of variables (x, y) a *dependence* and say that a run r *exhibits* the dependence (x, y) if the value of y after execution of r depends on the initial value of x (cf. Section 7.1 for the formal definition). Unfortunately, we cannot use dependences themselves as abstract domain because, in general, we cannot obtain the dependences of a parallel composition of run sets from the dependences of the components (cf. Section 7.2). Therefore, an abstraction employing just dependences cannot be sound and complete at the same time. We need to collect more information in the abstract domain.

The basic idea is to collect not only dependences but sequences of dependences (*dependence sequences*) that can successively be exhibited by a run. For example, the run $r_1 = \langle c := b, e := d \rangle$ has $\langle (b, c), (d, e) \rangle$ as one of its dependence sequences. This dependence sequence plays a dual role: on the one hand, it captures the potential of r_1 to exhibit the dependence (b, e) if a parallel run fills the gap between c and d (like, e.g., $r_2 = \langle d := c \rangle$) and, on the other hand, its potential to successively fill the gaps (b, c) and (d, e) in a parallel run (like, e.g., in $r_3 = \langle b := a, d := c, f := e \rangle$.

Further information must be collected. To see why, compare the run $r_4 = \langle b := 0, c := b, e := d, e := 0 \rangle$ with r_1. Unlike r_1, r_4 does *not* have the potential to exhibit the dependence (b, e) if a parallel run fills the gap between c and d, but it is still able to successively fill the gaps (b, c) and (d, e) in a parallel run. The difference is that in r_4, unlike in r_1, the part of the run before b is read and after e is written is not transparent for b and e, respectively. Therefore, we refine dependence sequences to *dependence traces* in which we record in addition to a dependence trace by two Boolean values, whether the parts of the run before the source variable of the first dependence is read and after the target variable of the final dependence is written are transparent for these variables. Run r_1 for instance has the dependence trace $(1, \langle (b,c), (d,e) \rangle, 1)$ which r_4 has not, but both share the dependence trace $(0, \langle (b,c), (d,e) \rangle, 0)$. In order to allow a proper propagation of transparency information in sequential composition, we furthermore collect in the abstraction the set of variables for which a transparent run exists.

According to these ideas, we can abstract a set of (non-atomic) runs R to a pair (T_R, D_R) consisting of the set of variables

$$T_R = \{x \mid \exists r \in R : r \text{ is transparent for } x\}$$

and the set of dependence traces

$$D_R = \{\tau \mid \exists r \in R : \tau \text{ is a dependence trace of } r\}.$$

On this abstraction of run sets, we can indeed define abstract operators that precisely mirror the operators on sets of non-atomic runs that are used in the constraint systems of Section 5.5. However, we are not yet done. The problem is, that this abstract domain is not effective, because D_R can be infinite. In order to obtain an effective domain, we have to go one step further.

For this purpose, we define a subsumption order, written $\sqsubseteq$, on transition traces. The intuition is that a transition trace τ is subsumed by another transition trace τ' if τ' has fewer gaps than τ—we write this as $\tau \sqsubseteq \tau'$ (cf. Section 7.4). Intuitively, τ' is more useful than τ in forming dependences. We then collect for a run set only the transition traces that are maximal with respect to the order $\sqsubseteq$. This set forms an antichain with respect to $\sqsubseteq$. It is not hard to show that all $\sqsubseteq$-maximal dependence traces of a run set are *short* in a certain sense made precise in Section 7.6. As there are only finitely many short dependence traces this makes the abstract domain finite, such that we can effectively perform fixpoint calculations.

Summarizing, the abstract domain consists of pairs (D, T) where D is an $\sqsubseteq$-antichain of short dependence traces and T is a set of variables. It is not hard to define on this domain abstract counterparts to the sequential composition operator and to the pre- and post-operator on run sets and to show that these abstract operators are precise abstractions of the concrete ones. It is also straightforward to abstract the run sets associated with base edges precisely.

The interleaving operator, however, poses some complication. The natural way to compose two transition traces τ and τ' concurrently is to use τ to fill gaps in τ' and vice versa. This was our motivation for considering transition traces in the first place; a precise formalization of this idea is given through the relation C in Section 7.11.1. However, if τ'' is a transition trace obtained in this way from a transition trace τ of a run r and a transition trace τ' of a run r', it is not obvious that there is always a run constructed by interleaving r and r' that has τ'' as one of its transition traces. Otherwise the abstraction would be imprecise. Indeed this is not true for run sets derived from an atomic interpretation of base statements but we can show it for the run sets appearing with a non-atomic interpretation.

On the other hand, short transition traces can be obtained from non-short ones in this way. There is thus some reason to suspect that we cannot obtain all $\sqsubseteq$-maximal dependence traces of the interleaving $R_1 \otimes R_2$ of two run sets from the $\sqsubseteq$-maximal dependence traces of the components. This would make the abstract operator unsound. Fortunately, we can show that this is not the case. The main insight is covered by a shortening lemma, Lemma 7.11.3.

As an auxiliary notion we introduce a further order on dependence traces, called the *implication order* which is written as $\leq$. Its name is justified by the fact that any run r that has τ as a dependence trace also has τ' as a dependence trace, if $\tau \leq \tau'$. Therefore, the implication order captures implied knowledge about dependence traces of runs, hence its name. The implication order is crucial in particular for a concise formulation of the shortening lemma mentioned above.

In the remainder of this chapter we elaborate these topics in detail.

7.1 Transparency and Dependences

A run r is called *transparent* for a variables a if it does not contain an assignment with a as left hand side variable. Thus, a run is transparent for a if its execution is guaranteed not to change the value held by a.

Example 7.1.1. The run $\langle a := 0, b := c \rangle$ is transparent for all variables except a and b, in particular for c.   □

A *dependence* is a pair $d = (x, y)$ of program variables $x, y \in X$. We call x the *source variable* and y the *destination variable* of d. A run r is said to *exhibit* dependence (x, y), $r \vdash (x, y)$ for short, if there are variables $a_0, \ldots, a_l$, $l > 0$, expressions $e_1, \ldots, e_l$, and (sub-) runs $r_0, \ldots, r_l$ such that

1. $r = r_0 \cdot \langle a_1 := e_1 \rangle \cdot r_1 \cdot \langle a_2 := e_2 \rangle \cdot r_2 \cdot \ldots \cdot \langle a_l := e_l \rangle \cdot r_l$;
2. $a_0 = x$, $a_l = y$;
3. e_i contains a_{i-1} for $i = 1, \ldots, l$; and
4. r_i is transparent for a_i for $i = 0, \ldots, l$.

We also say "(x, y) is a dependence of r" in this case.

Example 7.1.2. Run $\langle b := a, c := b, e := 0, f := e \rangle$ exhibits the dependences (a, b), (a, c), and (b, c) but not the dependence (e, f) because e is killed by the assignment $e := 0$ before it is read.   □

7.2 Dependence Traces

In general, the dependences of the interleaving $R_1 \otimes R_2$ of two sets of runs cannot directly be inferred from the dependences of the component run sets R_1 and R_2. As an example, consider the two sets of runs $R_1 := \{\langle b := a, d := c \rangle\}$ and $R_2 := \{\langle b := a \rangle, \langle d := c \rangle\}$. Both exhibit just the dependences (a, b) and (c, d). But the interleaving of R_1 with $R_3 := \{\langle c := b \rangle\}$ contains the run $\langle b := a, c := b, d := c \rangle$ that exhibits the dependence (a, d) while there is no run in the interleaving of R_2 and R_3 that exhibits this dependence.

Thus, an abstraction of sets of runs that faithfully mirrors dependences must collect more information than just dependences. We propose to employ *dependence traces* that are defined in the remainder of this section.

The basic idea is to collect not just dependences but sequences of dependences that can successively be exhibited by a run. For example, we would record the sequences $\varphi = \langle (a, b), (c, d) \rangle$ for the run $r_1 = \langle b := a, d := c \rangle$ from R_1 but not for R_2. Intuitively, φ shows us that r_1 could exhibit a dependence from a to d if a parallel component fills the gap from b to c. Dually, it also indicates that r_1 can successively fill the gaps (a, b) and (c, d).

A *dependence sequence* is a sequence $\varphi = \langle (x_1, y_1), \ldots, (x_k, y_k) \rangle$, $k \geq 0$, of dependences. Note that we allow the empty dependence sequence ε. We write $\overleftarrow{\varphi}$ for x_1 and $\overrightarrow{\varphi}$ for y_k, if $\varphi \neq \varepsilon$; if $\varphi = \varepsilon$, $\overleftarrow{\varphi}$ and $\overrightarrow{\varphi}$ are undefined. We denote the set of dependence sequences by DS.

Example 7.2.1. $\varphi = \langle (a, b), (c, d) \rangle$ is a dependence sequence with $\overleftarrow{\varphi} = a$ and $\overrightarrow{\varphi} = d$. □

Further information must be collected. As explained in the introduction to this chapter we must distinguish between runs like $r_2 = \langle a := 0, b := a, d := c \rangle$ and r_1 above. Unlike r_1, r_2 does *not* have the potential to exhibit dependence (a, d) if a parallel run fills the gap between b and c, but like r_1 it can successively fill the gaps (a, b) and (c, d) in a parallel run. The crucial difference is that in r_2 the part of the run before a is read is not transparent for the source variable of the first dependence, viz. a. A similar difference can arise for the target variable of the final dependence. Therefore, we refine dependence sequences to *dependence traces*.

A *dependence trace* is a triple $\tau = (\iota, \varphi, \kappa)$ consisting of Boolean values $\iota, \kappa \in \mathbb{B} = \{0, 1\}$ coding initial and final transparency and a dependence sequence φ. We assume that $\iota = 0$ and $\kappa = 0$ if $\varphi = \varepsilon$. The set of dependence traces is denoted by DT:

$$\mathsf{DT} = \{(\iota, \varphi, \kappa) \in \mathbb{B} \times \mathsf{DS} \times \mathbb{B} \mid \varphi = \varepsilon \Rightarrow (\iota = 0 \wedge \kappa = 0)\}.$$

A run r is said to *exhibit* dependence trace $\tau = (\iota, \langle (x_1, y_1), \ldots, (x_k, y_k) \rangle, \kappa)$, $r \vdash \tau$ for short, if there are sub-runs $t_0, \ldots, t_k, r_1, \ldots, r_k$, such that

1. $r = t_0 \cdot r_1 \cdot t_1 \cdot r_2 \cdots r_k \cdot t_k$;
2. r_i exhibits dependence (x_i, y_i) for $i = 1, \ldots, k$;
3. $\iota = 1$ implies that t_0 is transparent for x_1; and
4. $\kappa = 1$ implies that t_k is transparent for y_k.

In this case, we call $t_0 \cdot r_1 \cdot t_1 \cdot r_2 \cdots r_k \cdot t_k$ a *decomposition* of r that witnesses $r \vdash \tau$. Note that $r \vdash (0, \varepsilon, 0)$ holds for all runs r as witnessed by the trivial decomposition $t_0 = r$. The trivial dependence trace $(0, \varepsilon, 0)$ allows us to distinguish the dependence trace abstraction of the empty run set from the abstraction of non-empty run sets. Instead of saying "r exhibits τ" we often use the phrase "τ is a dependence trace of r".

Example 7.2.2. Run r_1 exhibits the dependence trace $(1, \langle (a, b), (c, d) \rangle, 1)$ in contrast to r_2. Both runs share the dependence trace $(0, \langle (a, b), (c, d) \rangle, 0)$. □

Example 7.2.3. Consider the following run:

$$r = \langle a := 0, b := a, c := b, c := 0, f := e, e := 0 \rangle .$$

One of the dependence traces of r is $\tau = (0, \langle (a, c), (e, f) \rangle, 1)$ as witnessed by the decomposition $r = t_0 \cdot r_1 \cdot t_1 \cdot r_2 \cdot t_2$ where

$$\langle \underbrace{a := 0,}_{t_0} \underbrace{b := a, c := b,}_{r_1} \underbrace{c := 0,}_{t_1} \underbrace{f := e,}_{r_2} \underbrace{e := 0}_{t_2} \rangle .$$

Another decomposition witnessing τ is

$$\langle \underbrace{a := 0,}_{t_0} \underbrace{b := a, c := b}_{r_1} \underbrace{}_{t_1 = \varepsilon}, \underbrace{c := 0, f := e, e := 0}_{r_2} \underbrace{}_{t_2 = \varepsilon} \rangle .$$

The run r has also many other dependence traces, e.g., $(1, \langle (b, c), (e, f) \rangle, 1)$ and $(1, \langle (e, f) \rangle, 1)$. □

Ultimately, we are interested in dependence traces without gaps that code complete transfers from one variable to another one, where a gap can either be a lack of initial or final transparency or a hole from y_i to x_{i+1}. Thus, the dependence traces of ultimate interest are those of the form $(1, \langle (x, y) \rangle, 1)$. They correspond to dependences.

Proposition 7.2.1. $r \vdash (1, \langle (x, y) \rangle, 1)$ *if and only if r exhibits dependence* (x, y). □

We can abstract a set R of runs to the set $D_R = \{ \tau \mid \exists r \in R : r \vdash \tau \}$ of compatible dependence traces and it is possible to define precise abstract operators on this abstraction.[1] However, D_R is in general infinite such this does not lead immediately to an effective domain.

---

[1] For sequential composition we also need the set of variables for which a transparent run exists in order to allow a proper propagation of the transparency bits.

Fortunately, it is not necessary to collect *all* compatible dependence traces in the abstraction, in order to describe the potential for forming dependences with a parallel context. It suffices to retain only certain short dependence traces in the abstraction that subsume the potential of all the other ones. A number of definitions and observations are necessary to make this precise. Before we turn to the technical development, let us illustrate this kind of subsumption by a small example.

Consider the two dependence traces $\tau_1 = (1, (a, b) \cdot (c, d) \cdot (e, f), 1)$ and $\tau_2 = (1, (a, d) \cdot (e, f), 1)$. Intuitively, both have the gap (d, e) but τ_1 has the additional gap (b, c). If a run r of a parallel context can successively fill the two holes in τ_1—i.e. if r is compatible with the dependence trace $\tau_3 = (0, (b, c) \cdot (d, e), 0)$—it can also fill the single hole in τ_2—i.e. r is then also compatible with $\tau_4 = (0, (d, e), 0)$. Two interesting relationships between dependence traces popped up in this discussion. On the one hand, τ is "subsumed" by τ' in the sense sketched above as it has fewer gaps. On the other hand τ_4 is "implied" by τ_3 as it has less dependences: any run having τ_3 as a dependence traces also has τ_4 as a dependence trace.

We now define two orders on the set of dependence traces that capture these two relationships, the "implication order" and the "subsumption order".

7.3 Implication Order

Let $\leq \subseteq \mathsf{DT} \times \mathsf{DT}$ be the smallest reflexive and transitive relation on the set of dependence traces that satisfies

1. $(\iota, \varphi \cdot \langle (x, y) \rangle \cdot \psi, \kappa) \leq (\iota, \varphi \cdot \psi, \kappa)$, if $\varphi \neq \varepsilon \vee \iota = 0$ and $\psi \neq \varepsilon \vee \kappa = 0$;
2. $(1, \varphi, \kappa) \leq (0, \varphi, \kappa)$; and
3. $(\iota, \varphi, 1) \leq (\iota, \varphi, 0)$.

Proposition 7.3.1. $\leq$ *is a partial order on* DT. *It is called the* implication order. $\qquad\square$

The implication order $\leq$ allows us to weaken the information in a dependence trace in two ways. First of all, we can omit dependences (1.); here we must be careful not to omit the first or last dependence if the corresponding transparency bit is set, as otherwise the transparency bit might become invalid. Secondly, we can weaken the information about transparency of the initial or final part of the run, by changing the transparency bits from 1 to 0 (2. & 3.).

The most appealing fact about $\leq$ is that it preserves compatibility, which justifies the name "implication order".

Proposition 7.3.2 ($\leq$ preserves compatibility). *Suppose* $r \vdash \tau$ *and* $\tau \leq \tau'$. *Then* $r \vdash \tau'$. $\qquad\square$

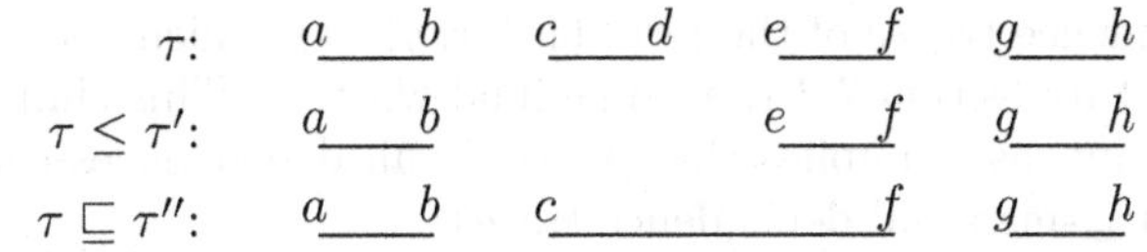

$$\begin{array}{llllllll}
\tau: & \underline{a \quad b} & \underline{c \quad d} & \underline{e \quad f} & \underline{g \quad h} \\
\tau \leq \tau': & \underline{a \quad b} & & \underline{e \quad f} & \underline{g \quad h} \\
\tau \sqsubseteq \tau'': & \underline{a \quad b} & c & \underline{ \; f} & \underline{g \quad h}
\end{array}$$

Fig. 7.1. Implication and subsumption order.

Example 7.3.1. Consider the dependence trace $\tau = (1, \langle (a,b), (c,d) \rangle, 0)$ of the run $r = \langle b := a, c := 0, d := c, d := 0 \rangle$. These are the dependence traces implied by τ:

$$\begin{aligned}
\tau_1 &= (0, \langle (a,b), (c,d) \rangle, 0) \\
\tau_2 &= (1, \langle (a,b) \rangle, 0) \\
\tau_3 &= (0, \langle (a,b) \rangle, 0) \\
\tau_4 &= (0, \langle (c,d) \rangle, 0) \\
\tau_5 &= (0, \varepsilon, 0)
\end{aligned}$$

i.e., we have $\tau \leq \tau_i$ for $i = 1, \ldots, 5$. All of them are dependence traces of r. But we do not have $\tau \leq \tau_6$ for $\tau_6 = (1, \langle (c,d) \rangle, 0)$. And indeed, τ_6 is not a dependence trace of r because variable c is killed before it is read in r.   □

7.4 Subsumption Order

A dependence trace with fewer gaps is more useful for the construction of dependences. We now define the *subsumption order* $\sqsubseteq \subseteq \mathsf{DT} \times \mathsf{DT}$. Intuitively, $\tau \sqsubseteq \tau'$ captures that τ' has fewer gaps than τ and thus subsumes the potential of τ for forming dependences with a cooperating parallel context. We define $\sqsubseteq$ as the smallest transitive and reflexive relation that satisfies

$$(\iota, \varphi \cdot \langle (x,y) \rangle \cdot \varphi' \cdot \langle (x',y') \rangle \cdot \varphi'', \kappa) \sqsubseteq (\iota, \varphi \cdot \langle (x,y') \rangle \cdot \varphi'', \kappa).$$

Fig. 7.1 illustrates the difference between the implication and the subsumption order. For simplicity, we only show the dependence sequences and omit the transparency bits. In the top row we show a dependence trace τ, in the middle row a dependence trace τ' that is implied by τ, and in the bottom row a dependence trace τ'' that subsumes τ. The implication order allows us to omit dependences (and weaken transparency bits). In contrast the subsumption order allows us to remove gaps.

It is obvious from the defining rule that a dependence trace τ' that properly subsumes another dependence trace τ embodies a strictly shorter dependence sequence. Therefore, $\sqsubseteq$ satisfies the ascending chain condition.

Proposition 7.4.1. $\sqsubseteq$ *is a partial order on* DT *that satisfies the ascending chain condition: every strictly increasing sequence* $\tau_1 \sqsubset \tau_2 \sqsubset \cdots$ *is finite.*   □

Note that dependence traces of the form $(1, \langle (x, y) \rangle, 1)$, which correspond to dependences by Proposition 7.2.1, are maximal w.r.t. $\sqsubseteq$. This simple observation is important, as it implies that we cover all dependences even when we only consider $\sqsubseteq$-maximal dependence traces.

7.5 A Lattice of Antichains

An *antichain* with respect to $\sqsubseteq$ (or $\sqsubseteq$-antichain for short) is a set $D \subseteq \mathsf{DT}$ of dependence traces satisfying

$$\neg \; \exists \tau, \tau' \in D : \tau \sqsubset \tau'.$$

We denote the set of $\sqsubseteq$-antichains by AC. We can lift the subsumption order to AC as follows:

$$D \sqsubseteq D' \quad :\Leftrightarrow \quad \forall \tau \in D \; \exists \tau' \in D' : \tau \sqsubseteq \tau'.$$

Thus, D' subsumes D, if every dependence trace in D is subsumed by some dependence trace in D'. We call $\sqsubseteq$ the *antichain order*. This is justified by the following lemma.

Lemma 7.5.1. $\sqsubseteq$ *is a partial order on* AC.

Proof. It is straightforward to show that $\sqsubseteq$ is reflexive and transitive. Let us show that $\sqsubseteq$ is also antisymmetric and hence a partial order.

Suppose $D \sqsubseteq D' \sqsubseteq D$. We show that $D \subseteq D'$, the reverse inclusion follows analogously. Suppose $\tau \in D$. Then there is $\tau' \in D'$ with $\tau \sqsubseteq \tau'$ as $D \sqsubseteq D'$. Because of $D' \sqsubseteq D$, there is $\tau'' \in D$ with $\tau' \sqsubseteq \tau''$. Thus, we have

$$D \ni \tau \sqsubseteq \tau' \sqsubseteq \tau'' \in D.$$

As D is an antichain, this implies that $\tau = \tau''$. Consequently, all these three dependence traces must be equal: $\tau = \tau' = \tau''$. But then $\tau = \tau' \in D'$. $\qquad \square$

A simple way to form an $\sqsubseteq$-antichain out of an arbitrary subset $D \subseteq \mathsf{DT}$ is to consider the set of $\sqsubseteq$-maximal elements in D. We denote this set by $D^\uparrow$:

$$D^\uparrow = \{\tau \in D \mid \neg \exists \tau' \in D : \tau \sqsubset \tau'\}.$$

The dependence traces in $D^\uparrow$ subsume all dependence traces in D. In this sense, no interesting information is lost when going from D to $D^\uparrow$.

Lemma 7.5.2 ($^\uparrow$ **subsumes**)**.** *For any* $\tau \in D$ *there is a* $\tau' \in D^\uparrow$ *such that* $\tau \sqsubseteq \tau'$.

Proof. The lemma follows easily with the ascending chain condition. $\qquad \square$

The operator $^\uparrow$ is a co-closure operator that yields $\sqsubseteq$-antichains:

Lemma 7.5.3 ($^\uparrow$ is a co-closure operator).

1. $D^\uparrow \subseteq D$.
2. $(D^\uparrow)^\uparrow = D^\uparrow$.
3. $D^\uparrow$ is an $\sqsubseteq$-antichain.
4. $(\cdot)^\uparrow$ is monotonic: $D \subseteq E$ implies $D^\uparrow \sqsubseteq E^\uparrow$.

Proof. The proof of these properties is straightforward. □

The $\sqsubseteq$-antichains together with the lifted subsumption order form a complete lattice.

Lemma 7.5.4. $(AC, \sqsubseteq)$ *is a complete lattice. The least upper bound (lub) of a subset* $\mathcal{D} \subseteq AC$ *is* $\bigsqcup \mathcal{D} := (\bigcup \mathcal{D})^\uparrow$ *and the least element of* $(AC, \sqsubseteq)$ *is* $\bot_{AC} := \emptyset$.

Proof. In order to show that $(AC, \sqsubseteq)$ is a complete lattice, it suffices to demonstrate that any subset $\mathcal{D} \subseteq AC$ has a least upper bound. We show that, as claimed in the lemma, $E := (\bigcup \mathcal{D})^\uparrow$ is indeed the least upper bound of $\mathcal{D}$.

Firstly, E is an upper bound of $\mathcal{D}$: we have to show that $D \sqsubseteq E$ for any $D \in \mathcal{D}$, which is seen as follows:

$\quad \tau \in D$

$\Rightarrow \quad [D \in \mathcal{D}, \text{definition of } \bigcup \mathcal{D}]$

$\quad \tau \in \bigcup \mathcal{D}$

$\Rightarrow \quad [\text{Lemma 7.5.2, definition } E]$

$\quad \exists \tau' \in E : \tau \sqsubseteq \tau'$.

Secondly, E is smaller than any other bound $\mathcal{D}$. Suppose F is an arbitrary upper bound of $\mathcal{D}$. Then $E \sqsubseteq F$ follows from the following chain of implications:

$\quad \tau \in E$

$\Rightarrow \quad [\text{Definition } E, \text{Lemma 7.5.3(1.)}]$

$\quad \tau \in \bigcup \mathcal{D}$

$\Rightarrow \quad [\text{Definition of } \bigcup \mathcal{D}]$

$\quad \exists D \in \mathcal{D} : \tau \in D$

$\Rightarrow \quad [D \sqsubseteq F \text{ as } F \text{ is an upper bound of } \mathcal{D}, \text{definition } \sqsubseteq]$

$\quad \exists \tau' \in F : \tau \sqsubseteq \tau'$.

The least element of $(AC, \sqsubseteq)$ is $\bot_{AC} = \bigsqcup \emptyset = (\emptyset)^\uparrow = \emptyset$. □

Let us consider another operator on sets of dependence traces, the downwards closure operator $(\cdot)^{\downarrow}$. It is defined for sets $D \in \mathsf{DT}$ by

$$D^{\downarrow} = \{\tau \in \mathsf{DT} \mid \exists \tau' \in D : \tau \sqsubseteq \tau'\}.$$

We can apply $(\cdot)^{\downarrow}$ in particular to antichains. Thus, we may consider $(\cdot)^{\downarrow}$ as an operator $(\cdot)^{\downarrow} : \mathsf{AC} \to 2^{\mathsf{DT}}$. It is not hard to see that $(\cdot)^{\downarrow}$ is monotonic.

Proposition 7.5.1. *Suppose $A, B \in \mathsf{AC}$. Then $A \sqsubseteq B$ implies $A^{\downarrow} \subseteq B^{\downarrow}$.* $\square$

$(\cdot)^{\uparrow}$ and $(\cdot)^{\downarrow}$ are approximate inverses of each other.

Lemma 7.5.5. *For any $D \in \mathsf{DT}$, we have $D^{\uparrow\downarrow} \supseteq D$ and $D^{\downarrow\uparrow} \subseteq D$. For any $A \in \mathsf{AC}$, we even have $A^{\downarrow\uparrow} = A$. As a consequence, $((\cdot)^{\uparrow}, (\cdot)^{\downarrow})$ is a Galois surjection from 2^{DT} to AC:*

$$2^{\mathsf{DT}} \overset{(\cdot)^{\uparrow}}{\underset{(\cdot)^{\downarrow}}{\rightleftarrows}} \mathsf{AC}$$

Proof. $D^{\uparrow\downarrow} \supseteq D$: By Lemma 7.5.2, there is, for any $\tau \in D$, a dependence trace $\tau' \in D^{\uparrow}$ such that $\tau \sqsubseteq \tau'$. This implies that $\tau \in D^{\uparrow\downarrow}$.

$D^{\downarrow\uparrow} \subseteq D$: If $\tau \in D^{\downarrow\uparrow}$, then τ is a maximal element in $D^{\downarrow}$. The maximal elements in $D^{\downarrow}$, however, must already be in D, as they cannot be added to D by lying strictly below another element of D.

$A^{\downarrow\uparrow} = A$: It remains to show that $A^{\downarrow\uparrow} \supseteq A$. Any $\tau \in A$ is maximal in $A^{\downarrow}$. Therefore, any such τ is also in $A^{\downarrow\uparrow}$. $\square$

The fact that $((\cdot)^{\uparrow}, (\cdot)^{\downarrow})$ is a Galois surjection from 2^{DT} into AC shows us that $\sqsubseteq$-antichains form a reasonable abstraction of sets of dependence traces. It also has other interesting consequences. First of all, it implies that $(\cdot)^{\uparrow}$ is universally disjunctive, which is important for ensuring that the abstraction mapping and the abstract operators defined later are universally disjunctive as well.

Proposition 7.5.2. $(\cdot)^{\uparrow} : 2^{\mathsf{DT}} \to \mathsf{AC}$ *is universally disjunctive ('distributive').* $\square$

Secondly, it shows us that we can present $(\mathsf{AC}, \sqsubseteq)$ isomorphically by downwards closed sets of dependence traces. From the theory of Galois connections, we know that the images of the upper and lower adjoint are isomorphic. This implies that $(\mathsf{AC}, \sqsubseteq)$, the image of $(\cdot)^{\uparrow}$, is isomorphic to the image of $(\cdot)^{\downarrow}$, which is the set of downwards closed sets of dependence traces ordered by set inclusion. Note that this isomorphism depends on the fact that the underlying subsumption order on dependence traces satisfies the ascending chain condition. Otherwise, Lemma 7.5.2 would fail and we would not have the property $D^{\uparrow\downarrow} \supseteq D$ that is crucial for the isomorphism between antichains and downwards closed sets.

For our purpose it is more convenient to work with antichains, because this leads to a more natural definition of the interleaving operator. If we work with downwards closed sets we may add dependence traces by means of downwards closure that are not exhibited by any run in the abstracted run set. These additional dependence traces do not represent actual potential of the run set and in order to avoid imprecision, we must ensure that they are not considered for inferring dependence traces of interleavings.

7.6 Short Dependence Traces

A dependence sequence $\varphi = \langle (x_1, y_1), \dots, (x_k, y_k) \rangle$ is called *short* if

1. all destination variables of dependences not counting the last one are distinct: for all $1 \le i < j < k$, $y_i \ne y_j$; and
2. all source variables of dependences not counting the first one are distinct: for all $1 < i < j \le k$, $x_i \ne x_j$.

A dependence trace $\tau = (\iota, \varphi, \kappa)$ is called *short* if the embodied dependence sequence φ is short. We write DTS for the set of short dependence traces:

$$\mathsf{DTS} = \{ \tau \in \mathsf{DT} \mid \tau \text{ is short} \}.$$

Example 7.6.1. Consider the run $r = \langle c := a, c := b, e := d \rangle$. One of its dependence traces is $\tau = (1, \langle (a, c), (b, c), (d, e) \rangle, 1)$, which is not short due to the repetition of variable c as a target variable. But run r has also the dependence trace $\tau' = (1, \langle (a, c), (d, e) \rangle, 1)$ which is short and subsumes τ. This is not a coincidence as we will see in a moment (Lemma 7.6.2).   □

We are interested in short dependence traces for two reasons. Firstly, there are only finitely many of them. This makes the abstract domain introduced in the next section finite as well and ensures that fixpoints for monotonic functions on this domain can be calculated effectively. The following lemma provides a formula for the cardinality of DTS and an asymptotic bound.

Lemma 7.6.1. *Let* $n = |X|$. *Then* $|\mathsf{DTS}| = 1 + 4n^2 n!^2 \sum_{i=0}^{n} \frac{1}{i!^2} = \mathcal{O}(n^{2n+2})$.

Proof. By the pigeonhole principle, a dependence sequence cannot contain more than $n + 1$ dependences without violating the condition of shortness.

Let $i \in \{0, \dots, n\}$. For forming a dependence sequence $\langle d_0, \dots, d_i \rangle$ of length $i + 1$ in a dependence trace, we can choose arbitrary program variables as source variable of d_0 and as destination variable of d_i; there are n^2 ways of doing this. We can choose the remaining source variables of $d_1, \dots, d_i$ as an arbitrary i-permutation of the variables in X. (Recall that an i-permutation of X is an ordered sequence of i elements of X, with no element appearing more than once in the sequence). The same holds for the remaining destination variables of $d_0, \dots, d_{i-1}$. As there are $\frac{n!}{(n-i)!}$ i-permutations [13], there are thus $n^2(\frac{n!}{(n-i)!})^2$ short dependence sequences of length $i+1$. There are four possible choices for the transparency bits in a dependence trace with a given non-empty dependence sequence. In addition we have a single dependence trace with an empty dependence sequence, viz. $(0, \varepsilon, 0)$. Summing up, the number of short dependence traces is thus

$$1 + 4 \sum_{i=0}^{n} \left(n^2 \left(\frac{n!}{(n-i)!} \right)^2 \right) = 1 + 4n^2 n!^2 \sum_{i=0}^{n} \frac{1}{(n-i)!^2} = 1 + 4n^2 n!^2 \sum_{i=0}^{n} \frac{1}{i!^2}.$$

Using the well-known fact that $n! \leq n^n$ and bounding the sum by

$$\sum_{i=0}^{n} \frac{1}{i!^2} \leq \sum_{i=0}^{n} \frac{1}{i!} \leq \sum_{i=0}^{\infty} \frac{1}{i!} = e$$

the asymptotic bound $\mathcal{O}(n^{2n+2})$ follows.   □

The asymptotic bound $\mathcal{O}(n^{2n+2})$ for $|\mathsf{DTS}|$ is rather rough as it involves the rather bad estimate n^n for $n!$ but suffices for our purposes. Using for instance Stirling's approximation [13] for the factorial function, we could obtain tighter bounds.

The second reason why we are interested in short dependence traces is that they suffice to capture the potential of runs to aid in forming dependences 'up to subsumption' as the following lemma shows.

Lemma 7.6.2 (Short dependence traces subsume). *Let* $r \vdash \tau$. *Then there is a short dependence trace* τ' *with* $r \vdash \tau'$ *and* $\tau \sqsubseteq \tau'$.

Proof. Suppose $r \vdash \tau = (\iota, \langle (x_1, y_1), \ldots, (x_k, y_k) \rangle, \kappa)$. We describe a shortening procedure that can be iterated until a short dependence trace is obtained.

Suppose τ is not already short. Let us assume that Condition 1. is violated; if Condition 2. is violated we can proceed analogously. Then there are indices i, j, $1 \leq i < j < k$, with $y_i = y_j$. Consider the dependence trace τ' obtained from τ by removing the middle part $\langle (x_{i+1}, y_{i+1}), \ldots, (x_j, y_j) \rangle$ of the dependence sequence:

$$\tau' := (\iota, \langle (x_1, y_1), \ldots, (x_i, y_i), (x_{j+1}, y_{j+1}), \ldots, (x_k, y_k) \rangle, \kappa).$$

It is not hard to see that both $\tau \sqsubseteq \tau'$ and $\tau \leq \tau'$. By Proposition 7.3.2 the latter implies $r \vdash \tau'$.   □

We still have to see that we can obtain the short dependence traces of a composed set of runs from the short dependence traces of the argument run sets. This is particularly challenging for run sets obtained by interleaving and will be the topic of Sections 7.8–7.12.

Shortening a dependence trace w.r.t. either $\leq$ or $\sqsubseteq$ results again in a short dependence trace.

Lemma 7.6.3 ($\leq$ and $\sqsubseteq$ preserve shortness). *If τ is short and $\tau \leq \tau'$ or $\tau \sqsubseteq \tau'$, then τ' is short.*

Proof. All pairs of source or target variables in τ' are also pairs of target variables in τ if $\tau \leq \tau'$ or $\tau \sqsubseteq \tau'$. $\qquad\square$

We denote the set of antichains of short dependence traces by ACS:

$$\mathsf{ACS} = \{D \in \mathsf{AC} \mid D \subseteq \mathsf{DTS}\}.$$

Lemma 7.6.2 implies that $\sqsubseteq$-maximal dependence traces of a run (or run set) are always short. Therefore, if we restrict attention to short dependence traces of a run or run set, we still capture all maximal dependence traces. By working with ACS instead of AC, we code this knowledge into the domain. In particular, we do not lose dependences because the dependence traces of the form $(1, \langle(a, b)\rangle, 1)$ that correspond to dependences are trivially short.

Lemma 7.6.4. $(\mathsf{ACS}, \sqsubseteq)$ *is a complete sub-lattice of* $(\mathsf{AC}, \sqsubseteq)$. *Its height is* $|\mathsf{DTS}| + 1 = \mathcal{O}(n^{2n+2})$ *where* $n = |X|$.

Proof. Suppose $\mathcal{D} \subseteq \mathsf{ACS}$. In order to prove that $(\mathsf{ACS}, \sqsubseteq)$ is a complete sub-lattice of $(\mathsf{AC}, \sqsubseteq)$ we have to show that $\bigsqcup \mathcal{D} \in \mathsf{ACS}$, i.e. that $\bigsqcup \mathcal{D} \subseteq \mathsf{DTS}$:

$$\underset{\uparrow}{\bigsqcup \mathcal{D}} \;=\; \underset{\uparrow}{(\bigcup \mathcal{D})^{\uparrow}} \;\subseteq\; \underset{\uparrow}{\bigcup \mathcal{D}} \;\subseteq\; \mathsf{DTS}.$$
$$\text{[Lem. 7.5.4]} \quad \text{[Lem. 7.5.3]} \quad [\mathcal{D} \subseteq \mathsf{ACS}]$$

We can restrict the downwards closure operator to short dependence traces, i.e. redefine it by $D^{\downarrow} = \{\tau \in \mathsf{DTS} \mid \exists \tau' \in D : \tau \sqsubseteq \tau'\}$ for $D \subseteq \mathsf{DTS}$. It follows as in Lemma 7.5.5 that $((\cdot)^{\uparrow}, (\cdot)^{\downarrow})$ is a Galois surjection from 2^{DTS} into ACS:

$$2^{\mathsf{DTS}} \underset{(\cdot)^{\downarrow}}{\overset{(\cdot)^{\uparrow}}{\rightleftharpoons}} \mathsf{ACS}$$

As a consequence $(\mathsf{ACS}, \sqsubseteq)$ is isomorphic to the lattice of downwards closed subsets of DTS, ordered by set inclusion. The latter is a sub-lattice of $(2^{\mathsf{DTS}}, \subseteq)$. Hence its height (and thus the height of $(\mathsf{ACS}, \sqsubseteq)$) cannot be larger than the height of $(2^{\mathsf{DTS}}, \subseteq)$ which is $|\mathsf{DTS}| + 1$.

On the other hand, we can construct an ascending chain of size $|\mathsf{DTS}| + 1$. Let $(x_1, \ldots, x_{|\mathsf{DTS}|})$ be a topological sort of $(\mathsf{DTS}, \sqsubseteq)$, i.e., a list containing all elements of DTS such that $x_i \sqsubseteq x_j$ implies $i \leq j$ for all $i, j \in \{1, \ldots, |\mathsf{DTS}|\}$. Then we can define a chain of length $\mathsf{DTS} + 1$ by choosing $A_0 = \emptyset$ and $A_i = (A_{i-1} \cup \{x_i\})^{\uparrow}$ for $i = 1, \ldots, |\mathsf{DTS}|$. $A_{i-1} \sqsubseteq A_i$ is obvious, and $A_{i-1} \neq A_i$ holds because $A_{i-1} \subseteq \{x_1, \ldots, x_{i-1}\}$, which is seen by a straightforward induction. Thus, x_i is maximal in $A_{i-1} \cup \{x_i\}$ due to the topological sort property.

Lemma 7.6.1 gives the asymptotic bound $|\mathsf{DTS}| + 1 = \mathcal{O}(n^{2n+2})$. $\qquad\square$

7.7 The Abstract Domain

Let us now define the abstract domain. The values of the abstract domain AD are pairs (T, D) consisting of a set $T \subseteq X$ of variables and an $\sqsubseteq$-antichain D of short dependence traces:

$$AD = 2^X \times ACS.$$

In the applications the dependence traces in D form the more interesting piece of information. T represents the variables for which a transparent run exists. This information is necessary in order to allow a proper propagation of initial and final transparency information in sequential contexts. The order on the abstract domain, which we also denote by the symbol $\sqsubseteq$, is defined as the lift of the inclusion order on the T component and the antichain order $\sqsubseteq$ on the D component: $(T, D) \sqsubseteq (T', D')$ iff

1. $T \subseteq T'$ and
2. $D \sqsubseteq D'$.

$(AD, \sqsubseteq)$ is the product lattice of the complete lattices $(2^X, \subseteq)$ and $(ACS, \sqsubseteq)$ and hence also a complete lattice. Both of these lattices have $\emptyset$ as their least element. Hence, $(\emptyset, \emptyset)$ is the least element of $\sqsubseteq$.

Lemma 7.7.1. $(AD, \sqsubseteq)$ *is a complete lattice with least element* $(\emptyset, \emptyset)$. *Its height is* $\mathcal{O}(n^{2n+2})$ *where* $n = |X|$.

Proof. It only remains to prove the asymptotic bound for the height. The height of AD is the sum of the height of $(2^X, \subseteq)$, which is $n + 1$, and the height of $(ACS, \sqsubseteq)$, which is $\mathcal{O}(n^{2n+2})$ by Lemma 7.6.4. This implies the stated bound. □

Let us now define an abstraction mapping $\alpha : NR \to AD$ that captures the intuition how non-atomic run sets are abstracted to values from AD:

$$\begin{aligned}
\alpha(R) &= (T_R, D_R), \text{ where} \\
T_R &= \{x \in X \mid \exists r \in R : r \text{ is transparent for } x\} \text{ and} \\
D_R &= \{\tau \in DT \mid \exists r \in R : r \vdash \tau\}^\uparrow.
\end{aligned}$$

Before we proceed, let us show that this is a proper definition.

Lemma 7.7.2. α *is well-defined.*

Proof. We have to show two things for an arbitrary $R \in NR$:

1. D_R consists of short dependence traces.
2. D_R is an $\sqsubseteq$-antichain.

Ad 1.: Assume there is $\tau \in D_R$ that is not short. Then there is $r \in R$ with $r \vdash \tau$. By Lemma 7.6.2, there is a *short* dependence trace τ' with $r \vdash \tau$ and $\tau \sqsubseteq \tau'$. In particular $\tau' \in \{\tau \in \mathsf{DT} \mid \exists r \in R : r \vdash \tau\}$ and, as τ' is short and τ is not, we even have $\tau \sqsubset \tau'$. But this shows that τ is not maximal in $\{\tau \in \mathsf{DT} \mid \exists r \in R : r \vdash \tau\}$ and hence is not a member of D_R, a contradiction.

Ad 2.: This is ensured by Lemma 7.5.3(4.). $\qquad\qquad\qquad\qquad\qquad\square$

The abstraction $\alpha(R)$ of a run set R is induced by the following abstraction $\beta(r)$ of the single runs $r \in R$:

$$
\begin{aligned}
\beta(r) &= (T_r, D_r)\,, \text{ where}\\
T_r &= \{x \in X \mid r \text{ is transparent for } x\} \text{ and}\\
D_r &= \{\tau \in \mathsf{DT} \mid r \vdash \tau\}^{\uparrow}\,.
\end{aligned}
$$

Lemma 7.7.3. *Suppose $R \in \mathsf{NR}$. Then $\alpha(R) = \bigsqcup\{\beta(r) \mid r \in R\}$.*

Proof. We have $\bigsqcup\{\beta(r) \mid r \in R\} = (\bigcup_{r \in R} T_r, \bigsqcup_{r \in R} D_r)$. It is obvious that $T_R = \bigcup_{r \in R} T_r$. On the other hand, we have $\bigsqcup_{r \in R} D_r = (\bigcup_{r \in R}\{\tau \mid r \vdash \tau\}^{\uparrow})^{\uparrow}$, by Lemma 7.5.4. It is not hard to show that this equals D_R by considering the $\sqsubseteq$- and the $\sqsupseteq$-direction separately. $\qquad\qquad\square$

The fact that α is induced by an abstraction on single runs has nice consequences.

Proposition 7.7.1. α *is monotonic: $R \subseteq R'$ implies $\alpha(R) \sqsubseteq \alpha(R')$.* $\qquad\square$

Proposition 7.7.2. α *is universally disjunctive.* $\qquad\qquad\qquad\qquad\square$

The latter property is crucial for precision of the abstract interpretation of constraint systems, cf. Chapter 8, and shows us that α provides a proper abstraction of run sets by being the lower adjoint of a Galois connection. For completeness let us introduce the corresponding upper adjoint. It is $\gamma : \mathsf{AD} \to \mathsf{NR}$, defined by

$$
\gamma(T, D) = \{r \mid T_r \subseteq T,\ D_r \sqsubseteq D\}\,.
$$

Proposition 7.7.3. (α, γ) *is a Galois connection between* NR *and* AD:
$$
\mathsf{NR} \underset{\gamma}{\overset{\alpha}{\rightleftarrows}} \mathsf{AD}\,.
$$
$\qquad\qquad\qquad\qquad\qquad\qquad\qquad\qquad\qquad\qquad\qquad\qquad\qquad\qquad\square$

We leave the proof that γ is well-defined and forms a Galois connection with α to the reader.

In the sections that follow we define composition operators on AD and show that they are precise abstractions of the corresponding operators on NR. We start with the pre- and the post-operator that are rather simple. Then we discuss sequential composition. Afterwards we consider the most interesting and challenging operator: interleaving. Finally, we discuss the abstract semantics of base edges.

7.8 Pre-operator

We define the (abstract) pre-operator, $pre^\# : \mathsf{AD} \to \mathsf{AD}$, as follows:

$$pre^\#(T, D) = \begin{cases} (\emptyset, \emptyset), & \text{if } D = \emptyset \\ (X, \{(\iota, \varphi, \kappa) \in \mathsf{DT} \mid (\iota, \varphi, 0) \in D\}), & \text{if } D \neq \emptyset. \end{cases}$$

Lemma 7.8.1. $pre^\#$ *is well-defined: for any* $(T, D) \in \mathsf{AD}$, $pre^\#(T, D) \in \mathsf{AD}$.

Proof. The only property that is not obvious is that $A := \{(\iota, \varphi, \kappa) \in \mathsf{DT} \mid (\iota, \varphi, 0) \in D\}$ is an antichain of short dependence traces. First of all, any dependence trace $(\iota, \varphi, \kappa) \in A$ inherits being short from the dependence trace $(\iota, \varphi, 0) \in D$ that induces its inclusion in A. Secondly, assume that there are distinct dependence traces $\tau, \tau' \in A$ with $\tau \sqsubseteq \tau'$. By the definition of the subsumption order, the transparency bits in τ and τ' must coincide, i.e. we can write them in the form $\tau = (\iota, \varphi, \kappa)$ and $\tau' = (\iota, \varphi', \kappa)$. From $\tau \sqsubseteq \tau'$ it follows that also $(\iota, \varphi, 0) \sqsubseteq (\iota, \varphi', 0)$. But then $(\iota, \varphi, 0)$ and $(\iota, \varphi', 0)$ are two distinct comparable dependence traces in D, which is a contradiction to D being an antichain. Hence $pre^\#(T, D)$ must be an antichain of short dependence traces. $\square$

The crucial observation for the adequacy of the definition of $pre^\#$ is this.

Lemma 7.8.2. $r \vdash (\iota, \varphi, 0)$ *if and only if there is a prefix* r' *of* r *with* $r' \vdash (\iota, \varphi, \kappa)$.

Proof. Let $\varphi = \langle (x_1, y_1), \dots, (x_k, y_k) \rangle$.

'$\Rightarrow$': Suppose $r \vdash (\iota, \varphi, 0)$. If $\kappa = 0$, we can choose $r' = r$. So assume $\kappa = 1$. Choose a decomposition $t_0 \cdot r_1 \cdots r_k \cdot t_k$ of r that witnesses $r \vdash (\iota, \varphi, 0)$. Let $r' = t_0 \cdot r_1 \cdots r_k$. Then, clearly, r' is a prefix of r and $t_0 \cdot r_1 \cdots r_k \cdot t'_k$ with $t'_k = \varepsilon$ is a decomposition of r' that witnesses $r' \vdash (\iota, \varphi, 1)$.

'$\Leftarrow$': Suppose r' is a prefix of r with $r' \vdash (\iota, \varphi, \kappa)$. Choose r'' with $r = r' \cdot r''$, and let $t_0 \cdot r_1 \cdots r_k \cdot t_k$ be a decomposition of r' that witnesses $r' \vdash (\iota, \varphi, \kappa)$. Then $t_0 \cdot r_1 \cdots r_k \cdot t'_k$ with $t'_k = t_k \cdot r''$ is a decomposition of r that witnesses $r \vdash (\iota, \varphi, 0)$. $\square$

We can now show that the abstract pre-operator is a precise abstraction of the concrete pre-operator.

Theorem 7.8.1 (Abstract pre-operator is precise). *Suppose* $R \in \mathsf{NR}$. *Then* $\alpha(pre(R)) = pre^\#(\alpha(R))$.

Proof. If $R = \emptyset$, then $\alpha(pre(R)) = \alpha(\emptyset) = (\emptyset, \emptyset) = pre^\#(\emptyset, \emptyset) = pre^\#(\alpha(R))$. So let us assume $R \neq \emptyset$.

By unfolding the definitions, we see that $\alpha(pre(R)) = (T_{pre(R)}, D_{pre(R)})$ with

$$T_{pre(R)} = \{x \mid \exists r, r' \in \mathsf{Runs} : r \cdot r' \in R \wedge r \text{ is transparent for } x\}$$
$$D_{pre(R)} = \{\tau \mid \exists r, r' \in \mathsf{Runs} : r \cdot r' \in R \wedge r \vdash \tau\}^{\uparrow}.$$

In order to evaluate the right hand side, note first that D_R is non-empty: there is a run $r \in R$ and any such run satisfies $r \vdash (0, \varepsilon, 0)$; moreover, $(0, \varepsilon, 0)$ is $\sqsubseteq$-maximal and hence contained in D_R. Consequently, the second case applies in the definition of $pre^{\#}$ and we have $pre^{\#}(\alpha(R)) = pre^{\#}(T_R, D_R) = (X, D)$ with

$$D = \{(\iota, \varphi, \kappa) \in \mathsf{DT} \mid (\iota, \varphi, 0) \in D_R\}^{\uparrow}.$$

Thus, we have to show $T_{pre(R)} = X$ and $D_{pre(R)} = D$.

$T_{pre(R)} \subseteq X$ is trivial. In order to see the reverse inclusion, i.e. that $T_{pre(R)}$ contains any $x \in X$, choose an arbitrary $r \in R$ and observe that the empty run ε is a prefix of r that is transparent for any variable x.

The following chain of implications shows $D_{pre(R)} \sqsubseteq D$:

$(\iota, \varphi, \kappa) \in D_{pre(R)}$

$\Rightarrow$ [Equation above, Lemma 7.5.3(1.)]
$\exists r, r' \in \mathsf{Runs} : r \cdot r' \in R \wedge r \vdash (\iota, \varphi, \kappa)$

iff [Lemma 7.8.2]
$\exists r \in R : r \vdash (\iota, \varphi, 0)$

iff [Set comprehension]
$(\iota, \varphi, 0) \in \{\tau \in \mathsf{DT} \mid \exists r \in R : r \vdash \tau\}$

$\Rightarrow$ [Lemma 7.5.2, definition D_R]
$\exists \tau' \in D_R : (\iota, \varphi, 0) \sqsubseteq \tau'$

$\Rightarrow$ [See below]
$\exists \tau \in D : (\iota, \varphi, \kappa) \sqsubseteq \tau$.

The reasoning for the last step is as follows. The subsumption order $\sqsubseteq$ is concerned only with removing gaps from the dependence sequence φ in a dependence trace but leaves the initial and final transparency information untouched. Hence, the dependence trace $\tau' \in D_R$ with $(\iota, \varphi, 0) \sqsubseteq \tau'$ must have the form $\tau' = (\iota, \psi, 0)$. But then $\tau := (\iota, \psi, \kappa) \in D$ and $(\iota, \varphi, \kappa) \sqsubseteq (\iota, \psi, \kappa)$.

Finally, we show $D \sqsubseteq D_{pre(R)}$:

$(\iota, \varphi, \kappa) \in D$

$\Rightarrow$ [Above equation for D, Lemma 7.5.3(1.)]
$(\iota, \varphi, 0) \in D_R$

$\Rightarrow$ [Definition of D_R, Lemma 7.5.3(1.)]
$\exists r \in R : r \vdash (\iota, \varphi, 0)$

iff [Lemma 7.8.2]
$\exists r, r' : r \cdot r' \in R \wedge r \vdash (\iota, \varphi, \kappa)$

iff   [Set comprehension]

$(\iota, \varphi, \kappa) \in \{\tau \in \mathsf{DT} \mid \exists r, r' : r \cdot r' \in R \wedge r \vdash \tau\}$

$\Rightarrow$ [Lemma 7.5.2]

$\exists \tau \in \{\tau \in \mathsf{DT} \mid \exists r, r' : r \cdot r' \in R \wedge r \vdash \tau\}^{\uparrow} : (\iota, \varphi, \kappa) \sqsubseteq \tau$

iff   [Above equation for $D_{pre(R)}$]

$\exists \tau \in D_{pre(R)} : (\iota, \varphi, \kappa) \sqsubseteq \tau$.

This completes the proof.   □

7.9 Post-operator

We define the (abstract) post-operator, $post^{\#} : \mathsf{AD} \to \mathsf{AD}$, in complete analogy to the pre-operator as follows:

$$post^{\#}(T, D) = \begin{cases} (\emptyset, \emptyset), & \text{if } D = \emptyset \\ (X, \{(\iota, \varphi, \kappa) \in \mathsf{DT} \mid (0, \varphi, \kappa) \in D\}), & \text{if } D \neq \emptyset. \end{cases}$$

By symmetry to the pre-operator we obtain that the post operator is well-defined and a precise abstraction of the post-operator on non-atomic run sets.

Theorem 7.9.1 (Abstract post-operator is precise). *Suppose $R \in \mathsf{NR}$. Then $\alpha(post(R)) = post^{\#}(\alpha(R))$.*   □

7.10 Sequential Composition

The *(abstract) sequential composition operator*, $;^{\#} : \mathsf{AD} \times \mathsf{AD} \to \mathsf{AD}$, which we write as an infix operator, is defined by

$$(T, D);^{\#}(T', D') = (T \cap T', (D; D')^{\uparrow}),$$

where

$$D; D' = \{(\iota, \varphi, \kappa) \in D \mid \kappa = 1 \Rightarrow \vec{\varphi} \in T'\} \tag{7.1}$$

$$\cup \{(\iota, \varphi, \kappa) \in D' \mid \iota = 1 \Rightarrow \overleftarrow{\varphi} \in T\} \tag{7.2}$$

$$\cup \{(\iota, \varphi \cdot \psi, \kappa) \in \mathsf{DTS} \mid (\iota, \varphi, 0) \in D, (0, \psi, \kappa) \in D'\} \tag{7.3}$$

$$\cup \{(\iota, \varphi \cdot \langle (x, z) \rangle \cdot \psi, \kappa) \in \mathsf{DTS} \mid \tag{7.4}$$

$$\exists y : (\iota, \varphi \cdot \langle (x, y) \rangle, 1) \in D, (1, \langle (y, z) \rangle \cdot \psi, \kappa) \in D'\}.$$

Before we explain the intuition underlying this definition we show that $;^{\#}$ is well-defined.

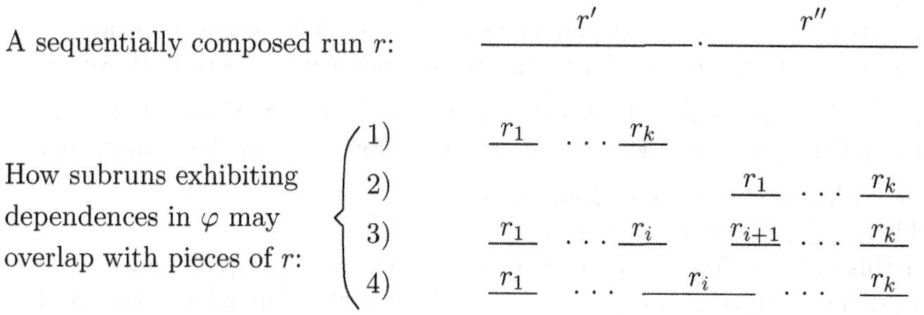

A sequentially composed run r:

$$\frac{\quad r' \quad}{} \cdot \frac{\quad r'' \quad}{}$$

How subruns exhibiting
dependences in φ may
overlap with pieces of r:

$$\left\{ \begin{array}{l} 1) \\ 2) \\ 3) \\ 4) \end{array} \right.$$

1) $\quad \frac{r_1}{} \quad \dots \quad \frac{r_k}{}$

2) $\qquad\qquad\qquad \frac{r_1}{} \quad \dots \quad \frac{r_k}{}$

3) $\quad \frac{r_1}{} \quad \dots \quad \frac{r_i}{} \quad \frac{r_{i+1}}{} \quad \dots \quad \frac{r_k}{}$

4) $\quad \frac{r_1}{} \quad \dots \quad \frac{r_i}{} \quad \dots \quad \frac{r_k}{}$

Fig. 7.2. Intuition of sequential composition.

Lemma 7.10.1. *The abstract sequential composition operator $;^{\#}$ is well-defined.*

Proof. We have to show that $(D; D')^{\uparrow} \in \mathsf{ACS}$ for all $D, D' \in \mathsf{ACS}$, i.e. that $(D; D')^{\uparrow}$ is an $\sqsubseteq$-antichain of short dependence traces.

It is easy to see that $D; D'$ (and hence its subset $(D; D')^{\uparrow}$) contains only short dependence traces: the first two sets contain only dependence traces from D or D', which consequently are short, and the constructions in the third and fourth set are explicitly restricted to contain short dependence traces. The application of the $^{\uparrow}$-operator ensures that $(D; D')^{\uparrow} \in \mathsf{ACS}$ is an $\sqsubseteq$-antichain. $\qquad\square$

Obviously, a run $r = r' \cdot r''$ composed of two runs r' and r'' is transparent for a variable x if and only if both r' and r'' are. Therefore, transparency information must be intersected in a sequential composition.

Let us explain the intuition underlying the definition of $D; D'$. Suppose given a run $r = r' \cdot r''$ which is composed of two runs $r' \in D$ and $r'' \in D'$ that use distinct virtual variables ($\text{virtual}(r') \cap \text{virtual}(r'') = \emptyset$). Assume that $\tau = (\iota, \varphi, \kappa)$ with $\varphi = \langle d_1, \dots, d_k \rangle$ is a dependence trace of r. Each d_i in φ is a dependence of a sub-piece r_i of r; we can choose the r_i as short as possible (i.e., such that it starts with an assignment that reads the source variable of d_i and ends with an assignment to the destination variable of d_i). There are four possibilities, how these sub-pieces can be situated in r as illustrated in Fig. 7.2:

1) all of them can lie in r';
2) all of them can lie in r'';
3) there is an i, $1 \le i < k$, such that $r_1, \dots, r_i$ lie in r' and $r_{i+1}, \dots, r_k$ lie in r'';
4) there is an i such that r_i overlaps with the join point of r' and r''.

These four cases are handled by the four sets appearing in the definition of $D; D'$:

1) in this case, τ is also a dependence trace of r'. Vice versa, dependence traces $\tau' = (\iota', \varphi', \kappa')$ of r' give rise to dependence traces of r. However, if $\kappa' = 1$, no statement that kills $\overrightarrow{\varphi'}$, the destination variable of the last dependence in φ', is allowed after r_k. Therefore, r' must be transparent for $\overrightarrow{\varphi'}$; hence the side condition in set (7.1).

2) this case is symmetric to case 1).

3) in this case, r' has the dependence trace $(\iota, \langle d_1, \dots, d_i \rangle, 0)$ and r'' the dependence trace $(0, \langle d_{i+1}, \dots, d_k \rangle, \kappa)$. Vice versa, dependence traces of r' and r'' of this form give rise to a dependence trace of r.

4) choose variables $x, z \in X$ such that $d_i = (x, z)$. Sub-run r_i accomplishes the transfer from x to z via certain intermediate variables. One of these intermediate variables, say y, must bridge the joint point between r' and r'' (i.e., it is assigned to in r', read from in r'' and not killed in between). As r and r' use distinct virtual variables, y must be a program variable: $y \in X$. Then $(s, \langle d_1, \dots, d_{i-1}, (x, y) \rangle, 1)$ is a dependence trace of r' and $(1, \langle (y, z), d_{i+1}, \dots, d_k \rangle, \kappa)$ is a dependence trace of r''. The bit 1 as final component of τ' and first component of τ'' is justified, as y is not killed from the place where it is assigned to in r' and read in r''. Similarly, dependences of r' and r'' of the above form give rise to a dependence trace of r.

It is not hard to see that in all four cases the dependence traces of r' and/or r'' in question are short and $\sqsubseteq$-maximal if τ is and, vice versa, that each short and $\sqsubseteq$-maximal dependence trace of r can be composed of short and $\sqsubseteq$-maximal dependence traces of r' and r'' in the described way.

Lemma 7.10.2 (Abstract sequential composition is precise).
Suppose $R, S \in \mathsf{NR}$. Then $\alpha(R \,;\, S) = \alpha(R) \,;^{\#} \alpha(S)$.

Proof. By formalizing the intuition described above. $\square$

7.11 Interleaving

Transparency information for the interleaving $R \otimes S$ of two run sets R and S is easy to obtain from transparency information of the components: a transparent run for a variable x exists in $R \otimes S$ if and only if each component set contains a transparent run. Therefore, the transparency information in T_R and T_S must simply be intersected.

It is far more interesting to consider the dependence traces in $D_{R \otimes S}$ as the two threads modeled by R and S can cooperate in order to exhibit dependences. More specifically, a dependence (u, v) can be composed of complementary dependence sequences of two runs $r \in R$ and $s \in S$, e.g., as illustrated here:

Deps. of r: $u = x_1 \rightarrow y_1 \quad x_2 \rightarrow y_2 \quad x_3 \rightarrow y_4 \quad \cdots \quad x_{k-1} \rightarrow y_{k-1} \quad x_k \rightarrow y_k = v$
Deps. of s: $\qquad\quad y_1 \rightarrow x_2 \quad y_2 \rightarrow x_3 \qquad \cdots \qquad\quad y_{k-1} \rightarrow x_k$

Of course such a combination of complementary dependence sequences can also start and/or end with a dependence of s. And, as a border case, one of the dependence sequences can be empty; the other then just consists of a single dependence. Before we define the abstract interleaving operator, we present in the next section the general definition of when two dependence sequences complement each other to a single dependence and introduce a relation C that extends this definition to dependence traces.

7.11.1 Complementary Dependence Traces

Let $\varphi, \psi \in \mathsf{DS}$ be two dependence sequences (one of them can be empty) and $u, v \in X$. Choose variables such that $\varphi = \langle (x_1, y_1), \ldots, (x_k, y_k) \rangle$, $k \geq 0$. We say that ψ *complements* φ to (u, v) if one of the following cases applies:

1. $\varphi \neq \varepsilon$, $u = \overleftarrow{\varphi}$, $v = \overrightarrow{\varphi}$, and $\psi = \langle (y_1, x_2), \ldots, (y_{k-1}, x_k) \rangle$;
2. $\varphi \neq \varepsilon$, $\psi \neq \varepsilon$, $u = \overleftarrow{\varphi}$, $v = \overrightarrow{\psi}$, and $\psi = \langle (y_1, x_2), \ldots, (y_{k-1}, x_k), (y_k, v) \rangle$;
3. $\varphi \neq \varepsilon$, $\psi \neq \varepsilon$, $u = \overleftarrow{\psi}$, $v = \overrightarrow{\varphi}$, and $\psi = \langle (u, x_1), (y_1, x_2), \ldots, (y_{k-1}, x_k) \rangle$; or
4. $\psi \neq \varepsilon$, $u = \overleftarrow{\psi}$, $v = \overrightarrow{\psi}$, and $\psi = \langle (u, x_1), (y_1, x_2), \ldots, (y_{k-1}, x_k), (y_k, v) \rangle$.

Intuitively, ψ complements φ to (u, v) if the two of them can alternately be combined to a gap-free transfer from u to v. The different cases are distinguished by whether the first read in this gap-free transfer comes from φ (cases 1/2) or ψ (cases 3/4) and whether the last write is in φ (cases 1/3) or ψ (cases 2/4).

Now, consider a dependence trace τ of a run $t \in R \otimes S$ which is an interleaving of the runs $r \in R$, $s \in S$. Then every single dependence in τ must be obtained in the above described fashion from pieces of dependence traces of r and s. We, therefore, generalize this notion of completion to dependence traces as follows. Suppose given dependence traces τ, τ_0, τ_1, where $\tau = (\iota, \langle (x_1, y_1), \ldots, (x_k, y_k) \rangle, \kappa)$, $\tau_0 = (\iota_0, \varphi, \kappa_0)$, $\tau_1 = (\iota_1, \psi, \kappa_1)$. Then we say that τ_1 complements τ_0 to τ, $C(\tau_0, \tau_1, \tau)$ for short, if there are dependence sequences $\varphi_1, \ldots, \varphi_k, \psi_1, \ldots, \psi_k$ such that

1. $\varphi = \varphi_1 \cdot \ldots \cdot \varphi_k$ and $\psi = \psi_1 \cdot \ldots \cdot \psi_k$;
2. ψ_i complements ϕ_i to (x_i, y_i) for $i = 1, \ldots, k$.
3. $\iota = 1$ implies $\iota_0 = 1$ and ψ_1 complements φ_1 to (x_1, y_1) according to cases 1 and 2, or $\iota_1 = 1$ and ψ_1 complements φ_1 according to cases 3 and 4; and
4. $\kappa = 1$ implies $\kappa_0 = 1$ and ψ_k complements φ_k to (x_k, y_k) according to cases 1 and 3, or $\kappa_1 = 1$ and ψ_k complements φ_k according to cases 2 and 4.

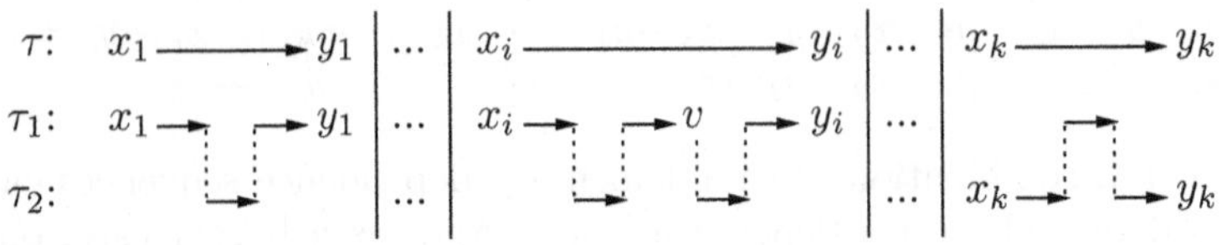

Fig. 7.3. Complementary dependence traces.

The typical situation of two dependence traces τ_0 and τ_1 that complement each other to a dependence trace τ is illustrated in Fig. 7.3. For clarity we omit the transparency bits. The dashed vertical lines indicate equality of variables.

A number of elementary properties of the relation C are collected in the following lemma.

Lemma 7.11.1 (Basic properties of C). *Suppose $\tau, \tau_0, \tau_1 \in$ DT. Then*

1. *C is symmetric in the first two parameters: $C(\tau_0, \tau_1, \tau)$ if and only if $C(\tau_1, \tau_0, \tau)$.*
2. *$(0, \varepsilon, 0)$ is a 'neutral element': $C((0, \varepsilon, 0), \tau, \tau)$.*
3. *In particular, $C((0, \varepsilon, 0), (0, \varepsilon, 0), (0, \varepsilon, 0))$.*

Proof. Left to the reader. □

7.11.2 Interleaving Operator

We are now in the position to define the *(abstract) interleaving operator,* $\otimes^{\#} : $ AD $\times$ AD $\to$ AD, which we write again as an infix operator:

$$(T, D) \otimes^{\#} (T', D') = (T \cap T', \{\tau'' \in \text{DTS} \mid \exists \tau \in D, \tau' \in D' : C(\tau, \tau', \tau'')\}^{\uparrow}).$$

By restricting the set construction to short dependence traces and applying the $(\cdot)^{\uparrow}$ operator, the interleaving operator is trivially well-defined. The goal of the remainder of this section is to show that it is a precise abstraction of the interleaving operator on sets of non-atomic runs.

Theorem 7.11.1 (Abstract interleaving operator is precise).
Suppose $R, S \in$ NR. Then $\alpha(R \otimes S) = \alpha(R) \otimes^{\#} \alpha(S)$.

The proof is deferred to Section 7.11.5. Before that, we establish a number of lemmas that capture the main insights underlying the proof.

7.11.3 Soundness Lemmas

The lemmas in this section are concerned with the soundness of the abstract interleaving composition operator, i.e. they are crucial for the proof that $\alpha(R \otimes S) \sqsubseteq \alpha(R) \otimes^{\#} \alpha(S)$ for any two run sets R, S. The critical point here is to guarantee that our definition of the abstract interleaving operator includes enough dependence traces.

As a first step, we show that each dependence trace of some interleaving of two runs r, s can also be obtained by combining two dependence traces of the component runs r and s via the relation C.

Let $r, s, t \in$ Runs with $\mathsf{virtual}(r) \cap \mathsf{virtual}(s) = \emptyset$ and $\tau \in \mathsf{DT}$.

Lemma 7.11.2. *Suppose $t \in r \otimes s$ and $t \vdash \tau$. Then there are $\tau_r, \tau_s \in \mathsf{DT}$ with $r \vdash \tau_r$, $s \vdash \tau_s$, and $C(\tau_r, \tau_s, \tau)$.*

Proof. Assume that t is an interleaving of r and s and $\tau = (\iota, \langle d_1, \ldots, d_k \rangle, \kappa)$ is a dependence trace of t. Each d_i is a dependence of a certain sub-run t_i of t and each t_i is an interleaving of certain sub-runs of r and s.

From t_i we can construct dependence traces φ_i and ψ_i of these sub-runs of r and s such that φ_i complements ψ_i to dependence d_i. This is described below. Then $\varphi_1 \cdot \ldots \cdot \varphi_k$ and $\psi_1 \cdot \ldots \cdot \psi_k$ are dependence sequences of r and s, resp., and we can choose transparency bits $\iota_r, \kappa_r, \iota_s, \kappa_s \in \mathbb{B}$ such that $\tau_r = (\iota_r, \varphi_1 \cdot \ldots \cdot \varphi_k, \kappa_r)$ and $\tau_s = (\iota_s, \psi_1 \cdot \ldots \cdot \psi_k, \kappa_s)$ are dependence traces of r and s, resp., such that $C(\tau_r, \tau_s, \tau)$ holds. Specifically, we choose $\iota_r = \iota$ if the first assignment instance involved in the mediation of d_1 belongs to r and $\iota_s = \iota$ if it belongs to s, and similarly for the final transparency bits and the last assignment instance involved in the mediation of d_k. All other transparency bits are chosen 0.

Let us now explain how to construct the dependence sequences φ_i and ψ_i mentioned above. Choose program variables x, y such that $d_i = (x, y)$. Sub-run t_i of t exhibits d_i via certain assignment instances $a_j := e_j$, $j = 1, \ldots, l$. In particular, $a_l = y$. Each of these assignment instances lies either in a sub-piece of r or a sub-piece of s. Let us consider the case that the first assignment instance $a_1 := e_1$ lies in a sub-piece of r; the case that it lies in a sub-piece of s is analogous. We can then find indices $0 < j_0 < j_1 < \ldots < j_n$ such that $a_j := e_j$ lies in a sub-piece of r if $j_m < j \le j_{m+1}$ for an *even* $m \in \{0, \ldots, n-1\}$ and in a sub-piece of s otherwise. In particular, for any $j \in \{j_1, \ldots, j_{n-1}\}$ one of the assignments instances $a_j := e_j$ and $a_{j+1} := e_{j+1}$ lies in a sub-piece of r and the other one in a sub-piece of s. This implies that a_j must be a program variable, because it appears in e_{j+1} and $\mathsf{virtual}(r) \cap \mathsf{virtual}(s) = \emptyset$. Choose now

$$
\begin{aligned}
\varphi_i &= \langle (x, a_{j_1}), (a_{j_2}, a_{j_3}), \ldots, (a_{j_{n-2}}, a_{j_{n-1}}) \rangle, \\
\psi_i &= \langle (a_{j_1}, a_{j_2}), (a_{j_3}, a_{j_4}), \ldots, (a_{j_{n-1}}, y) \rangle
\end{aligned}
$$

if n is even and

$$
\begin{aligned}
\varphi_i &= \langle (x, a_{j_1}), (a_{j_2}, a_{j_3}), \ldots, (a_{j_{n-1}}, y) \rangle, \\
\psi_i &= \langle (a_{j_1}, a_{j_2}), (a_{j_3}, a_{j_4}), \ldots, (a_{j_{n-2}}, a_{j_{n-1}}) \rangle
\end{aligned}
$$

if n is odd. Then φ_i and ψ_i are dependence sequences of the sub-runs of r and s that comprise t_i and, obviously, φ_i complements ψ_i to d_i. $\qquad \square$

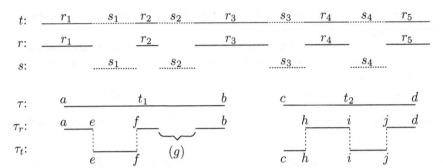

Fig. 7.4. Dependence traces of interleavings are induced by complementary dependence traces of the components.

Example 7.11.1. Fig. 7.4 illustrates the construction in the proof. The run t is an interleaving of the runs r and s. We can thus decompose r and s into sub-runs such that t is obtained by alternately shuffling these sub-runs together; in the example $r = r_1 \cdot r_2 \cdot r_3 \cdot r_4 \cdot r_5$, $s = s_1 \cdot s_2 \cdot s_3 \cdot s_4$, and $t = r_1 \cdot s_1 \cdot r_2 \cdot s_2 \cdot r_3 \cdot s_3 \cdot r_4 \cdot s_4 \cdot r_5$.

Let us assume that $\tau = (\iota, \langle (a,b), (c,d) \rangle, \kappa)$ is a dependence trace of t. Then there are sub-runs t_1 and t_2 of t that exhibit the two dependences (a,b) and (c,d), e.g., as shown in the figure. These sub-runs overlap in a certain way with the decompositions of r and s; in the example in the figure, for instance, t_1 overlaps with a postfix of r_1, all of s_1, r_2, s_2, and a prefix of r_3. The dependence (a,b) is exhibited via certain intermediate assignments $a_i := e_i$ (not shown in the figure); we call these assignments *crucial* in the following.

There may be sub-runs of r and/or s that overlap with t_i but do not contain a crucial assignment. Such sub-runs must be transparent for the variable that transfers the dependence at this moment and can be ignored. In our example, r_2 is such a sub-run and g is the variable that transfers the dependence while r_2 is executed.

Whenever two successive crucial assignments lie in sub-pieces of different runs, the dependence must be transfered in a program variable between these assignments because r and s do not share virtual variables. In the figure, e.g., e is the variable that transfers the dependence from the last crucial assignment in r_1 to the first crucial assignment in s_1 and f transfers it from the last crucial assignment in s_1 to the first crucial assignment in r_2. From these variables we can construct dependence traces τ_r and τ_s of r and s such that $C(\tau_r, \tau_s, \tau)$ holds. In Fig. 7.4, for instance, we have $\tau_r = (\iota, \langle (a,e), (f,b), (h,i), (j,d) \rangle, \kappa)$ and $\tau_s = (0, \langle (e,f), (c,h), (i,j) \rangle, 0)$. $\square$

Lemma 7.11.2 ensures that combining dependence traces of component runs via C is fundamentally rich enough to give us all dependence traces of potential interleavings. However, in our abstract domain, we do not collect

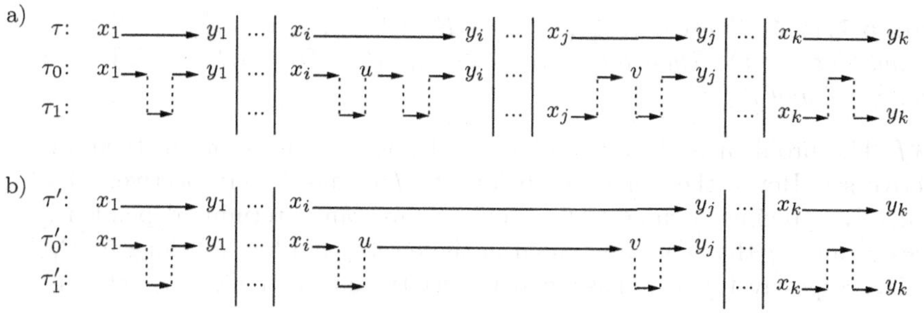

Fig. 7.5. Removing gaps in a component dependence trace.

all dependence traces but only the *maximal* ones. Therefore, we only combine the maximal dependence traces of component runs in the definition of interleaving, which is the best we can do with the available information. Can we really obtain all the *maximal* dependence traces just from the *maximal* dependence traces of the components?

The next lemma provides us with a kind of shortening rule that is crucial for the proof that maximal dependence traces of component run sets suffice to infer the maximal dependence traces of their interleaving.

Suppose $\tau_0, \tau_0', \tau_1, \tau \in \mathsf{DT}$.

Lemma 7.11.3. *Suppose $C(\tau_0, \tau_1, \tau)$ and $\tau_0 \sqsubseteq \tau_0'$. Then there are dependence traces $\tau_1', \tau' \in \mathsf{DT}$ such that $\tau_1 \leq \tau_1'$, $\tau \sqsubseteq \tau'$, and $C(\tau_0', \tau_1', \tau')$. By symmetry of C (Lemma 7.11.1(1)) an analogous property holds with the roles of τ_0 and τ_1 exchanged.*

Proof. The proof idea is illustrated in Fig. 7.5. The diagram in a) shows the typical situation of dependence traces τ_0, τ_1 and τ with $C(\tau_0, \tau_1, \tau)$. For clarity the transparency bits are omitted. The diagram in b) shows a typical dependence trace τ_0' with $\tau_0 \sqsubseteq \tau_0'$. It is obtained from τ_0 by removing all gaps between the target variable u of a certain dependence d in τ_0 and the destination variable v of a later dependence e. We can remove all the dependences from τ_1 that are used to fill some or all of these gaps in $C(\tau_0, \tau_1, \tau)$. This results in a dependence trace τ_1' with $\tau_1 \leq \tau_1'$ as shown in b). Then the dependence traces τ_0' and τ_1' complement each other to a dependence trace τ' with $\tau \leq \tau'$ as shown. As border cases, we may have $\tau_0' = \tau_0$, if none of the gaps between d and e is filled in $C(\tau_0, \tau_1, \tau)$, or $\tau' = \tau$ if d and e are used in $C(\tau_0, \tau_1, \tau)$ in the same dependence of τ. But this does not invalidate our reasoning as $\sqsubseteq$ and $\leq$ are reflexive. □

By applying this shortening rule iteratively, we obtain the following lemma that is of direct use in the proof of Theorem 7.11.1.

Lemma 7.11.4. *Suppose $\tau_r \in \{\tau \mid \exists r \in R : r \vdash \tau\}$, $\tau_s \in \{\tau \mid \exists s \in S : s \vdash \tau\}$, and $C(\tau_r, \tau_s, \tau)$. Then there are $\tau_r' \in D_R$, $\tau_s' \in D_S$, and $\tau' \in \mathsf{DT}$ with $C(\tau_r', \tau_s', \tau')$ and $\tau \sqsubseteq \tau'$.*

Proof. The problem is that τ_r and τ_s need not be $\sqsubseteq$-maximal in their respective set. Hence they may not belong to D_R and D_S, respectively. By iteratively applying Lemma 7.11.3, however, we can determine dependence traces $\tau_r^\uparrow$ and $\tau_s^\uparrow$ that are $\sqsubseteq$-maximal in these sets (and hence belong to D_R and D_S, respectively) as well as a dependence trace $\tau^\uparrow$ with $C(\tau_r^\uparrow, \tau_s^\uparrow, \tau^\uparrow)$ and $\tau \sqsubseteq \tau^\uparrow$:

We start with $(\tau_r^\uparrow, \tau_s^\uparrow, \tau^\uparrow) := (\tau_r, \tau_s, \tau)$. This initialization trivially ensures $\tau_r^\uparrow \in \{\tau \mid \exists r \in R : r \vdash \tau\}$, $\tau_s^\uparrow \in \{\tau \mid \exists s \in S : s \vdash \tau\}$, $C(\tau_r^\uparrow, \tau_s^\uparrow, \tau^\uparrow)$, and $\tau \sqsubseteq \tau^\uparrow$, which is an invariant of the loop we describe in the following.

If $\tau_r^\uparrow$ is not $\sqsubseteq$-maximal in $\{\tau \mid \exists r \in R : r \vdash \tau\}$, we can choose a dependence trace $\tau_r' \in \{\tau \mid \exists r \in R : r \vdash \tau\}$ which is strictly larger: $\tau_r^\uparrow \sqsubset \tau_r'$. Then, by Lemma 7.11.3, there are τ_s' and τ' with $\tau_s^\uparrow \leq \tau_s'$, $\tau \sqsubseteq \tau^\uparrow \sqsubseteq \tau'$, and $C(\tau_r', \tau_s', \tau')$. By Proposition 7.3.2, $\tau_s' \in \{\tau \mid \exists r \in R : r \vdash \tau\}$, hence the invariant remains valid. We then set $(\tau_r^\uparrow, \tau_s^\uparrow, \tau^\uparrow) := (\tau_r', \tau_s', \tau')$. We can proceed analogously, if $\tau_s^\uparrow$ is not maximal in $\{\tau \mid \exists s \in S : s \vdash \tau\}$.

This shortening procedure is applied iteratively until both $\tau_r^\uparrow$ and $\tau_s^\uparrow$ are $\sqsubseteq$-maximal in their respective sets. Termination is guaranteed, because in each step either the dependence sequence in $\tau_r^\uparrow$ or in $\tau_s^\uparrow$ becomes shorter and the dependence sequence in the other dependence trace does not become longer. □

7.11.4 Completeness Lemmas

The lemmas in this section are concerned with completeness of the interleaving operator, i.e. they are important for the proof that $\alpha(R \otimes S) \sqsupseteq \alpha(R) \otimes^\# \alpha(S)$ for any two non-atomic run sets R, S. They crucially depend on runs being non-atomic.

A dependence of a non-atomic run r must involve a virtual variable at a certain stage as assignments that have program variables on both the left- and the right-hand-side do not occur in non-atomic runs. But when the execution of r is in such a stage, no parallel thread can disturb propagation of the dependence because parallel threads do not interfere on virtual variables. This observation underlies the proof of the following lemma.

Lemma 7.11.5. *Suppose r, s are runs with $\mathsf{virtual}(r) \cap \mathsf{virtual}(s) = \emptyset$, and $x, y \in X$. If r exhibits (x, y) then there is a run $t \in r \otimes s$ that exhibits (x, y).*

Proof. Suppose (x, y) is a dependence of r. This means that r can be written in the form $r = r_0 \cdot \langle a_1 := e_1 \rangle \cdot r_1 \cdot \langle a_2 := e_2 \rangle \cdot r_2 \cdots \cdots r_{l-1} \cdot \langle a_l := e_l \rangle \cdot r_l$ as in the definition of "r exhibits (x, y)". Then in particular e_1 contains the variable x. As x is a program variable, this implies by the form of assignments appearing in runs that a_1 must be a virtual variable (cf. the definition of Asg).

As $\mathsf{virtual}(r) \cap \mathsf{virtual}(s) = \emptyset$, s must thus be transparent for a_1. Hence the run $t \in r \otimes s$ defined by

$$t := r_0 \cdot \langle a_1 := e_1 \rangle \cdot s \cdot r_1 \cdot \langle a_2 := e_2 \rangle \cdot r_2 \cdot \ldots \cdot r_{l-1} \cdot \langle a_l := e_l \rangle \cdot r_l$$

still exhibits dependence (x, y).   □

Note that this argument crucially depends on the assumption about the form of assignments in runs that derives from the assumption that assignments execute non-atomically. If assignments execute atomically, the above lemma is no longer valid.

Example 7.11.2. Consider the parallel execution of the two straight-line programs $\pi_1 = (y := x)$ and $\pi_2 = (x := 0\,;y := 0)$.

If assignment statements execute atomically, there are just three possible runs,

1) $\langle x := 0, y := 0, y := x \rangle$,
2) $\langle x := 0, y := x, y := 0 \rangle$, and
3) $\langle y := x, x := 0, y := 0 \rangle$.

None of these runs exhibits dependence (x, y) because either x is killed before $y := x$ is executed as in 1) and 2), or y is killed after $y := x$ is executed as in 2) and 3).

If, on the other hand, assignment statements may execute non-atomically, then the two initialization statements in π_2 could well be executed after x is read but before y is written. This is witnessed by the run

4 $\langle v := x, x := 0, y := 0, y := v \rangle$,

where v is a virtual variable, in our model of non-atomic execution. In contrast to the runs 1)-3), run 4) exhibits dependence (x, y).   □

Lemma 7.11.5 provides an intuitive explanation why precise analysis of parallel programs is simpler if we assume non-atomic execution of assignments. Under this assumption dependences once generated by a thread cannot be definitely destroyed by its environment. Thus, an analysis that collects positive information about potential dependences is precise. (In order to do this in a ¡ compositional fashion it must collect more information, namely (maximal, short) dependence traces. If we analyze with respect to the assumption that assignments execute atomically, there is a complex interplay between the way dependences are generated by a thread and the order of re-initializations performed by its environment as illustrated by the above example. Therefore, an analysis that just collects positive information is doomed to be imprecise.

Lemma 7.11.6. *Suppose* r_0, r_1 *are runs with* $\mathsf{virtual}(r_0) \cap \mathsf{virtual}(r_1) = \emptyset$ *and* τ_0, τ_1, τ *are dependence traces with* $r_0 \vdash \tau_0$, $r_1 \vdash \tau_1$, *and* $C(\tau_0, \tau_1, \tau)$. *Then there is a run* $r \in r_0 \otimes r_1$ *such that* $r \vdash \tau$.

Proof. For notational convenience, we discuss the case that the dependence sequence in τ consists of just a single dependence; the generalization to arbitrary dependence sequences is left to the reader. Let $\tau = (\iota, \langle(u, v)\rangle, \kappa)$. Furthermore, let $\tau_0 = (\iota_0, \phi, \kappa_0)$ and $\tau_1 = (\iota_1, \psi, \kappa_1)$.

Let us assume that case 2 in the definition of $C(\tau_0, \tau_1, \tau)$ applies; the other cases are similar. Then we can choose variables $u = x_1, \ldots, x_{k+1} = v$ such that

$$\varphi = \langle(x_1, y_1), \ldots, (x_k, y_k)\rangle \quad \text{and} \quad \psi = \langle(y_1, x_2), \ldots, (y_k, x_{k+1})\rangle,$$

and it is $\iota_0 = 1$ if $\iota = 1$ and $\kappa_1 = 1$ if $\kappa = 1$. As $r_0 \vdash \tau_0$ and $r_1 \vdash \tau_1$ we can write r_0 and r_1 in the form

$$r_0 = t_0^0 \cdot r_1^0 \cdot t_1^0 \cdot r_2^0 \cdots t_{k-1}^0 \cdot r_k^0 \cdot t_k^0 \quad \text{and} \quad r_1 = t_0^1 \cdot r_1^1 \cdot t_1^1 \cdot r_2^1 \cdots t_{k-1}^1 \cdot r_k^1 \cdot t_k^1$$

such that

1) r_i^0 exhibits (x_i, y_i) and r_i^1 exhibits (y_i, x_{i+1}) for $i = 1, \ldots, k$;
2) t_0^0 is transparent for u if $\iota = 1$ (and hence $\iota_0 = 1$); and
3) t_k^1 is transparent for v if $\kappa = 1$ (and hence $\kappa_1 = 1$).

The run $r_1^0 \cdot r_1^1 \cdot r_2^0 \cdot r_2^1 \cdots r_k^0 \cdot r_k^1$ clearly exhibits dependence (u, v), but in order to construct an interleaving of r_0 and r_1, we must also execute the intermediate code pieces t_i^j. Fortunately, each of the dependences realized by some r_i^j must involve a virtual variable; and, while the transfer is in such a stage, code pieces of the other run, r_{1-j}, can safely be executed without destroying the dependence, due to the disjointness of the virtual variables used in r_0 and r_1. Thus, we can execute each code piece t_i^1 at such a stage of execution of r_{i+1}^0 and, similarly, t_i^0 during such a stage of r_i^1. The rest of the proof pursues this argument more formally.

By Lemma 7.11.5, there are interleavings $s_i^0 \in r_i^0 \otimes t_{i-1}^1$ and $s_i^1 \in r_i^1 \otimes t_i^0$ such that, for $i = 1, \ldots, k$, s_i^0 still exhibits (x_i, y_i) and s_i^1 still exhibits (y_i, x_{i+1}). Then the run $r := t_0^0 \cdot s_1^0 \cdot s_1^1 \cdot s_2^0 \cdot s_2^1 \cdots s_k^0 \cdot s_k^1 \cdot t_k^1$ is an interleaving of r_0 and r_1 (i.e. $r \in r_1 \otimes r_2$). On the other hand, $r \vdash \tau$ because $s_1^0 \cdot s_1^1 \cdot s_2^0 \cdot s_2^1 \cdots s_k^0 \cdot s_k^1$ exhibits dependence (u, v) and items 2) and 3) above give the transparency properties. □

Like Lemma 7.11.5, Lemma 7.11.6 fails to hold if assignments execute atomically as illustrated by the following example.

Example 7.11.3. Consider the two programs $\pi_1 = (y := x)$ and $\pi_2 = (x := 0; y := 0; z := y)$ and the three dependence traces $\tau_1 = (1, \langle(x, y)\rangle, 1)$, $\tau_2 = (1, \langle(y, z)\rangle, 1)$, and $\tau = (1, \langle(x, z)\rangle, 1)$.

If assignments execute atomically, π_1 has only the run $r_1 = \langle y := x\rangle$ and π_2 has only the run $r_2 = \langle x := 0, y := 0, z := y\rangle$. Clearly, τ_1 is a dependence trace of r_1 and τ_2 is a dependence trace of r_2, independently of whether assignments execute atomically or not. Moreover, $C(\tau_1, \tau_2, \tau)$ holds.

But only the following four runs are possible interleavings of r_1 and r_2:

1) $\langle x := 0, y := 0, z := y, y := x \rangle$,
2) $\langle x := 0, y := 0, y := x, z := y \rangle$,
3) $\langle x := 0, y := x, y := 0, z := y \rangle$, and
4) $\langle y := x, x := 0, y := 0, z := y \rangle$.

It is not hard to see that τ is not exhibited by any of these runs.

If, on the other hand, assignments do not execute atomically, there are also runs like

5) $\langle v := x, x := 0, y := 0, y := v, u := y, z := u \rangle$,

where u, v are virtual variables, which exhibits dependence trace τ.   □

7.11.5 Proof of Theorem 7.11.1

We can now put the pieces together and prove Theorem 7.11.1. By unfolding the definitions, we have

$$\begin{aligned} \alpha(R \otimes S) &= (T_{R \otimes S}, D_{R \otimes S}) \text{ and} \\ \alpha(R) \otimes^\# \alpha(S) &= (T_R \cap T_S, D), \end{aligned}$$

where $D = \{\tau \in \mathsf{DTS} \mid \exists \tau_R \in D_R, \tau_S \in D_S : C(\tau_R, \tau_S, \tau)\}^\uparrow$. Consequently, we have to show $T_{R \otimes S} = T_R \cap T_S$ and $D_{R \otimes S} = D$.

"$T_{R \otimes S} \subseteq T_R \cap T_S$": If $x \in T_{R \otimes S}$, then there is a run $t \in R \otimes S$ that is transparent for x. By definition, t is an interleaving of runs $r \in R$ and $s \in S$. These runs r, s must then also be transparent for x. Thus, $x \in T_R \cap T_S$.

"$T_{R \otimes S} \supseteq T_R \cap T_S$": If $x \in T_R \cap T_S$, then there are runs $r \in R$ and $s \in S$ that are transparent for x. By bounded renaming of virtual variables these runs can be chosen such that they do not share virtual variables. Then all interleavings of these two runs are in $S \otimes R$, and all of them are transparent for x. Thus, $x \in T_{R \otimes S}$.

"$D_{R \otimes S} \sqsubseteq D$": In order to show this relationship, assume that we are given $\tau \in D_{R \otimes S}$. Then we have, by the definition of $D_{R \otimes S}$ and Lemma 7.5.3(1.):

$$\exists t \in R \otimes S : t \vdash \tau$$

iff   [Definition $R \otimes S$]

$$\exists r \in R, s \in S, t \in r \otimes s : t \vdash \tau$$

$\Rightarrow$ [Lemma 7.11.2]

$$\exists r \in R, s \in S, \tau_r, \tau_s \in \mathsf{DT} : r \vdash \tau_r \land s \vdash \tau_s \land C(\tau_r, \tau_s, \tau)$$

$\Rightarrow$ [Shunting, set comprehension]

$$\exists \tau_r \in \{\tau \mid \exists r \in R : r \vdash \tau\}, \tau_s \in \{\tau \mid \exists s \in S : s \vdash \tau\} : C(\tau_r, \tau_s, \tau).$$

$\Rightarrow$ [Lemma 7.11.4]
$$\exists \tau_r \in D_R, \tau_s \in D_S, \tau' \in \mathsf{DT} : C(\tau_r, \tau_s, \tau') \wedge \tau \sqsubseteq \tau'$$

iff   [Set comprehension, see below]
$$\exists \tau' \in \{\tau \in \mathsf{DTS} \mid \exists \tau_R \in D_R, \tau_S \in D_S : C(\tau_R, \tau_S, \tau)\} : \tau \sqsubseteq \tau'$$

$\Rightarrow$ [Definition D, Lemma 7.5.2]
$$\exists \tau' \in D : \tau \sqsubseteq \tau'.$$

In the step marked "see below", we must prove for "$\Rightarrow$" that τ' can be chosen as a *short* dependence trace, which is *not* true for this step in isolation. But, it is true under the assumption that $\tau \in D_{R \otimes S}$ which underlies the whole calculation: as a consequence of this assumption τ is *short* and this implies that any τ' with $\tau \sqsubseteq \tau'$ must also be short (Lemma 7.6.3). A calculation, in which this step is valid in isolation, requires to furnish each of the preceeding predicates with the conjunct $\tau \in D_{R \otimes S}$, which would clutter the calculation.

"$D_{R \otimes S} \sqsupseteq D$": This is shown by the following chain of implications:

$\tau \in D$

$\Rightarrow$ [Definition of D, Lemma 7.5.3(1.)]
$$\exists \tau_R \in D_R, \tau_S \in D_S : C(\tau_R, \tau_S, \tau)$$

$\Rightarrow$ [Definition D_R, D_S, Lemma 7.5.3(1.)]
$$\exists r \in R, s \in S, \tau_R, \tau_S : r \vdash \tau_R \wedge s \vdash \tau_S \wedge C(\tau_R, \tau_S, \tau)$$

iff   [By bounded renaming of virtual variables in s]
$$\exists r \in R, s \in S, \tau_R, \tau_S :$$
$$r \vdash \tau_R \wedge s \vdash \tau_S \wedge C(\tau_R, \tau_S, \tau) \wedge \mathsf{virtual}(r) \cap \mathsf{virtual}(s) = \emptyset$$

$\Rightarrow$ [Lemma 7.11.6, definition $R \otimes S$]
$$\exists t \in R \otimes S : t \vdash \tau$$

iff   [Set comprehension]
$$\tau \in \{\tau \in \mathsf{DT} \mid \exists r \in R \otimes S : r \vdash \tau\}$$

$\Rightarrow$ [Lemma 7.5.2, definition $D_{R \otimes S}$]
$$\exists \tau' \in D_{R \otimes S} : \tau \sqsubseteq \tau'.$$

This ends the proof of Theorem 7.11.1.   □

7.12 Base Edges

In Chapter 6 we discussed that the atomicity assumptions about assignments may vary and that this gives rise to different definitions of the non-atomic run sets $[\![x := e]\!]$ assigned to an assignment statement $x := e$. Fortunately, all reasonable choices result in the same abstraction which is given by the following definition:

$$[\![x := e]\!]^{\#} \;=\; (X \setminus \{x\}, \{(\iota, \langle (y, x) \rangle, \kappa) \mid \iota, \kappa \in \mathbb{B},\ y \text{ appears in } e\})\,.$$

Whatever atomicity assumption we are working with, all runs in $[\![x := e]\!]$ will contain certain auxiliary assignments to virtual variables and a single assignment to x. No program variable except x will ever be the target of an assignment in a run in $[\![x := e]\!]$. Hence, all non-atomic runs are transparent just for the program variables in $X \setminus \{x\}$, which explains the adequacy of the first component of $[\![x := e]\!]^{\#}$. Moreover, it implies that no dependence trace of a non-atomic run can embody a dependence sequence that is longer than one or has a destination variable different from x. Each reasonable non-atomic run induces the same dependences between program variables as $x := e$, hence the induced dependences are (y, x) where y is a variable appearing in e. Moreover, no reasonable run kills a variable in e before it reads it or kills x after it has written it, which implies that the transparency bits can be chosen arbitrarily.

All dependence traces included in the second component of $[\![x := e]\!]^{\#}$ are trivially short and $\sqsubseteq$-maximal. Thus, $[\![x := e]\!]^{\#}$ is well-defined..

Proposition 7.12.1. $\alpha([\![x := e]\!]) = [\![x := e]\!]^{\#}$. $\qquad\qquad\qquad\qquad$ $\square$

Statement **skip** has just the single run ε, which is obviously transparent for all variables and has just the dependence trace $(0, \varepsilon, 0)$. Hence, we define $[\![\mathbf{skip}]\!]^{\#} = (X, \{(0, \varepsilon, 0)\})$.

Proposition 7.12.2. $\alpha([\![\mathbf{skip}]\!]) = [\![\mathbf{skip}]\!]^{\#}$. $\qquad\qquad\qquad\qquad$ $\square$

We define the abstract interpretation of a base edge e of the underlying flow graph as the interpretation of the statement $A(e)$ associated with e: $[\![e]\!]^{\#} = [\![A(e)]\!]^{\#}$.

Proposition 7.12.3. $\alpha([\![e]\!]) = [\![e]\!]^{\#}$ for all base edges e. $\qquad\qquad$ $\square$

7.13 Running Time

In this section we show that we can compute the abstract operations $pre^{\#}$, $post^{\#}$, $;^{\#}$, and $\otimes^{\#}$ in time $2^{p(|X|)}$, where $p(x)$ is a polynomial. We emphasize that we do *neither* intend to develop efficient implementations of the operations *nor* to present a very precise analysis. The results of this section will mainly be used in order to establish the qualitative complexity statement that the algorithms developed later run in exponential time. We are, however, interested in uncovering the parameter of exponential growth: it is the number of program variables $|X|$ rather than the size of the parallel flow graph.

Let us investigate the most expensive operation, interleaving, to some detail. First of all, we recall its definition from Section 7.11:

$$(T, D) \otimes^{\#} (T', D') \; = \; (T \cap T', D''^{\uparrow}),$$

where $D'' = \{\tau'' \in \mathsf{DTS} \mid \exists \tau \in D, \tau' \in D' : C(\tau, \tau', \tau'')\}$. The sets T and T' are subsets of X, the set of program variables. Computing the intersection of T and T' is cheap: if we represent these sets as bit-strings (of length $|X|$), we can clearly calculate the intersection in time $\mathcal{O}(|X|)$ by looking through the bit-strings for T and T' once.

D and D' are antichains of short dependence traces, hence $D, D' \subseteq \mathsf{DTS}$. By Lemma 7.6.1, the cardinality of DTS and hence of D and D' is $\mathcal{O}(|X|^{2|X|+2})$. This clearly is $\mathcal{O}(2^{p_0(|X|)})$ for some polynomial $p_0(x)$. We can hence consider at most $\mathcal{O}(2^{2p_0(|X|)})$ pairs of dependence traces τ and τ' when computing D''. For each fixed pair of dependence traces τ, τ' all dependence traces τ'' with $C(\tau, \tau', \tau'')$ can be determined in time $\mathcal{O}(2^{p_1(|X|)})$ for some polynomial $p_1(x)$. We leave it to the reader to invent some procedure for this task that realizes this rather rough bound. Even a very naive procedure that lists all short dependence traces τ'' and then checks for each listed dependence trace whether $C(\tau, \tau', \tau'')$ holds will do. The observation that τ, τ', and τ'' are short, and hence the length of their dependence sequences is bounded by $|X| + 1$ is helpful. As a consequence, we can calculate D'' in time $\mathcal{O}(2^{2p_0(|X|)+p_1(|X|)})$. Again $\mathcal{O}(2^{p_0(|X|)})$ is an asymptotic bound for the size of D'' because $D'' \subseteq \mathsf{DTS}$. It is, therefore, not hard to see that $D''^{\uparrow}$, the second component of $(T, D) \otimes^{\#} (T', D')$, can be computed from D'' in time $\mathcal{O}(2^{p_2(|X|)})$ for some polynomial $p_2(x)$. Hence the overall cost of computing $(T, D) \otimes^{\#} (T', D')$ is $\mathcal{O}(2^{p(|X|)})$ for some polynomial $p(x)$.

By similar considerations we can show that the other operations can be computed in time $\mathcal{O}(2^{p(|X|)})$ too.

Lemma 7.13.1. *The operations $\mathrm{pre}^{\#}$, $\mathrm{post}^{\#}$, $;^{\#}$, and $\otimes^{\#}$ can be computed in time $\mathcal{O}(2^{p(|X|)})$ for some polynomial $p(x)$.* $\square$

7.14 Discussion

In this chapter, we have defined an abstraction of sets of non-atomic runs from which the dependences exhibited by the abstracted run sets can be read off. Specifically, run sets are abstracted to antichains of short dependence traces that capture the potential to exhibit dependences in cooperation with a parallel environment. The abstraction also records the set of program variables for which a transparent run exists in the abstracted run set. This information is needed in order to propagate the transparency bits of the dependence traces properly in sequential contexts.

We have defined abstract interpretations of the operations and constants used in the constraint systems of Chapter 5.5 and have shown that they precisely abstract the corresponding operations on sets of non-atomic runs. Therefore, the least solution of the constraint systems of Section 5.5 over the resulting abstract lattice $(\mathsf{AD}, \sqsubseteq)$ consists of the precise abstractions of the run sets characterized by these constraint systems. As the lattice $(\mathsf{AD}, \sqsubseteq)$ is finite, it can be computed effectively by fixpoint iteration. We can use this least solution in order to effectively determine the dependences exhibited by the characterized run sets. This allows us, in particular, to determine the dependences exhibited by bridging runs in procedural parallel flow graphs. This information can in turn be used to detect all copy constants and eliminate faint code completely, which is explained in detail in the next chapter.

In summary, the dependence traces abstraction provides us with a means to perform precise interprocedural dependence analysis in parallel programs.

8. Detecting Copy Constants and Eliminating Faint Code

In this chapter we show that we can detect copy constants and eliminate faint code in parallel flow graphs completely—relative to the non-atomic semantics of Chapter 6. The basic idea is to evaluate the constraint system for bridging runs from Chapter 5 over the complete lattice $(\mathsf{AD}, \sqsubseteq)$ from the previous chapter and to exploit this information.

The least solution of a constraint system over some domain corresponds in a straightforward way to the least fixpoint of a function on this domain derived from the constraints. We have seen that the abstract counterparts of the operators and constants appearing in the constraint systems in Chapter 5 precisely abstract the corresponding operators on non-atomic run sets. Moreover, the abstraction mapping $\alpha : \mathsf{NR} \rightarrow \mathsf{AD}$ is universally disjunctive (Proposition 7.7.2). As commonly known in the area of abstract interpretation [14, 15], this implies that the least solution of the constraint systems over domain AD consists just of the abstractions of the least solution over domain NR. More formally, the facts recalled above ensure that the premises of the Transfer Lemma (Lemma 3.3.1, Page 39) hold for the functions f and g derived from the concrete and abstract interpretation of the constraint systems over non-atomic runs and over AD, respectively, and the transfer function γ that component-wise maps the concrete interpretation x of each variable X of the constraint system to its abstraction $\alpha(x)$. As AD is finite, we can compute the least solution of the constraint system for (non-atomic) bridging runs over lattice AD effectively by fixpoint iteration. From the computed values we can read off in particular all the dependences of the bridging runs: if $\alpha(R) = (T, D)$ is the precise abstraction of a set R of (non-atomic) runs then (x, y) is a dependence of a run in R if and only if $(1, \langle (x, y) \rangle, 1) \in D$ (Proposition 7.2.1).

Based on this information we can detect copy constants and eliminate faint code. In this chapter we develop corresponding algorithms with an exponential worst case running time. (More precise statements about the dependence of their running time from the different input parameters are provided by Theorem 8.3.1.) Indeed the point here is *not* to develop efficient algorithms—we will see in the next chapter that all these problems are intractable already for loop-free parallel programs—the point is that these problems can be solved effectively at all. This comes as a surprise, because the

---

Algorithm 8.1.

Input: A parallel flow graph as defined in Chapter 5, a program point $v \in N$ and
    a program variable $y \in X$.
Output: "yes" if y is a copy constant at v; "no" otherwise.
Method:
    1) Compute—by standard fixpoint iteration—the least solution over domain
       $(\mathsf{AD}, \sqsubseteq)$ of the constraint system for bridging runs to program point v;
       this gives us a value $\mathsf{B}_v^{\#}[u]$ for each program point u; as a by-product this
       computation determines $\mathsf{R}^{\#}[v]$.
    2) Set $I[w] := \{x \mid (1, \langle (x,y) \rangle, 1) \in \mathsf{B}_v^{\#}[w].2\}$ for each program point $w \in N$.
    3) Set $flag :=$ false and $val :=$ unset.
    4) If $y \in \mathsf{R}^{\#}[v].1$ or if there is $x \in X$ with $(1, \langle (x,y) \rangle, 1) \in \mathsf{R}^{\#}[v].2$ then
       $flag :=$ true.
    5) For all base edges $e = (u, w)$ annotated by an assignment statement $x := e$
       with $x \in I[w]$:
       5.1) If e is a composite expression then $flag :=$ true;
       5.2) If e is a constant expression then
              if $val =$ unset then $val := e$ else if $val \neq e$ then $flag :=$ true.
    6) If $flag$ then output "no" else output "yes".

Fig. 8.1. An algorithm that detects copy constants in parallel programs.

corresponding problems are uncomputable, if we assume atomic execution of assignments (Chapter 4).

Without further ado, we present, in the remainder of this chapter, the algorithms for detection of copy constants (Section 8.1) and faint-code elimination (Section 8.2). While we do not perform formal correctness proofs for these algorithms, we argue (hopefully convincingly) that the presented algorithms solve the respective problems. In our opinion a more formal argumentation would obscure rather than clarify matters here. After the presentation of the algorithms, we analyze their asymptotic running time in Section 8.3 and finish the chapter with some concluding remarks. Throughout this chapter we assume that execution of base statements is non-atomic.

8.1 Copy-Constant Detection

A variable x is a *copy-constant* at a program point u if it gets assigned the same value on all runs reaching u either through a constant assignment (like in $\langle x := 42 \rangle$) or a constant assignment followed by copying assignments (like in $\langle z := 42, y := z, x := y \rangle$). Of course the runs may contain other assignments also that do not influence the final value of x (like in $\langle x := 42, y := a + b \rangle$). Thus, in copy constant detection only assignments of the simple form $x := k$, where k is a constant or variable, are interpreted, all other forms of assignments (e.g. $x := y + 1$) are (conservatively) assumed to make x non-constant [83].

Algorithm 8.1 in Fig. 8.1 reads a parallel flow graph, a program point $v \in N$, and a program variable $y \in X$ and decides whether y is a copy constant at v or not. For this purpose it first computes (in Steps 1 and 2) for each program point w the set

$$I[w] = \{x \mid e_{Main} \Longrightarrow c_w \stackrel{r}{\Longrightarrow} c_v, At_w(c_w), At_v(c_v), \hat{r} \text{ exhibits dep. } (x,y)\} \,.$$

Intuitively, $I[w]$ is the set of variables that can influence the value of y at v when some computation is at w. Clearly, in $I[w]$ dependences of bridging runs from w to v are considered. By solving the constraint system for bridging runs from Section 5 over the domain $(\mathsf{AD}, \sqsubseteq)$ (Step 1), we can compute the dependence traces of bridging runs; they are given by the second component of the value $\mathsf{B}_v^\#[w]$ that is computed. From the dependence traces we can read off the dependences by Proposition 7.2.1 and hence determine $I[w]$ (Step 2). The fixpoint computation in Step 1 determines as a by-product the abstraction $\mathsf{R}^\#[v]$ of the runs reaching v because the constraint system for bridging runs embodies the one for reaching runs.

The rest of the algorithm is based on the following observation: variable y is *not* a copy constant at v if and only if one of the following is true:

a) there is a variable x the initial value of which can influence y at v;
b) there is a base edge $e = (u, w)$ annotated by an assignment $x := e$ with a composite expression e on the right hand side such that x's value at w can influence y's value at v;
c) there are two distinct base edges $e = (u, w)$ and $e' = (u', w')$ each of them annotated by a constant assignment $x := c$ and $x' := c'$, respectively, such that both x at w and x' at w' can influence y at v and $c \neq c'$.

In Step 3-6 we check whether one of these conditions is true. We use a Boolean variable *flag* that is initialized to false and is set to true once we encounter a reason for y not being a copy constant at v. Step 4 tests whether condition a) is true: it sets *flag* if the initial value of y can flow to v ($y \in \mathsf{R}^\#[v].1$) or if the initial value of some variable x can influence y at v via a chain of assignments $((1, \langle (x,y) \rangle, 1) \in \mathsf{R}^\#[v].2)$. Step 5 is concerned with conditions b) and c). Each base edge is examined in turn. Step 5.1 tests whether b) holds. In order to check c), we memorize in a variable *val* the value of the constant assignment that can influence y at w encountered first. In order to check c) we simply compare the value of constant assignments encountered later with the value memorized in *val*. Variable *val* is initialized with a special value unset that indicates that we have not seen a constant assignment so far. Finally, Step 6 outputs the answer.

Of course we could stop the algorithm immediately, once the flag is set to true. Moreover, we can output the value stored in *val* as additional information, if we have identified y as a copy constant at v. It is the value guaranteed for y at v. It may happen that *val* has still the value unset; this indicates that v is an unreachable program point.

Algorithm 8.2.

Input: A parallel flow graph as defined in Chapter 5; a mapping $R : N \rightarrow 2^X$ that associates each program point u with the set of variables relevant at u.

Output: An updated edge annotation A_{new} of the parallel flow graph in which faint code is eliminated.

Method:
    1) Initialize the new annotation of flow graph edges: $A_{\text{new}} := A$.
    2) For each base edge $e \in$ Base: $A_{\text{new}}[e] :=$ **skip**.
    3) For each $v \in N$ with $R(v) \neq \emptyset$:
        3.1) Compute—by standard fixpoint iteration—the least solution over domain $(\text{AD}, \sqsubseteq)$ of the constraint system for bridging runs to program point v; this gives us a value $\mathsf{B}_v^{\#}[u]$ for each program point u.
        3.2) Set $I[w] := \{x \mid \exists y \in R(v) : (1, \langle(x, y)\rangle, 1) \in \mathsf{B}_v^{\#}[u].2\}$ for each program point $w \in N$.
        3.3) For each base edge $e = (\_, w) \in$ Base with $A[e] = (x := t)$:
            if $x \in I[w]$ then $A_{\text{new}}[e] := (x := t)$.
    4) Output the new edge annotation A_{new}.

Fig. 8.2. An algorithm that eliminates faint code in parallel programs.

We conclude:

Theorem 8.1.1. *Algorithm 8.1 solves the interprocedural copy constant detection problem in parallel flow graphs relative to non-atomic interpretation of base statements.* □

8.2 Faint-Code Elimination

A variable x is *live* at a program point p if there is a run from p to the end of the program in which x is used before it is overwritten. By referring to [25], Horwitz et. al. [32] define a variable x as *truly live* at a program point p if there is a run from p to the end of the program on which x is used in a truly live context before being defined, where a truly live context means: in a predicate, or in a call to a library routine, or in an expression whose value is assigned to a truly live variable. True liveness can be seen as a refinement of the ordinary liveness property. We call a use of a variable x in a predicate or call to a library routine a *relevant use* of x.

Assignments to variables that are not truly live at the program point just after the assignment are called *faint*. Intuitively, faint assignments can not influence any predicate in the program or call of a library routine. Thus, they cannot influence the observable behavior of the program (except of producing run-time errors) and may safely be eliminated from the program. This is called *faint code elimination*.

Faint code elimination is a stronger form of the classic transformation of dead-code elimination [56]. Indeed, any assignment that is dead is also faint

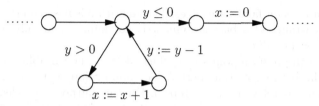

Fig. 8.3. An assignment that is faint but not dead.

but not vice versa. The paradigmatic example is shown in Fig. 8.3. The value computed by $x := x + 1$ in the loop is immediately overwritten after the loop and thus never used in a relevant context. Hence $x := x + 1$ is faint. However, it is not dead because x is potentially (non-relevantly) used by the same statement in the next iteration of the loop. Thus, faint code elimination in general can eliminate more code from a program.

Faint code elimination is based on information about the relevant uses of variables. Typically, this information is derived from the library calls and the conditions in the program. As our view of a program, a parallel flow graph, is an abstraction of the actual program in which library calls as well as conditions are invisible, we assume that we are given this information explicitly in the form of a mapping $R : N \rightarrow 2^X$; for each program point $u \in N$, $R(u)$ is the set of variables directly relevant at u.

Example 8.2.1. In a given program we might find a printf statement, e.g.,

```
printf("x+y=%d", x+y);
```

In the abstract flow graph view of the program this statement gives rise to a skip edge $e = (u, v)$. Then both x and y are relevant at u, hence $R(u) = \{x, y\}$.

Similarly, we might find a branching statement, e.g.,

```
if (z > x*y) then {...} else {...}
```

In the abstract flow graph view of the program this if-statement gives rise to two skip-edges (u, v) and (u, w); u is the start node for the flow graph for the whole if-statement; at v the flow graph for the then part and at w the flow graph for the else part is found. In this case, we have $R(u) = \{x, y, z\}$.   □

Algorithm 8.2 in Fig. 8.2 reads a parallel flow graph and a mapping $R : N \rightarrow 2^X$ as described above. Based on this information it calculates an updated version of the edge annotation mapping of the given flow graph in which faint code is eliminated, i.e., faint instances of base statements are replaced by skip.

First the new edge annotation mapping is initialized by the original edge annotation (Step 1) and all annotations of base edges are removed, i.e. replaced by skip (Step 2). The rest of the algorithm restores the original edge annotation for the non-faint base edges. The algorithm is based on the simple idea that an instance of a base statement is not faint if and only if it can influence a relevant value.

We explore all program points v at which at least one variable is relevant and restore the base edges that perform a computation that can influence a variable y that is relevant at v (Step 3). For this purpose we calculate in Steps 3.1 and 3.2 for all program points w the following set $I[w]$:

$$\{x \mid e_{Main} \Longrightarrow c_w \overset{r}{\Longrightarrow} c_v, At_w(c_w), At_v(c_v), \exists y \in R(v) : \hat{r} \text{ exhibits } (x, y)\}.$$

Intuitively, $I[w]$ contains the variables that can influence the value of a relevant variable y at v when some computation is at w. The computation is analogous to the one of the similar set $I[w]$ in Algorithm 8.1; therefore, we omit a detailed explanation. Step 3.3 restores the annotation of those base edges that assign to a variable that can influence a relevant variable at v from the target node of the base edge. Finally, Step 4 outputs the computed new edge annotation mapping.

We conclude:

Theorem 8.2.1. *Algorithm 8.2 solves the interprocedural faint code elimination problem in parallel flow graphs relative to non-atomic interpretation of base statements.*   □

8.3 Running Time

In this section we analyze the asymptotic running time of the algorithms from the previous sections. Specifically, we show that the algorithms run in time exponential in the number of program variables, $|X|$, and polynomial in the size of the parallel flow graph. The latter is measured by the parameters $|N|$, the number of program points, $|E|$, the number of edges, and $|\mathsf{Proc}|$, the number of procedures.

In both algorithms the bulk of the work is done during the least fixpoint computation(s) for the constraint system(s) for bridging runs over the domain $(AD, \sqsubseteq)$. Let us, first of all, determine an asymptotic bound for the complexity of such a fixpoint computation. As we are heading for a rough bound only, we assume that the least fixpoint is computed naively by standard fixpoint iteration: starting from an assignment of the bottom value to each variable appearing in the constraint system we iteratively determine a new assignment to the variables by re-evaluating all constraints until stabilization. Of course the asymptotic complexity of this naive fixpoint algorithm is bounded by the product of the maximal number of iterations and the maximal cost of a single step.

In each iteration except of the last one, at least one constraint variable must change its value. As values only increase during fixpoint iteration, each constraint variable can change its value at most $\mathcal{O}(|X^{2|X|+3})$ times, because $\mathcal{O}(|X|^{2|X|+3})$ is a bound for the height of AD by Lemma 7.7.1. Moreover, it is a simple counting exercise to show that the complete constraint system for bridging runs (it comprises the constraint systems for same-level runs, inverse same-level runs, reaching runs, etc.) has $\mathcal{O}(|\mathsf{Proc}| \cdot |N|)$ constraint variables.[1] Thus, we can have at most $\mathcal{O}(|\mathsf{Proc}| \cdot |N| \cdot |X|^{2|X|+3})$ iterations. This clearly is $\mathcal{O}(|\mathsf{Proc}| \cdot |N| \cdot 2^{p_0(|X|)})$ for some polynomial $p_0(x)$ in x.

Let us now bound the costs of a single iteration. In each iteration we must reevaluate all constraints. It is again a simple counting exercise to show that the complete constraint system for bridging runs has $\mathcal{O}(|N| \cdot |E|)$ constraints.[2] From Lemma 7.13.1 we know that all operations can be computed in time $\mathcal{O}(2^{p_1(|X|)})$ for some polynomial $p_1(x)$. As the number of operations in each single constraint is bounded, the cost of a single iteration is $\mathcal{O}(|N| \cdot |E| \cdot 2^{p_1(|X|)})$.

Summarizing:

Lemma 8.3.1. *The constraint system for bridging runs can be evaluated over domain* $(\mathsf{AD}, \sqsubseteq)$ *in time* $\mathcal{O}(|\mathsf{Proc}| \cdot |N|^2 \cdot |E| \cdot 2^{p(|X|)})$, *where* $p(x)$ *is a polynomial.* □

Let us now turn attention to the algorithms. Clearly, in the copy-constant detection algorithm, Algorithm 8.1, the bulk of the work is done in Step 1 such that the time taken for Step 1 majorizes the time taken for the other steps. Hence this algorithm runs in time $\mathcal{O}(|\mathsf{Proc}| \cdot |N|^2 \cdot |E| \cdot 2^{p(|X|)})$ by Lemma 8.3.1.

In the faint-code elimination algorithm, Algorithm 8.2, the work performed in Step 3.1 majorizes the work done in the other steps. Step 3.1 is executed at most $|N|$ times. Consequently, Algorithm 8.2 runs in time $\mathcal{O}(|\mathsf{Proc}| \cdot |N|^3 \cdot |E| \cdot 2^{p(|X|)})$.

Clearly, only those program variables are of interest in the algorithms that appear in the parallel flow graph. We can thus assume without loss of generality, that all program variables in X appear in the parallel flow graph. As the latter constitutes part of the input to all algorithm, the input size cannot be smaller than the size of X. Obviously, the same holds for Proc, N, and E such that the size of the input clearly bounds all the parameters appearing in above estimations. Hence all algorithms run in time exponential in the size of the input.

Theorem 8.3.1. *Algorithms 8.1 and 8.2 run in exponential time. More precisely, Algorithm 8.1 runs in time* $\mathcal{O}(|\mathsf{Proc}| \cdot |N|^2 \cdot |E| \cdot 2^{p(|X|)})$ *and Algorithm 8.2 in time* $\mathcal{O}(|\mathsf{Proc}| \cdot |N|^3 \cdot |E| \cdot 2^{p(|X|)})$. □

---

[1] This asymptotic bound holds in the special case where ASS1 and ASS2 are true as well as in the general case.

[2] Again this asymptotic bound holds for both the special and the general case.

Corollary 8.3.1. *Relative to non-atomic interpretation of base statements, the following two problems can be solved interprocedurally in parallel flow graphs in exponential time: (1) copy-constant detection and (2) faint-code elimination.*   □

8.4 Conclusion

We have shown in this chapter that we can detect copy constants and eliminate faint code in parallel flow graphs in exponential time, *if we do not assume that base statements execute atomically*. This should be contrasted to the result that all these problems are undecidable if assignment statements are assumed to execute atomically (Chapter 4). So, the (unrealistic) idealization from program verification "atomic execution of assignment statements" that presumably simplifies matters actually increases the difficulty of these problems from the point of view of program analysis: amazingly these problems become more tractable if we adopt a less idealized, more realistic view of execution.

These results raise the question whether there are also *efficient* algorithms for these problems. The answer to this question is 'no', unless P=NP, as we show in the next chapter.

9. Complexity in the Non-atomic Scenario

In the previous chapter, we have seen that we can detect all copy constants and eliminate faint code completely in parallel programs, if we abandon the assumption that base statements execute atomically. The presented algorithms run in exponential time, which raises the question whether there are also efficient algorithms for these problems. In this chapter we show that the answer is 'no', unless P=NP. In the conclusions of this monographs, Chapter 10, we sketch possible remedies and discuss directions of future research that may lead to algorithms of practical interest.

The hardness proofs from Chapter 4 rely on re-initialization of variables in order to ensure that runs which do not correspond to behavior to be simulated do not contribute to propagation. The example in Section 6.2 indicates that this technique does *not* work, if the assumption of atomic execution of base statements is abandoned. Indeed, the above analysis problems become decidable, which implies that the *un*-decidability proofs cannot be valid any more.

In Section 9.1 we exhibit a co-NP-hardness proof by means of a reduction from the well-known SAT-problem [12, 72] that applies to both flow analysis problems. This reduction was first presented in [58] where atomic execution of base statement has been assumed, but it remains valid if this assumption is abandoned [59]. Unlike the reductions in Chapter 4, it only relies on active propagation along copying assignments but not on re-initialization.

The hardness proof constructs loop-free programs and it is easy to see that the co-NP lower bound is indeed sharp for loop-free programs. We have not yet been able to fully characterize the complexity for the other classes: the general intraprocedural problem and the interprocedural problem. Up to now we have the EXPTIME upper bound through the algorithms from Chapter 8 and the NP lower bound through the SAT reduction from Section 9.1. A natural idea for an NP-easiness proof would be to show that non-constancy and non-faintness is always witnessed by runs of polynomial length. We show in Section 9.2 that this idea does *not* work. Specifically, we exhibit a family of programs in which the length of the shortest witnessing runs is exponential in the program size. This justifies the conjecture that the general intraprocedural problem does not belong to NP, i.e., cannot be solved by a non-deterministic algorithm that runs in polynomial time.

For ease of presentation we represent parallel programs in this chapter, like in Chapter 4, by syntactic programs rather than flow graphs.

9.1 The SAT-reduction

We now describe the SAT reduction. An instance of SAT is a conjunction $c_1 \wedge \ldots \wedge c_k$ of *clauses* $c_1, \ldots, c_k$. Each clause is a disjunction of *literals*; a literal l is either a variable x or a negated variable $\overline{x}$, where x ranges over some set of variables X. We write $\overline{X} = \{\overline{x_1}, \ldots, \overline{x_n}\}$ for the set of negated variables. It is straightforward to define when a *truth assignment* $T : X \rightarrow \mathbb{B}$, where $\mathbb{B} = \{\mathsf{tt}, \mathsf{ff}\}$ is the set of truth values, satisfies $c_1 \wedge \ldots \wedge c_k$. The SAT problem asks us to decide for each instance $c_1 \wedge \ldots \wedge c_k$ whether there is a satisfying truth assignment or not.

From a given SAT instance $c_1 \wedge \ldots \wedge c_k$ with k clauses over n variables $X = \{x_1, \ldots, x_n\}$ we construct a loop-free parallel program. In the program we use $k+1$ variables $z_0, z_1, \ldots, z_k$. Intuitively, validity of clause c_i is related to propagation from z_{i-1} to z_i.

For each literal $l \in X \cup \overline{X}$ we define a statement π_l that consists of a sequential composition of assignments of the form $z_i := z_{i-1}$ in increasing order of i. The assignment $z_i := z_{i-1}$ is in π_l if and only if the literal l makes clause i true. Formally, $\pi_l = \pi_l^k$, where

$$\pi_l^0 \stackrel{\text{def}}{=} \mathbf{skip}$$

$$\pi_l^i \stackrel{\text{def}}{=} \begin{cases} \pi_l^{i-1} ; z_i := z_{i-1}, & \text{if clause } c_i \text{ contains } l \\ \pi_l^{i-1}, & \text{if clause } c_i \text{ does not contain } l \end{cases}$$

for $i = 1, \ldots, k$. Now, consider the following program π:

> **procedure** *Main*;
> $z_0 := 1 ; z_1 := 0 ; \ldots ; z_k := 0$;
> $[(\pi_{x_1} \sqcap \pi_{\overline{x_1}}) \parallel \cdots \parallel (\pi_{x_n} \sqcap \pi_{\overline{x_n}})]$;
> $(z_k := 0 \sqcap \mathbf{skip})$;
> $\mathbf{write}(z_k)$
> **end**

Clearly, π can be constructed from the given SAT instance $c_1 \wedge \ldots \wedge c_k$ in polynomial time or logarithmic space.

It is not hard to see that the value 1 from the initialization of z_0 can be propagated to the final write statement if and only if the given SAT instance is satisfiable:

"If": On the one hand, we can construct from a satisfying truth assignment $T : X \rightarrow \mathbb{B}$ a run that propagates z_0's initialization to the write-statement. In each parallel component $\pi_{x_i} \sqcap \pi_{\overline{x_i}}$ we choose the left branch π_{x_i} if $T(x_i) = \mathsf{tt}$ and the right branch $\pi_{\overline{x_i}}$ otherwise. As T is a satisfying truth assignment,

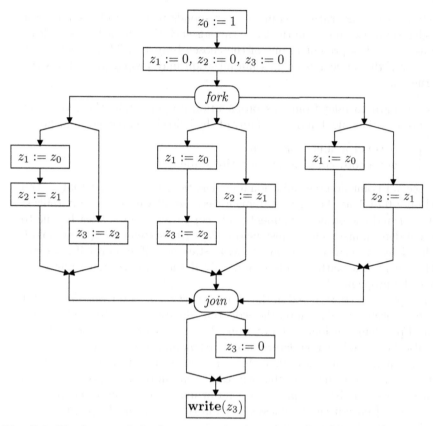

Fig. 9.1. The flow graph for $(x_1 \vee x_2 \vee x_3) \wedge (x_1 \vee \overline{x_2} \vee \overline{x_3}) \wedge (\overline{x_1} \vee x_2)$.

there will be, for any $i \in \{1, \ldots, k\}$, at least one assignment $z_i := z_{i-1}$ in one of the chosen branches. We interleave the branches now in such a way that the assignment(s) to z_1 are executed first, followed by the assignment(s) to z_2 etc. This results in a propagating run.

"Only if": On the other hand, a run can propagate the initialization value of z_0 to the write-statement only via copying from z_0 to z_1, from z_1 to z_2 etc., because all assignments have the form $z_i := z_{i-1}$. Such a run must contain an assignment $z_i := z_{i-1}$ for all $i = 1, \ldots, k$. From the way in which the non-deterministic choices are resolved in such a run we can easily construct a satisfying truth assignment.

Note that both directions hold independently from the atomicity assumption for assignment statements.

Example 9.1.1. Fig. 9.1 shows an example clause and program for illustration. Assignments to different variables are shown on different levels. Intuitively a satisfying truth assignment corresponds to a way of resolving the non-deterministic choices in the three threads such that at each level at least one assignment is present in one of the chosen branches. This is the case if and only if the value 1 from z_0's initialization may propagate to the write instruction.   □

It is not hard to infer from this propagation property that the given SAT instance is satisfiable if and only if any of the following two conditions holds:

1. $z_0 := 1$ is not a faint assignment.
2. z_k is not a copy constant at the write statement.

The second point deserves additional explanation. Observe first that z_k can hold only 0 or 1 at the write-statement because all variables are initialized by 0 or 1 and the other assignments only copy these values. Clearly, due to the non-deterministic choice just before the write-statement, z_k may hold 0 finally. Thus, z_k is a constant at the write-statement if and only if it cannot hold 1 there. The latter holds if and only if the initialization value of z_0 cannot be propagated.

The program constructed in the above reduction is loop-free and does not employ procedures. Therefore, the reduction already applies to the intraprocedural problems for loop-free programs. It is easy to see that the problems can also be solved in non-deterministic polynomial time for loop-free programs: a non-deterministic algorithms may guess two runs that witnesses non-constancy or a single run that witnesses non-faintness, respectively. Each of these runs can visit any program point at most once because the program is loop-free. Hence it can be guessed even in time linear in the program size.

These considerations prove:

Theorem 9.1.1. *Independently of the atomicity assumption for base statements, detecting copy constants and detecting faint code in loop-free parallel programs are co-NP-complete problems.*   □

Corollary 9.1.1. *Independently of the atomicity assumption, detecting copy constants and detecting faint code are co-NP-hard problems in arbitrary parallel programs.*   □

9.2 Towards Stronger Lower Bounds

A natural question is whether the lower bound provided by Corollary 9.1.1 for the three flow analysis problems, NP-hardness, is sharp, i.e., whether there are non-deterministic algorithms that run in polynomial time and solve the general intraprocedural (or even interprocedural) version of one (or both) of these problems. While we have not yet been able to settle this complexity question, we have achieved some progress towards an answer.

A natural approach for showing NP-easiness would be to exhibit a proof that shortest propagating runs are always of a length polynomial in the program size. This would guarantee that non-deterministic algorithms that guess runs witnessing non-constancy or non-faintness would run in polynomial time.

At first glance this approach seems promising, at least for the intraprocedural problem which has a fixed process architecture. One is tempted to believe that each assignment instance $x := e$ in the program can be used at most once for propagation in a *shortest* propagating run: if it is used twice in a propagating run r it seems possible to shorten this run. The intuition is that the thread T that contains this assignment instance $x := e$ could store the value to be propagated in a virtual variable v when $x := e$ is reached the first time in r; then it could wait until the environment has evolved to its state when $x := e$ is reached the second time in r. As virtual variables are private to P the evolution of the environment cannot affect the stored value. This reasoning seems similar to the intuition underlying Lemma 7.11.5 that is crucial for the completeness of the abstract interleaving operator $\otimes^{\#}$.

This intuition, however, is wrong as we show in Section 9.2.1. Specifically, we present an example program in which any propagating run must necessarily use a certain instance of an assignment twice. In Section 9.2.2 we exploit the construction of this example to exhibit a family of programs in which the length of shortest propagating runs grows exponentially with the program size. This proves that a non-deterministic algorithms that guesses witnessing runs is doomed to run in time exponential in the input size. While this does not rule out the possibility that small certificates other than witnessing runs exist, it justifies the conjecture that the two flow analysis problems that accompany us through this monograph probably do not belong to the class NP but that their complexity is higher. It is an open problem, whether the technique of these examples can be used to show better lower bounds than NP-hardness, e.g., PSPACE-hardness.

What is the error in the argument sketched above? It is that the thread T can prevent the environment from certain evolutions by waiting after it has stored the value to virtual variable v. For constructing programs in which this happens (like the ones shown in the remainder of this section), we can exploit the causality inherent in sequential and parallel composition and looping. Most importantly, we can exploit that the parallel composition operation synchronizes termination of the component threads.

9.2.1 Assignment Statements That Propagate Twice

Recall that a run r is said to *exhibit* dependence (x, y), $r \vdash (x, y)$ for short, if there are variables $a_0, \ldots, a_l$, $l > 0$, expressions $e_1, \ldots, e_l$, and (sub-) runs $r_0, \ldots, r_l$ such that

1. $a_0 = x$, $a_l = y$;
2. e_i contains a_{i-1} for $i = 1, \ldots, l$;

3. $r = r_0 \cdot \langle a_1 := e_1 \rangle \cdot r_1 \cdot \langle a_2 := e_2 \rangle \cdot r_2 \cdot \ldots \cdot \langle a_l := e_l \rangle \cdot r_l$; and
4. r_i is transparent for a_i for $i = 0, \ldots, l$.

If this is the case, we say that the run r *propagates from x to y via the assignments* $a_i := e_i$. When r is a run of a program π, the assignments with a program variable on their left hand side correspond to certain assignment statements in π. Then we say that the run propagates via these assignment statements.

We now present a program π that can exhibit the dependence (a, c), but in which any run that does so must use a certain assignment instance twice. Consider the following program π:

$$\mathbf{loop} \begin{pmatrix} x := b; \\ c := y; \\ x := a; \\ b := y; \\ x := 0 \end{pmatrix} \| \begin{pmatrix} y := x; \\ y := 0 \end{pmatrix} \mathbf{end}.$$

Program π can exhibit the dependence (a, c) even when assignments execute atomically (and hence also when they execute non-atomically): by iterating the loop twice and interleaving the two components of the parallel processes appropriately, we see that it has the run

1. Iteration: $x := b, c := y, \mathbf{x := a}, \mathbf{y := x}, \mathbf{b := y}, x := 0, y := 0,$
2. Iteration: $\mathbf{x := b}, \mathbf{y := x}, \mathbf{c := y}, x := a, b := y, x := 0, y := 0$

This run exhibits the dependence (a, c) via the assignments printed in bold face. The interesting point of this example is that—even when we assume non-atomic execution of assignments—there is no run that exhibits this dependence without copying via the assignment $y := x$ in the second parallel component twice. In order to see this, consider the following: as variable a is read only by the assignment $x := a$, a propagating run must use this assignment for propagation in some iteration of the loop, say in the k'th iteration. Before this iteration of the loop ends, x must be further propagated, because otherwise propagation is prohibited by the execution of $x := 0$. This can only happen in the second thread by means of $y := x$. Again, in order to successfully proceed with the propagation, y must be propagated before the end of the iteration of the loop, because otherwise $y := 0$ prohibits further propagation. Hence, $b := y$ must be executed before the end of the k'th loop iteration after complete execution of $y := x$. After the kth loop iteration, the value in b must be further propagated to c, which requires a second use of $y := x$.

Note that this example exploits the synchronous termination of the parallel composition operator as well as the causality inherent in sequential composition.

9.2.2 Propagating Runs of Exponential Length

The technique of the previous example can be iterated to construct a family of processes that require exponentially long runs to exhibit a particular dependence.

We inductively define processes P_i, $i \geq 0$. These processes have the ability to propagate from a variable a_i to a variable c_i. We will show below that the shortest runs that do so have length $\Omega(2^i)$.

$i = 0$: Process P_0 is defined as $c_0 := a_0$. It plays the role of the instruction $y := x$ in the previous example; a_0 corresponds to x and c_0 to y.

$i > 0$: For $i > 0$, the process P_i relies on the ability of P_{i-1} to propagate from a_{i-1} to c_{i-1}. The construction from Section 9.2.1 is used to enforce that P_{i-1} has to contribute two runs that propagates from a_{i-1} to c_{i-1} in any run of P_i that propagates from a_i to c_i. For this purpose an intermediate variable b_i is used. The definition of P_i is this:

$$
\mathbf{loop} \left(
\begin{array}{rcl}
a_{i-1} & := & b_i; \\
c_i & := & c_{i-1}; \\
a_{i-1} & := & a_i; \\
b_i & := & c_{i-1}; \\
a_{i-1} & := & 0
\end{array}
\right)
\;\Big\|\;
\left(
\begin{array}{l}
P_{i-1}; \\
c_{i-1} := 0
\end{array}
\right)
\mathbf{end}\,; \; b_i := 0
$$

We now prove by induction on i that process P_i has a run that propagates from a_i to c_i and that (for $i > 0$) any run of P_i that does so must include at least *two* runs of P_{i-1} that propagate from a_{i-1} to c_{i-1}. This proves the $\Omega(2^i)$ claim for the length of shortest propagating runs. In order to enable an inductive proof, the following additional property is proved simultaneously: any run of P_i finally kills all variables that it assigns to except of c_i, i.e.: if a run r of P_i can be written as $r = r_0 \cdot \langle x := e \rangle \cdot r_1$ with $x \neq c_i$ and $e \neq 0$, then r_1 can be written as $r_1 = r_2 \cdot \langle x := 0 \rangle \cdot r_3$.

For P_0 these properties are trivial. So suppose $i > 0$ and assume that the properties are valid for P_{i-1}. Let r be a shortest run of P_{i-1} with $r \vdash (a_{i-1}, c_{i-1})$. Then we can define a run s of P_i (with atomically executed assignments) in analogy to the run considered in the previous example:

1. Iter.: $a_{i-1} := b_i, c_i := c_{i-1}, \mathbf{a_{i-1} := a_i, r, b_i} := c_{i-1}, a_{i-1} := 0, c_{i-1} := 0,$
2. Iter.: $\mathbf{a_{i-1} := b_i, r, c_i} := c_{i-1}, a_{i-1} := a_i, b_i := c_{i-1}, a_{i-1} := 0, c_{i-1} := 0,$
Finally: $b_i := 0$

The parts in bold face show that $s \vdash (a_i, c_i)$. Obviously, this run contains r twice.

In order to see that any run s of P_i with $s \vdash (a_i, c_i)$ necessarily contains two runs of P_{i-1}, we argue similar to Section 9.2.1: as variable a_i is read only by the assignment $a_{i-1} := a_i$, a propagating run must use this assignment for propagation in some iteration of the loop, say in the k'th iteration. Before the k'th iteration of the loop ends, a_{i-1} must be read, because otherwise propagation is prohibited by the execution of $a_{i-1} := 0$. This can only happen in the second thread in a run r of P_{i-1}. By the induction hypothesis this run kills all variables except c_{i-1} finally, and c_{i-1} is also killed explicitly after the execution of P_{i-1} before the k'th iteration of the loop ends. Thus, successful propagation requires that r is a run that propagates to c_{i-1} and that afterwards $b_i := c_{i-1}$ is executed. In order to propagate from b_i to c_i in a later iteration of the loop, a further run of P_{i-1} that propagates from a_{i-1} to c_{i-1} is needed.

It remains to show that all runs of P_i kill all the variables they assign to except c_i. This is easy to see from the corresponding property for P_{i-1} and the places of the assignments $a_{i-1} := 0$, $c_{i-1} := 0$, and $b_i := 0$ in P_i.

These considerations justify the following conjecture.

Conjecture 9.2.1. For parallel programs, the intraprocedural copy-constant detection problem does not belong to co-NP. The same holds for faint-code elimination.

9.3 Summary

In this chapter we have seen that both detecting copy constants and eliminating faint code are intractable problems, even if the assumption that base statements execute atomically is abandoned. Both problems have been shown to be co-NP-hard by means of a reduction from the SAT problem. Unlike the reductions in (Chapter 4), this reduction applies under the assumption that assignments execute atomically as well as when this assumption is abandoned. Moreover, we have exhibited a family of example programs in which the length of shortest propagating runs is exponential in the program size. This indicates that the lower bound, NP-hardness, probably can be improved for the general intraprocedural problem as well as the interprocedural problem.

10. Conclusion

For fundamental recursion-theoretic reasons, program analyzers are doomed to give only approximate answers. By applying abstractions to programs, we can come to precisely defined, weaker analysis problems that can be solved exactly. By classifying such problems with the means provided by the theory of computational complexity, we hope to shed light on the trade-off between efficiency and precision for approximate analyzers and to uncover potential for more precise analysis algorithms.

In this monograph we studied various version of the constant propagation problem. More specifically, our contributions are the following:

1. We characterized the complexity of constant detection for a three-dimensional taxonomy of constants in *sequential* flow graphs on integer variables almost completely. The first dimension selects a subset of expressions that are interpreted precisely. The second dimension distinguishes between *must-* and *may-constants*; may-constants appear in two variations: single- and multiple-valued. In the third dimension we distinguish between programs with or without loops. May constants are related to reachability.

2. We showed that detection of copy constants in parallel programs is undecidable, PSPACE-complete, and NP-complete if we consider programs with procedures, without procedures, and without loops, respectively. These proofs rely on the standard assumption that base statements execute atomically. They reveal fundamental limits for precise analysis of parallel programs.

3. We then abandoned this atomic execution assumption. Surprisingly, this makes copy-constant detection decidable for programs with procedures although it remains intractable (co-NP-hard). Similar statements can be made for faint-code elimination. In order to show decidability we worked out a precise abstract interpretation of sets of runs (program executions). The worst-case running time of this algorithm is exponential in the number of global variables but polynomial in the parameters describing the program size.

From a practical perspective, our most interesting findings concern potential for the construction of algorithms. In the sequential case, we find that

polynomial constants are decidable and that Presburger constants can even
be detected in polynomial time. In the parallel case we could show that problems that are undecidable under the standard idealization of atomic execution
are in the reach of algorithmic techniques if more realistic atomicity assumptions are adopted. This in particular holds for the fundamental problem of
exact dependence analysis. While further work is necessary to construct algorithms that are efficient enough to be of practical use, our findings open
up potential for interesting future work.

The worst-case running-time of the algorithms in Chapter 8 is exponential.
Unfortunately, already the elementary operations are expensive, in particular
the abstract interleaving operator, such that we cannot hope that they would
perform well in practice if the number of variables is large. Nevertheless, we
believe that refinements of the technique underlying dependence traces can
lead to practically interesting algorithms with acceptable performance and
superior precision. Let us discuss possible targets for improvements.

While the running time of the algorithms is exponential in the number
of program variables, it is *polynomial in the program size*; cf. Theorem 8.3.1.
Hence, if the number of program variables is bounded, they are polynomial-
time algorithms. For a practical algorithm it is thus essential to keep the
number of the variables that are used in dependence trace construction small.
In order to keep the technical treatment manageable, we do not distinguish
between local and global variables of threads and procedures in the current
exposition. All variables are global and all of them are visible to each thread.
Therefore, we must include all variables into the precise interference analysis
provided by dependence traces. In practice, however, most variables are local
to threads and there are only a few global variables on which interference
can happen. A practical algorithm should take advantage of the distinction
between local and global variables. The idea is to design a combined analysis
that applies the expensive interference reasoning via dependence traces only
to really shared variables and uses a cheap sequential technique for propagation via other variables. Analysis with respect to such a domain promises
to be exponential only in the number of global variables, which is probably
small in practice.

We should also strive for a compact representation of the values in the
abstract domain AD. Each value comprises a set of variables T and an antichain of short dependence traces D. The set T may straightforwardly be
represented by a bit-vector. It is less clear, however, how to represent the antichain D adequately. Storing all the dependence traces in D explicitly, e.g.,
in a linked list, is probably not a good solution, because D can be large and
there is much redundancy. The run $\langle b := a, d := c, f := e \rangle$, for instance, has
the dependence trace $\tau = (1, \langle (a, b), (c, d), (e, f) \rangle, 1)$ but also the dependence
traces $(1, \langle (a, b), (c, d) \rangle, 1)$, $(1, \langle (a, b) \rangle, 1)$ and many others. In a certain sense
the latter dependence traces are implied by τ except of the transparency bits.
We should use a representation that employs sharing to compactly represent

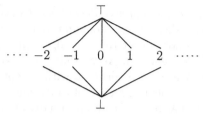

Fig. 10.1. A lattice for constant propagation.

all these dependence traces by a structure that is not much larger than τ alone and that allows a cheaper computation of the composition operators.

In flow analysis of sequential programs we mostly propagate informative values through the program. In constant propagation, for instance, we use values of a lattice like the one in Figure 10.1. The dependence traces domain, however, is a rather pure domain that treats interference in isolation. It is fitted to the computation of dependences only. Although it allows us to solve problems like copy-constant detection and faint-code elimination, the approach is indirect via bridging runs and involves even an iterated computation of dependence traces in the case of faint-code detection. It is interesting to invent and study more complex abstract domains that work with more informative values but rely on the idea of dependence traces to come to grips with interference. Ideally, such domains should be obtained by a modular extension of the dependence traces domain in order to isolate the interference-related reasoning from other semantic questions.

10.1 Future Research

Let us discuss some ideas for future research.

Complete the hierarchy of constants. An obvious target for future research are the two questions that remain open in the hierarchy of constants of Chapter 2: (1) we miss an upper bound for linear may-constants and (2) the upper and lower bound for polynomial must-constants do not coincide. Currently, we have decidability as an upper bound, as witnessed by the algorithm in Chapter 3, and PSPACE-hardness as a lower bound.

Investigate interprocedural hierarchy. It is interesting to study the hierarchy of constants in Chapter 2 also in sequential programs with procedures, i.e., the interprocedural problem. While we now know that Presburger constants can interprocedurally still be detected efficiently [65], it is an open problem whether polynomial constants remain decidable. In view of the negative results of Chapter 4 and 9 already for the weakest class of constants, copy constants, it is less interesting to generalize the results to parallel programs.

Research towards more practical analysis algorithms. Concerning analysis of parallel programs the dependence traces domain proposed in this monograph is only a first step. We do not expect that the algorithms in Chapter 8 run satisfactorily in practice. We believe, however, that variants of the dependence traces techniques can well lead to algorithms with acceptable performance and superior precision. The next three points mention again the possible targets for improvements that have already been motivated and discussed in more detail above.

Take advantage of local variables. We would like to study algorithms that take advantage of the distinction between local and global variables. The expensive dependence traces technique should be applied only to global variables and local variables should be treated by much cheaper sequential techniques. The two propagation methods must be intertwined because both types of variables can contribute to propagate information to a certain point in the program. This may make the resulting algorithms rather complicated.

Represent antichains compactly. It is important to find a compact representation of antichains of dependence traces on which the abstract operations can be computed more efficiently than on an explicit representation.

Specialized domains. It is worth inventing domains that work with more informative values than dependence traces. Such domains should enable us to perform, e.g., copy-constant detection by means of an abstraction of reaching runs rather than bridging runs. Thus, they would reveal closer connections to traditional analysis of sequential programs. Note, however, that in itself this does not imply a gain in efficiency (with respect to asymptotic running time) because the constraint systems for reaching runs and bridging runs both have $\mathcal{O}(|\mathsf{Proc}| \cdot |N|)$ constraint variables and $\mathcal{O}(|N| \cdot |E|)$ constraints.

More realistic programming languages. We should also consider application of the dependence traces technique to more realistic programming languages. In this monograph we studied the prototypic scenario of non-deterministic parallel flow graphs. Generalization to practical languages may lead to additional interesting problems.

Weak memory consistency models. Many modern implementations of multi-threaded programs provide only a weak memory consistency model that allows the implementation to change the order in which writes from one thread are observed in other threads [1, 75, 80, 48]. The reason is that weaker assumptions about the memory enable a multitude of software and hardware optimizations. A weak memory consistency model is another reason besides non-atomicity, why the idealistic atomicity assumptions adopted in classic program verification and in our reductions in Chapter 4 are unrealistic. We conjecture that the dependence traces abstraction is sound and complete also under most if not all weak memory consistency models. This would emphasize the importance of dependence traces.

A. A Primer on Constraint-Based Program Analysis

Constraint-based program analysis provides a framework for developing analyses and arguing about their correctness and completeness. In this chapter we describe the idea underlying constraint-based program analysis. As a running example we use forward dataflow analysis in (non-procedural, sequential) flow graphs and consider constant propagation in particular.

Definition A.0.1. *A flow graph is a structure $G = (N, E, A, \mathbf{s}, \mathbf{e})$ with node set N, edge set $E \subseteq N \times N$, a unique start node $\mathbf{s} \in N$, and a unique end node $\mathbf{e} \in N$. The mapping $A : E \to \mathsf{Asg} \cup \{\mathbf{skip}\}$ associates each edge with an assignment statement $x := e \in \mathsf{Asg}$ or with the statement $\mathbf{skip}$. Edges represent the branching structure and the statements of a program, while nodes represent program points.*

Program analysis problems are concerned with answering questions about certain sets of runs. A *run* is a sequence of atomic action; in a sequential context we can think of an action simply as an edge of the flow graph. A forward dataflow analysis, for instance, is concerned with the runs that reach program points from the start point of the program.

Definition A.0.2. *Let $G = (N, E, A, \mathbf{s}, \mathbf{e})$ be a flow graph and $w \in N$ a program point. A run reaching w is a sequence of edges $\langle e_1, \ldots, e_k \rangle$ with $e_i = (u_i, v_i) \in E$ such that $u_1 = \mathbf{s}$, $v_k = w$, and $v_i = u_{i+1}$ for $1 \le i < k$. In addition ε, the empty sequence, is a run reaching $\mathbf{s}$, the start node. We write $R[u]$ for the set of runs reaching u.*

In constraint-based program analysis, we first set up a system of subset constraints that characterize the run sets of interest. Each constraint takes the form

$$X_i \supseteq E(X_1, \ldots, X_k),$$

where the variables X_i represent the run sets of interest plus, perhaps, some additional auxiliary run sets, and $E(X_1, \ldots, X_k)$ is a term in these variables that denotes a monotonic mapping on run sets. We can have more than one constraint per variable. It follows from the Knaster-Tarski fixpoint theorem [90] that such a constraint system always has a smallest solution. We choose the constraints such that their smallest solution comprises just the run sets of interest. This is meant by saying that the constraint system *characterizes* the run sets. Throughout this monograph, we obey the following convention: run sets of interest are denoted by letters in sans serif font and the corresponding variables in constraint systems by the same letter in italic font.

Let us consider as an example a constraint system for the reaching runs in a flow graph. We have one variable $R[u]$ for each program point $u \in N$ that represents $\mathsf{R}[u]$ and no auxiliary variables. The characterizing constraint system for reaching runs has a special constraint for the start node

$$[1] \quad R[\mathsf{s}] \supseteq \{\varepsilon\}$$

and one constraint for each edge $e = (u, v) \in E$:

$$[2] \quad R[v] \supseteq R[u] \cdot \{\langle (u, v) \rangle\} \,.$$

It is easy to see that the family $(\mathsf{R}[u])_{u \in N}$ of sets of reaching runs satisfies all these constraints. It is moreover not hard to prove by induction on the length of runs that if $(F_u)_{u \in N}$ is a family of run sets that solves this constraint system, then any run that reaches u must be contained in F_u. Together this implies that the smallest solution of this family of inequalities over run sets is indeed the family of sets of reaching runs.

On the right hand side of constraints, certain run sets and operations on run sets are used. We may conceive the constraint system abstractly as a system over a certain *signature* $Sig = (C, O)$ consisting of a set of constants C and a set of operator O, where each operator o has an associated arity $ar(o) \in \mathbb{N}$.

In the constraint system for reaching runs, for instance, the signature consists of one constant c_ε and a unary operator o_e; the constraint system is this:[1]

$$[1] \quad R[\mathsf{s}] \sqsupseteq c_\varepsilon$$
$$[2] \quad R[v] \sqsupseteq o_e(R[u]), \quad \text{if } (u, v) \in E$$

An *interpretation* I of the signature comprises a complete lattice $(\mathbb{D}, \sqsubseteq)$ and an assignment of a value $I(c) \in \mathbb{D}$ to each constant c and an (n-ary) operations $I(o) : \mathbb{D}^n \to \mathbb{D}$ to each n-ary operator o.

In the *standard* or *concrete interpretation* I, $\mathbb{D}$ is the power set of the set of runs, $\mathbb{D} = 2^{\mathsf{Runs}}$, the order is subset inclusion, $\sqsubseteq = \subseteq$, and the interpretation of the constants and operators is as in the concrete constraint system. Thus, the least solution of the constraint-system comprises the run sets of interest. The concrete interpretation for the signature underlying the reaching runs

---

[1] The reader may consider it more natural to read the second constraint as

$$[2'] \quad R[v] \sqsupseteq R[u] \,; c_e, \quad \text{if } (u, v) \in E$$

where c_e is a constant and ; is a binary operator. While this alternative interpretation is legitimate in principle, it does not lead to an efficient intraprocedural analysis algorithm.

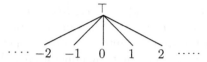

Fig. A.1. Hasse diagram of the co-flat order on $\mathbb{Z} \cup \{\top\}$.

in flow graphs, for instance, is this: $I(c_\varepsilon) = \{\varepsilon\} \in 2^{\mathsf{Runs}}$ for constant c_ε and $I(o_e) = (\lambda R : R \cdot \{\langle e \rangle\}) \in (2^{\mathsf{Runs}} \to 2^{\mathsf{Runs}})$ for unary operator o_e.

In constraint-based program analysis we obtain the analysis result by solving the constraint system over an *abstract lattice* $(\mathbb{D}^\#, \sqsubseteq^\#)$ and a *nonstandard or abstract interpretation* $I^\#$ of the constants and operators over $(\mathbb{D}^\#, \sqsubseteq^\#)$. Typically, $\mathbb{D}^\#$ is a finite-height lattice such that the constraint system can be effectively solved by standard fixpoint iteration.

In order to specify a forward dataflow analysis, we choose a finite-height lattice $(\mathbb{D}^\#, \sqsubseteq^\#)$ of *dataflow facts* and a value $d_0 \in \mathbb{D}^\#$ that represents the fact valid at the start of the program, and associate with each flow graph edge e a monotonic *transfer function* $[\![e]\!]^\# : \mathbb{D}^\# \to \mathbb{D}^\#$ that describes the effect of execution of edge e on dataflow facts. Often the latter is given via the annotation of edges by statements. The members of $\mathbb{D}^\#$ represent, depending on the specific analysis, potential run-time properties of program points. The order, $\sqsubseteq^\#$, captures information contents: smaller values represents more accurate (more precise) information. In particular, the top value, $\top_{\mathbb{D}^\#}$, represents absence of information. Note that our interpretation of the order is dual to the traditional one.

Example A.0.1 (Simple constant propagation). Let us discuss so-called *simple constant propagation.* Here the lattice is $\mathbb{D}_{\mathrm{sc}} = (\mathit{Var} \to (\mathsf{Val} \cup \{\top\})) \cup \{\bot\}$, where *Var* is the set of variables occurring in the program and Val is the set from which variables draw their value at run-time.[2] $\bot$ is an artificial bottom element that is added in order to make $\mathbb{D}_{\mathrm{sc}}$ a complete lattice. The other values are *abstract states* $d : \mathit{Var} \to (\mathsf{Val} \cup \{\top\})$. An abstract state assigns to each variable $x \in \mathit{Var}$ either a value $c \in \mathsf{Val}$—in this case x is guaranteed to be a constant of value c—or the special value $\top$—in this case x's value at run-time is unknown.

The order on $\mathbb{D}_{\mathrm{sc}}$ is defined as follows: $\bot \sqsubseteq d$ for all $d \in \mathbb{D}_{\mathrm{sc}}$ and, for abstract states $d, d, d \sqsubseteq d'$ iff for all $x \in \mathit{Var}$, $d'(x) = \top$ or $d(x) = d'(x)$. That is, the order is the lift of the co-flat order on $\mathsf{Val} \cup \{\top\}$ extended by $\bot$ as a bottom element. The co-flat order on $\mathsf{Val} \cup \{\top\}$ is illustrated by the Hasse diagram in Fig. A.1 for $\mathsf{Val} = \mathbb{Z}$.

The initial value is $d_0 = (\lambda x : \top)$—at the start of the program we have no knowledge about the value of the variables.

The transfer functions are induced by the statements: $[\![e]\!]^\# = [\![A(e)]\!]_{\mathrm{sc}}$, where $[\![\mathbf{skip}]\!]_{\mathrm{sc}}(d) = d$, i.e., $[\![\mathbf{skip}]\!]$ is the identity on $\mathbb{D}_{\mathrm{sc}}$, and $[\![x := e]\!]_{\mathrm{sc}}$

---

[2] For simplicity, we assume that all variables have the same type.

is defined by $[\![x := e]\!]_{sc}(\bot) = \bot$ and $[\![x := e]\!]_{sc}(d) = d[x \mapsto e^d]$ for abstract states d. The standard way of defining e^d, the value of expression d in abstract state d, is by extending the standard interpretation of operators from Val to $\mathsf{Val} \cup \{\top\}$ in a strict way, i.e., such that each operation yields $\top$ if any of its arguments is $\top$.[3]   □

The entities that specify a forward dataflow analysis induce a non-standard interpretation of the signature underlying the constraint system for reaching runs: the interpretation works on the lattice $(\mathbb{D}^{\#}, \sqsubseteq^{\#})$ of dataflow facts; constant c_{ε} is interpreted by $I^{\#}(c_{\varepsilon}) = d_0$, and the operator o_e by the transfer function associated with edge e: $I^{\#}(o_e) = [\![e]\!]^{\#}$. The smallest solution of the constraint system for reaching runs over this non-standard interpretation can effectively be computed by fixpoint iteration. It is called the *MFP-solution* in dataflow analysis parlance. We denote the value computed for variable $R[v]$ by $\mathsf{MFP}[v]$ for each $v \in N$.

Example A.0.2 (Simple Constant Propagation). If, for the simple constant propagation framework, $\mathsf{MFP}[v] \neq \bot$ and $\mathsf{MFP}[v](x) = c \in \mathsf{Val}$ then x is called a *simple constant of value c* at program point v.   □

The theory of abstract interpretation allows us to argue that the non-standard interpretation gives us the desired analysis result. For this purpose, we define first an abstraction function $\alpha : \mathbb{D} \to \mathbb{D}^{\#}$ that describes the intended relationship between the concrete interpretation I and the abstract interpretation $I^{\#}$. In the standard setting this amounts to a relationship between run sets and analysis results.

We call α a *weak homomorphism* of the two interpretations I and $I^{\#}$ if

1. $\alpha(I(c)) \sqsubseteq^{\#} I^{\#}(c)$ for any constant $c \in C$ and
2. $\alpha(I(o))(d_1, \ldots, d_k) \sqsubseteq^{\#} I^{\#}(o)(\alpha(d_1), \ldots, \alpha(d_k))$ for any k-ary operator $o \in O$ and values $d_1, \ldots, d_k \in \mathbb{D}$.

Alternatively, we say in this case that the abstract operators and constants are *correct abstractions* of the concrete ones. Intuitively, α is a weak homomorphism if a computation on abstractions yields sound but maybe less accurate abstractions than a computation on concrete values.

We call α a *strong homomorphism* if 1. and 2. hold with $=$ in place of $\sqsubseteq^{\#}$. Alternatively, we say that the abstract operators and constants are *precise abstractions* of the concrete ones. Intuitively, α is a strong homomorphism if we get the same abstract information by computing on abstractions and concrete values.

A function $f : L \to L'$ between complete lattices L and L' is called *distributive (universally disjunctive)* if it distributes over arbitrary joins, i.e., if $f(\bigvee S) = \bigvee \{f(l) \mid l \in S\}$ for all $S \subseteq L$.

---

[3] For some operators, we could use a non-strict interpretation, if other arguments determine the value of the operation uniquely. For example, we could define that $0 \cdot \top = 0$.

For any variable X used in a given constraint system, let $X_c \in \mathbb{D}$ be the value assigned to variable X in the smallest solution over concrete interpretation I and $X_a \in \mathbb{D}^{\#}$ be the value assigned to X in the smallest solution over abstract interpretation $I^{\#}$. Then the crucial theorem can be formulated as follows:

Theorem A.0.1. *Suppose α is distributive.*

1. *If α is a weak homomorphism then $\alpha(X_c)\sqsubseteq^{\#}X_a$.*
2. *If α is a strong homomorphism then $\alpha(X_c) = X_a$.*   □

In forward dataflow analysis the relationship between the standard and the abstract interpretation is given by the *MOP-abstraction*. MOP stands for "<u>M</u>eet <u>O</u>ver all <u>P</u>aths". As our interpretation of the order is dual to the traditional one we define it here as a "join over all paths". Nevertheless, we use the term MOP that is very well-established in the literature.

In order to define the MOP-abstraction, the local interpretation $[\![e]\!] : \mathbb{D} \to \mathbb{D}$ of flow-graph edges is extended to runs by the natural definition

$$[\![\langle e_1,\ldots,e_k\rangle]\!] \stackrel{\text{def}}{=} [\![e_k]\!] \circ \ldots \circ [\![e_1]\!].$$

In particular, $[\![\varepsilon]\!] = (\lambda d \in \mathbb{D}^{\#} : d)$, the identity on $\mathbb{D}^{\#}$. Obviously, the information valid after execution of a particular run r is given by $[\![r]\!](d_0)$. The MOP-abstraction is now defined as $\alpha_{\mathsf{MOP}} : \mathbb{D} \to \mathbb{D}^{\#}$:

$$\alpha_{\mathsf{MOP}}(R) \stackrel{\text{def}}{=} \bigsqcup\{[\![r]\!](d_0) \mid r \in R\}.$$

With this definition, we clearly have

$$\alpha_{\mathsf{MOP}}(\mathsf{R}[v]) = \mathsf{MOP}[v] \stackrel{\text{def}}{=} \bigsqcup\{[\![r]\!](d_0) \mid r \in \mathsf{R}[v]\}.$$

That is, the set of reaching runs to v is abstracted to what is commonly called the *MOP-solution* in dataflow analysis, where it is used as the specification of what the analysis tries to compute or approximate. The intuition is that $\mathsf{MOP}[v]$ is the most precise abstract information we can guarantee whenever execution reaches program point v: we must be prepared to see any of the runs $r \in \mathsf{R}[v]$; the best we can say after a specific run r is $[\![r]\!](d_0)$; and the most precise value consistent with all these values is their join. Therefore, a sound analysis must compute for program point v a fact f with $\mathsf{MOP}[v]\sqsubseteq^{\#}f$, preferably $f = \mathsf{MOP}[v]$.

Example A.0.3 (Simple constant propagation). For the simple constant propagation framework, $\mathsf{MOP}[v] \neq \bot$ for each reachable program point $v \in N$. Let us assume that v is indeed reachable. If x is a constant of value $c \in \mathsf{Val}$ at program point v, i.e., holds c whenever execution reaches v, $\mathsf{MOP}[v](x) = c$. Otherwise, $\mathsf{MOP}[v](x) = \top$. Therefore, the MOP-solution of the simple constant propagation framework is a perfect reference point for judging soundness of constant propagation algorithms.   □

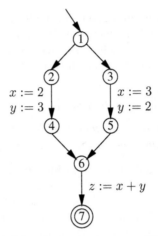

Fig. A.2. Non-distributivity of simple constant propagation.

It is not hard to prove that the MOP-abstraction is distributive. Furthermore, if all transfer functions $[\![e]\!]$ are monotonic, a very natural assumption we have made above, α_{MOP} is a weak homomorphism. By Theorem A.0.1 this means that the constraint-based analysis delivers sound results, a classic theorem by Kam and Ullman [38].

Theorem A.0.2 (Monotonic frameworks). *If all transfer functions $[\![e]\!]$, $e \in E$, are monotonic then* $\mathsf{MOP}[v] \sqsubseteq^{\#} \mathsf{MFP}[v]$ *for all* $v \in N$. $\qquad\square$

Example A.0.4. Theorem A.0.2 implies, in particular, that simple constant propagation yields sound results. If $\mathsf{MFP}[v](x) = c \in \mathsf{Val}$ for a program point $v \in N$ and a variable $x \in Var$, we can infer $\mathsf{MOP}[v](x) = c$ because $\mathsf{MOP}[v] \sqsubseteq \mathsf{MFP}[v]$. Therefore, x is indeed a constant of value c in this case. However, if $\mathsf{MFP}[v](x) = \top$ we cannot infer anything. $\qquad\square$

Ideally, we would like that MOP- and MFP-solution coincide. Indeed, if we pose stronger requirements on the transfer functions we obtain such a result: it is not hard to show that α_{MOP} is a strong homomorphism if all transfer functions $[\![e]\!]$ are universally disjunctive (distributive) and by Theorem A.0.1 this implies that the constraint-based analysis computes exactly the MOP-solution in this case. Thus, we obtain the classic theorem of Kildall [40] ensuring soundness and completeness of the MFP-solution for distributive frameworks.

Theorem A.0.3 (Distributive frameworks). *If all transfer functions $[\![e]\!]$, $e \in E$, are distributive then* $\mathsf{MOP}[v] = \mathsf{MFP}[v]$ *for all* $v \in N$. $\qquad\square$

The transfer functions in simple constant propagation are *not* distributive as illustrated by the program in Fig. A.2: while the MOP-solution assigns the value 5 to z at node 7, the MFP-solution loses precision at node 6 by assigning $\top$ to both x and y at node 6. Hence, the MFP-solution assigns the sound but imprecise value $\top$ to z at node 7. The reason is that $[\![z := x + y]\!]_{sc}$, the transfer function assigned to edge $(6, 7)$, is non-distributive. Let us write $[a, b, c]$ with $a, b, c \in \mathsf{Val} \cup \{\top\}$ for the abstract state that assigns a to x, b to y, and c to z. Then

$$[\![z := x + y]\!]_{sc}([2, 3, \top] \sqcup [3, 2, \top]) = [\![z := x + y]\!]_{sc}([\top, \top, \top]) = [\top, \top, \top]$$

but

$$[\![z := x + y]\!]_{sc}([2, 3, \top]) \sqcup [\![z := x + y]\!]_{sc}([3, 2, \top]) = [\top, \top, 5] \neq [\top, \top, \top].$$

It is possible to define distributive frameworks for constant propagation. A well-known example is copy-constant propagation in which composite expressions are not interpreted at all.

Example A.0.5 (Copy-constant propagation). In copy-constant propagation we use the same lattice as in simple constant propagation, the same order, and the same initial value. We modify, however, the transfer functions: composite expressions are no longer interpreted. Specifically, we define for composite expressions e, $[\![x := e]\!]_{cc}$ by $[\![x := e]\!]_{cc}(\bot) = \bot$ and $[\![x := e]\!]_{cc}(d) = d[x \mapsto \top]$. For all other base statements s, $[\![s]\!]_{cc} = [\![s]\!]_{sc}$. Note that besides of **skip**, only constant and copying assignments $x := v$, where v is a constant or variable, are interpreted, hence the name copy-constant propagation.

It is not hard to prove that the transfer functions of the copy-constant framework are universally disjunctive, Therefore, the MFP-solution of the copy constant propagation framework coincides with the MOP-solution. Of course we pay a price for this coincidence. The MOP-solution of the copy constant propagation framework no longer captures constancy at run-time precisely. In contrast to the MOP-solution of the simple constant propagation framework, it is itself a conservative approximation only.   □

There is no deep fundamental difference between the classic approach to dataflow analysis, which relies on equations, and the constraint-based approach that relies on inequalities. However, the constraint-based approach enables a more modular specification, as in any single inequality we can concentrate on one particular phenomenon, why a certain dataflow information must be weakened. An equational specification, on the other hand, forces us to consider all of them at the same time. Therefore constraint-based specifications are often clearer, in particular in more complex scenarios than intraprocedural analysis of sequential flow graphs like analysis of parallel flow graphs.

References

1. S. V. Adve and K. Gharachorloo. Shared memory consistency models: A tutorial. *IEEE Computer*, 29(12):66–76, December 1996.
2. A. V. Aho, R. Sethi, and J. D. Ullman. *Compilers: Principles, Techniques, and Tools*. Addison-Wesley, 1986.
3. K.-R. Apt and E.-R. Olderog. *Verification of Sequential and Concurrent Programs*. Springer-Verlag, 2nd edition, 1997.
4. K. R. Apt and G. D. Plotkin. Countable nondeterminism and random assignment. *Journal of the ACM*, 33(4):724–767, 1986.
5. J. C. M. Baeten and W. P. Weijland. *Process Algebra*. Cambridge Tracts in Theoretical Computer Science. Cambridge University Press, 1990.
6. A. Bouajjani and P. Habermehl. Constrained properties, semilinear systems, and Petri nets. In U. Montantari and V. Sassone, editors, *Concur '96*, volume 1119 of *Lecture Notes in Computer Science*. Springer-Verlag, 1996.
7. O. Burkart, D. Caucal, F. Moller, and B. Steffen. Verification on infinite structures. In J. Bergstra, A. Ponse, and S. Smolka, editors, *Handbook of Process Algebra*. Elsevier, 2001.
8. E. M. Clarke, M. Fujita, S. P. Rajan, T. Reps, S. Shankar, and T. Teitelbaum. Program slicing for VHDL. In *Correct hardware design and verification methods (Proceedings Charme'99)*, Bad Herrenalb, Germany, September 1999.
9. C. Click and K. D. Cooper. Combining analyses, combining optimizations. *ACM Transactions on Programming Languages and Systems*, 17(2):181–196, 1995.
10. M. Colón. Approximating the algebraic relational semantics of imperative programs. In R. Giacobazzi, editor, *International Symposium on Static Analysis (SAS 2004)*, volume 3148 of *Lecture Notes in Computer Science*, pages 296–311. Springer-Verlag, 2004.
11. M. Colón, S. Sankaranarayanan, and H. Sipma. Linear invariant generation using non-linear constraint solving. In *Computer Aided Verification (CAV 2003)*, pages 420–432. Springer Verlag, LNCS 2725, 2003.
12. S. A. Cook. The complexity of theorem-proving procedures. In *Proc. 3rd Ann. ACM Symp. on Theory of Computing*, pages 151–158, 1971.
13. T. H. Cormen, C. E. Leiserson, and R. L. Rivest. *Introduction to Algorithms*. The MIT Press, 1990.
14. P. Cousot and R. Cousot. Abstract interpretation: A unified lattice model for static analysis of programs by construction or approximation of fixpoints. In *Proceedings 4th POPL*, Los Angeles, California, January 1977.
15. P. Cousot and R. Cousot. Abstract interpretation frameworks. *J. Logic Computat.*, 4(2):511–547, 1992.
16. J. H. Davenport, Y. Siret, and E. Tournier. *Computer Algebra: Systems and Algorithms for Algebraic Computation*. Academic Press, 1988.
17. E. W. Dijkstra. *A Discipline of Programming*. Prentice Hall, 1976.

18. J. Esparza and J. Knoop. An automata-theoretic approach to interprocedural data-flow analysis. In *FoSSaCS '99*, volume 1578 of *Lecture Notes in Computer Science*, pages 14–30. Springer-Verlag, 1999.

19. J. Esparza and A. Podelski. Efficient algorithms for pre* and post* on interprocedural parallel flow graphs. In *ACM International Conference on Principles of Programming Languages (POPL)*, pages 1–11, 2000.

20. C. Fischer and R. LeBlanc. *Crafting a Compiler*. Benjamin/Cummings Publishing Co., Inc., Menlo Park, CA, 1988.

21. N. Francez. *Program Verification*. Addison-Wesley Publishing Company, 1992.

22. M. R. Garey and D. S. Johnson. *Computers and Intractability: A Guide to the Theory of NP-Completeness*. W. H. Freeman and Company, 1978.

23. K. O. Geddes, S. R. Czapor, and G. Labahn. *Algorithms for Computer Algebra*. Kluwer, 1992.

24. R. Giacobazzi, F. Ranzato, and F. Scozzari. Making abstract interpretations complete. *Journal of the ACM*, 47(2):361–416, 2000.

25. R. Giegerich, U. Möncke, and R. Wilhelm. Invariance of approximative semantics with respect to program transformations. In *GI 11. Jahrestagung*, volume 50 of *Informatik Fachberichte*, pages 1–10. Springer-Verlag, 1981.

26. D. Grunwald and H. Srinivasan. Data flow equations for explicitly parallel programs. In *Proceedings of the ACM SIGPLAN Symposium on Principles of Parallel Programming (PPOPP'93)*, pages 159–168, 1993. SIGPLAN Notices, 28(7).

27. S. Gulwani and G. C. Necula. Discovering affine equalities using random interpretation. In *30th ACM Symposium on Principles of Programming Languages (POPL)*, pages 74–84, New Orleans, LA, January 2003. ACM Press.

28. S. Gulwani and G. C. Necula. Precise interprocedural analysis using random interpretation. In J. Palsberg and M. Abadi, editors, *32th ACM Symposium on Principles of Programming Languages (POPL)*, pages 324–337, Long Beach, California, January 2005. ACM Press.

29. J. Hatcliff, J. Corbett, M. Dwyer, S. Sokolowski, and H. Zheng. A formal study of slicing for multi-threaded programs with JVM concurrency primitives. In A. Cortesi and G. Filé, editors, *Static Analysis – SAS'99*, volume 1694 of *Lecture Notes in Computer Science*, pages 1–18. Springer-Verlag, 1999.

30. M. S. Hecht. *Flow Analysis of Computer Programs*. Elsevier North-Holland, 1977.

31. J. E. Hopcroft and J. D. Ullman. *Introduction to Automata Theory, Languages and Computation*. Addison-Wesley, 1979.

32. S. Horwitz, T. Reps, and M. Sagiv. Demand interprocedural dataflow analysis. Technical Report TR-1283, Computer Sciences Department, University of Wisconsin, Madison, WI, August 1995.

33. inmos limited. *Occam2 Reference Manual*. Prentice Hall International, first edition, 1988.

34. inmos limited. *Transputer Instruction Set – A Compiler Writer's Guide*. Prentice Hall International, first edition, 1988.

35. M. Iwaihara, M. Nomura, S. Ichinose, and H. Yasuura. Program slicing on VHDL descriptions and its applications. In *Proc. 3rd Asian Pacific Conference Hardware Description Languages (APCHDL'96)*, pages 132–139, Bangalore, January 1996.

36. D. S. Johnson. A catalog of complexity classes. In J. van Leeuwen, editor, *Handbook of Theoretical Computer Science. Volume A: Algorithms and Complexity*, pages 67–161. Elsevier Science Publishers B.V., 1990.

37. N. D. Jones and S. S. Muchnick. Complexity of flow analysis, inductive assertion synthesis, and a language due to Dijkstra. In [57], chapter 12, pages 380–393.

38. J. B. Kam and J. D. Ullman. Monotone data flow analysis frameworks. Technical Report 169, Department of Electrical Engineering, Princeton University, Princeton, NJ, 1975.

39. M. Karr. Affine relationships among variables of a program. *Acta Informatica*, 6:133–151, 1976.

40. G. A. Kildall. A unified approach to global program optimization. In *Conf. Rec. 1st ACM Symposium on Principles of Programming Languages POPL'73*, pages 194–206, 1973.

41. J. Knoop. Parallel constant propagation. In D. Pritchard and J. Reeve, editors, *4th European Conference on Parallel Processing (Euro-Par)*, volume 1470 of *Lecture Notes in Computer Science*, pages 445–455. Springer-Verlag, 1998.

42. J. Knoop and O. Rüthing. Constant propagation on the value graph: Simple constants and beyond. In *CC'2000*, volume 1781 of *Lecture Notes in Computer Science*, pages 94–109, Berlin, Germany, 2000. Springer-Verlag.

43. J. Knoop and B. Steffen. The interprocedural coincidence theorem. In P. P. U. Kastens, editor, *Proceedings of the 4th International Conference on Compiler Construction (CC'92), Paderborn (Germany)*, volume 641 of *Lecture Notes in Computer Science (LNCS)*, pages 125–140, Heidelberg, Germany, 1992. Springer-Verlag.

44. J. Knoop, B. Steffen, and J. Vollmer. Parallelism for free: Efficient and optimal bitvector analyses for parallel programs. *ACM Transactions on Programming Languages and Systems*, 18(3):268–299, 1996.

45. D. Kozen. Lower bounds for natural proof systems. In *Proc. 18the Ann. Symp. on Foundations of Computer Science*, pages 254–266, Long Beach, CA, 1977. IEEE Computer Society.

46. W. Landi. Undecidability of static analysis. *ACM Letters on Programming Languages and Systems*, 1(4):323–337, 1992.

47. D. Lugiez and P. Schnoebelen. The regular viewpoint on PA-processes. *Theoretical Computer Science*, 274(1-2):89–115, 2002.

48. J. Manson, W. Pugh, and S. V. Adve. The Java memory model. In J. Palsberg and M. Abadi, editors, *Proceedings 32nd ACM Symposium on Principles of Programming Languages (POPL 2005)*, pages 378–391, Long Beach, California, 2005. ACM Press.

49. Mathematics of Program Construction Group. Fixed-point calculus. *Information Processing Letters*, 53(3):131–136, 1995.

50. Y. V. Matiyasevich. *Hilbert's Tenth Problem*. The MIT Press, 1993.

51. R. Mayr. *Decidability and Complexity of Model Checking Problems for Infinite-State Systems*. PhD thesis, TU München, 1998.

52. A. Melton, D. A. Schmidt, and G. E. Strecker. Galois connections and computer science applications. In D. Pitt, S. Abramsky, A. Poigné, and D. Rydeheard, editors, *Category Theory and Computer Programming*, volume 240 of *LNCS*, pages 299–312. Springer-Verlag, 1985.

53. L. I. Millett and T. Teitelbaum. Issues in slicing PROMELA and its applications to model checking, protocol understanding, and simulation. *International Journal on Software Tools for Technology Transfer*, 2(4):343–349, 2000.

54. M. Minsky. *Computation: Finite and Infinite Machines*. Prentice-Hall, 1967.

55. B. Mishra. *Algorithmic Algebra*. Springer-Verlag, 1993.

56. S. S. Muchnick. *Advanced Compiler Design and Implementation*. Morgan Kaufmann Publishers, San Francisco, California, 1997.

57. S. S. Muchnick and N. D. Jones, editors. *Program Flow Analysis: Theory and Applications*. Prentice Hall, Engelwood Cliffs, New Jersey, 1981.

58. M. Müller-Olm. The complexity of copy constant detection in parallel programs. In A. Ferreira and H. Reichel, editors, *STACS 2001 (18th Annual Symposium on Theoretical Aspects of Computer Science)*, volume 2010 of *Lecture Notes in Computer Science*, pages 490–501. Springer, 2001.

59. M. Müller-Olm. Precise interprocedural dependence analysis of parallel programs. *Theoretical Computer Science*, 311:325–388, 2004.

60. M. Müller-Olm and O. Rüthing. The complexity of constant propagation. In D. Sands, editor, *ESOP 2001 (10th European Symposium on Programming)*, volume 2028 of *Lecture Notes in Computer Science*, pages 190–205. Springer, 2001.

61. M. Müller-Olm and H. Seidl. On optimal slicing of parallel programs. In *STOC 2001 (33th Annual ACM Symposium on Theory of Computing)*, pages 647–656, Hersonissos, Crete, Greece, July 2001. ACM SIGACT, ACM Press.

62. M. Müller-Olm and H. Seidl. Polynomial constants are decidable. In M. Hermenegildo and G. Puebla, editors, *SAS 2002 (Static Analysis of Systems)*, volume 2477 of *Lecture Notes in Computer Science*, pages 4–19. Springer, 2002.

63. M. Müller-Olm and H. Seidl. Computing polynomial program invariants. *Information Processing Letters*, 91(5):233–244, 2004.

64. M. Müller-Olm and H. Seidl. A note on Karr's algorithm. In *31st Int. Coll. on Automata, Languages and Programming (ICALP)*, pages 1016–1028. Springer Verlag, LNCS 3142, 2004.

65. M. Müller-Olm and H. Seidl. Precise interprocedural analysis through linear algebra. In *31st ACM Symp. on Principles of Programming Languages (POPL)*, pages 330–341, 2004.

66. M. Müller-Olm and H. Seidl. Analysis of modular arithmetic. In *European Symposium on Programming (ESOP)*, pages 46–60. Springer Verlag, LNCS 3444, 2005.

67. M. Müller-Olm and H. Seidl. Checking Herbrand equalities and beyond. In *Verification, Model Checking, and Abstract Interpretation (VMCAI)*, pages 79–96. Springer Verlag, LNCS 3385, 2005.

68. M. Müller-Olm, H. Seidl, and B. Steffen. Interprocedural analysis of Herbrand equalities. In *European Symposium on Programming (ESOP)*, pages 31–45. Springer Verlag, LNCS 3444, 2005.

69. R. Muth and S. Debray. On the complexity of flow-sensitive dataflow analysis. In *POPL'2000*, pages 67–81, Boston, MA, 2000. ACM.

70. F. Nielson, H. R. Nielson, and C. Hankin. *Principles of Program Analysis*. Springer-Verlag, 1999.

71. S. Owicki and D. Gries. An axiomatic proof technique for parallel programs. *Acta Informatica*, 6:319–340, 1976.

72. C. H. Papadimitriou. *Computational Complexity*. Addison-Wesley, 1994.

73. G. D. Plotkin. A structured approach to operational semantics. Technical Report DAIMI FN-19, Aarhus University, Comput. Sci. Dept., 1981.

74. W. Pugh. The Omega test: a fast and practical integer programming algorithm for dependence analysis. In *Supercomputing '91*, pages 4–13, Albuquerque, NM, 1991. IEEE Computer Society Press.

75. W. Pugh. Fixing the Java memory model. In *Proceedings of the ACM 1999 Java Grande Conference*, San Francisco, CA, June 1999.

76. W. Pugh and D. Wonnacott. Constraint-based array dependence analysis. *ACM Transactions on Programming Languages and Systems*, 20(3):635–678, 1998.

77. G. Ramalingam. Context-sensitive synchronization-sensitive analysis is undecidable. *ACM Transactions on Programming Languages and Systems*, 22(2):416–430, 2000.

78. J. R. Reif and H. R. Lewis. Symbolic evaluation and the global value graph. In *Conf. Rec. 4th ACM Symposium on Principles of Programming Languages POPL'77*, pages 104–118, Los Angeles, CA, January 1977.

79. H. G. Rice. Classes of recursively enumerable sets and their decision probems. *Trans. AMS*, 89:25–59, 1953.

80. M. Rinard. Analysis of multithreaded programs. In P. Cousot, editor, *Static Analysis of Systems (SAS 2001)*, volume 2126 of *Lecture Notes in Computer Science*, pages 1–19. Springer-Verlag, 2001.

81. E. Rodríguez-Carbonell and D. Kapur. An abstract interpretation approach for automatic generation of polynomial invariants. In R. Giacobazzi, editor, *International Symposium on Static Analysis (SAS 2004)*, volume 3148 of *Lecture Notes in Computer Science*, pages 280–295. Springer-Verlag, 2004.

82. E. Rodríguez-Carbonell and D. Kapur. Program verification using automatic generation of invariants. In K. A. Zhiming Liu, editor, *1st International Colloquium on Theoretical Aspects of Computing (ICTAC'04)*, volume 3407 of *Lecture Notes in Computer Science*, pages 325–340. Springer-Verlag, 2005.

83. M. Sagiv, T. Reps, and S. Horwitz. Precise interprocedural dataflow analysis with applications to constant propagation. *Theoretical Computer Science*, 167(1–2):131–170, 1996.

84. S. Sankaranarayanan, H. B. Sipma, and Z. Manna. Non-linear loop invariant generation using Gröbner bases. In *POPL '04: Proceedings of the 31st ACM SIGPLAN-SIGACT symposium on Principles of programming languages*, pages 318–329, New York, NY, USA, 2004. ACM Press.

85. H. Seidl and B. Steffen. Constraint-based inter-procedural analysis of parallel programs. *Nordic Journal of Computing*, 7(4):371 – 400, 2001. Special issue for ESOP'2000.

86. M. Sharir and A. Pnueli. Two approaches to interprocedural data flow analysis. In [57], chapter 7, pages 189–233.

87. B. Steffen. Optimal run time optimization – proved by a new look at abstract interpretations. In H. Ehrig, R. Kowalski, G. Levi, and U. Montanari, editors, *Proceedings of the 2nd International Joint Conference on Theory and Practice of Software Development (TAPSOFT'87), Pisa (Italy)*, volume 249 of *Lecture Notes in Computer Science (LNCS)*, pages 52–68, Heidelberg, Germany, March 1987. Springer-Verlag.

88. B. Steffen, B. Jay, and M. Mendler. Compositional characterization of observable program properties. *International Journal on Theoretical Computer Science and Applications*, 26(5):403–424, 1992.

89. B. Steffen and J. Knoop. Finite constants: Characterizations of a new decidable set of constants. *Theoretical Computer Science*, 80(2):303–318, 1991.

90. A. Tarski. A lattice-theoretical fixpoint theorem and its application. *Pacific Journal of Mathematics*, 5:285–309, 1955.

91. R. N. Taylor. Complexity of analyzing the synchronization structure of concurrent programs. *Acta Informatica*, 19:57–84, 1983.

92. F. Tip. A survey of program slicing techniques. *Journal of Programming Languages*, 3(3):121–189, September 1995.

93. M. N. Wegman and F. K. Zadeck. Constant propagation with conditional branches. *ACM Transactions on Programming Languages and Systems*, 13(2), 1991.

94. M. Weiser. Program slicing. *IEEE Transactions on Software Engineering*, 10(4):352–357, 1984.

95. F. Winkler. *Polynomial Algorithms*. Springer-Verlag, 1996.

Lecture Notes in Computer Science

For information about Vols. 1–4142

please contact your bookseller or Springer

Vol. 4190: R. Larsen, M. Nielsen, J. Sporring (Eds.), Medical Image Computing and Computer-Assisted Intervention – MICCAI 2006, Part I. XXXVVIII, 949 pages. 2006.

Vol. 4189: D. Gollmann, J. Meier, A. Sabelfeld (Eds.), Computer Security – ESORICS 2006. XI, 548 pages. 2006.

Vol. 4188: P. Sojka, I. Kopeček, K. Pala (Eds.), Text, Speech and Dialogue. XIV, 721 pages. 2006. (Sublibrary LNAI).

Vol. 4187: J.J. Alferes, J. Bailey, W. May, U. Schwertel (Eds.), Principles and Practice of Semantic Web Reasoning. XI, 277 pages. 2006.

Vol. 4186: C. Jesshope, C. Egan (Eds.), Advances in Computer Systems Architecture. XIV, 605 pages. 2006.

Vol. 4185: R. Mizoguchi, Z. Shi, F. Giunchiglia (Eds.), The Semantic Web – ASWC 2006. XX, 778 pages. 2006.

Vol. 4184: M. Bravetti, M. Núñez, G. Zavattaro (Eds.), Web Services and Formal Methods. X, 289 pages. 2006.

Vol. 4183: J. Euzenat, J. Domingue (Eds.), Artificial Intelligence: Methodology, Systems, and Applications. XIII, 291 pages. 2006. (Sublibrary LNAI).

Vol. 4182: H.T. Ng, M.-K. Leong, M.-Y. Kan, D. Ji (Eds.), Information Retrieval Technology. XVI, 684 pages. 2006.

Vol. 4180: M. Kohlhase, OMDoc – An Open Markup Format for Mathematical Documents [version 1.2]. XIX, 428 pages. 2006. (Sublibrary LNAI).

Vol. 4179: J. Blanc-Talon, W. Philips, D. Popescu, P. Scheunders (Eds.), Advanced Concepts for Intelligent Vision Systems. XXIV, 1224 pages. 2006.

Vol. 4178: A. Corradini, H. Ehrig, U. Montanari, L. Ribeiro, G. Rozenberg (Eds.), Graph Transformations. XII, 473 pages. 2006.

Vol. 4177: R. Marín, E. Onaindía, A. Bugarín, J. Santos (Eds.), Current Topics in Aritficial Intelligence. XIII, 621 pages. 2006. (Sublibrary LNAI).

Vol. 4176: S.K. Katsikas, J. Lopez, M. Backes, S. Gritzalis, B. Preneel (Eds.), Information Security. XIV, 548 pages. 2006.

Vol. 4175: P. Bücher, B.M.E. Moret (Eds.), Algorithms in Bioinformatics. XII, 402 pages. 2006. (Sublibrary LNBI).

Vol. 4174: K. Franke, K.-R. Müller, B. Nickolay, R. Schäfer (Eds.), Pattern Recognition. XX, 773 pages. 2006.

Vol. 4173: S. El Yacoubi, B. Chopard, S. Bandini (Eds.), Cellular Automata. XV, 734 pages. 2006.

Vol. 4172: J. Gonzalo, C. Thanos, M. F. Verdejo, R.C. Carrasco (Eds.), Research and Advanced Technology for Digital Libraries. XVII, 569 pages. 2006.

Vol. 4169: H.L. Bodlaender, M.A. Langston (Eds.), Parameterized and Exact Computation. XI, 279 pages. 2006.

Vol. 4168: Y. Azar, T. Erlebach (Eds.), Algorithms – ESA 2006. XVIII, 843 pages. 2006.

Vol. 4167: S. Dolev (Ed.), Distributed Computing. XV, 576 pages. 2006.

Vol. 4166: J. Górski (Ed.), Computer Safety, Reliability, and Security. XIV, 440 pages. 2006.

Vol. 4165: W. Jonker, M. Petković (Eds.), Secure, Data Management. X, 185 pages. 2006.

Vol. 4163: H. Bersini, J. Carneiro (Eds.), Artificial Immune Systems. XII, 460 pages. 2006.

Vol. 4162: R. Královič, P. Urzyczyn (Eds.), Mathematical Foundations of Computer Science 2006. XV, 814 pages. 2006.

Vol. 4161: R. Harper, M. Rauterberg, M. Combetto (Eds.), Entertainment Computing - ICEC 2006. XXVII, 417 pages. 2006.

Vol. 4160: M. Fisher, W.v.d. Hoek, B. Konev, A. Lisitsa (Eds.), Logics in Artificial Intelligence. XII, 516 pages. 2006. (Sublibrary LNAI).

Vol. 4159: J. Ma, H. Jin, L.T. Yang, J.J.-P. Tsai (Eds.), Ubiquitous Intelligence and Computing. XXII, 1190 pages. 2006.

Vol. 4158: L.T. Yang, H. Jin, J. Ma, T. Ungerer (Eds.), Autonomic and Trusted Computing. XIV, 613 pages. 2006.

Vol. 4156: S. Amer-Yahia, Z. Bellahsène, E. Hunt, R. Unland, J.X. Yu (Eds.), Database and XML Technologies. IX, 123 pages. 2006.

Vol. 4155: O. Stock, M. Schaerf (Eds.), Reasoning, Action and Interaction in AI Theories and Systems. XVIII, 343 pages. 2006. (Sublibrary LNAI).

Vol. 4154: Y.A. Dimitriadis, I. Zigurs, E. Gómez-Sánchez (Eds.), Groupware: Design, Implementation, and Use. XIV, 438 pages. 2006.

Vol. 4153: N. Zheng, X. Jiang, X. Lan (Eds.), Advances in Machine Vision, Image Processing, and Pattern Analysis. XIII, 506 pages. 2006.

Vol. 4152: Y. Manolopoulos, J. Pokorný, T. Sellis (Eds.), Advances in Databases and Information Systems. XV, 448 pages. 2006.

Vol. 4151: A. Iglesias, N. Takayama (Eds.), Mathematical Software - ICMS 2006. XVII, 452 pages. 2006.

Vol. 4150: M. Dorigo, L.M. Gambardella, M. Birattari, A. Martinoli, R. Poli, T. Stützle (Eds.), Ant Colony Optimization and Swarm Intelligence. XVI, 526 pages. 2006.

Vol. 4149: M. Klusch, M. Rovatsos, T.R. Payne (Eds.), Cooperative Information Agents X. XII, 477 pages. 2006. (Sublibrary LNAI).

Vol. 4148: J. Vounckx, N. Azemard, P. Maurine (Eds.), Integrated Circuit and System Design. XVI, 677 pages. 2006.

Vol. 4147: M. Broy, I.H. Krüger, M. Meisinger (Eds.), Automotive Software – Connected Services in Mobile Networks. XIV, 155 pages. 2006.

Vol. 4146: J.C. Rajapakse, L. Wong, R. Acharya (Eds.), Pattern Recognition in Bioinformatics. XIV, 186 pages. 2006. (Sublibrary LNBI).

Vol. 4144: T. Ball, R.B. Jones (Eds.), Computer Aided Verification. XV, 564 pages. 2006.

Vol. 4143: R. Lämmel, J. Saraiva, J. Visser (Eds.), Generative and Transformational Techniques in Software Engineering. X, 471 pages. 2006.